Intimate Class Acts

Intimate Class Acts

Friendship and Desire in Indian and Pakistani Women's Fiction

Maryam Mirza

OXFORD
UNIVERSITY PRESS

OXFORD
UNIVERSITY PRESS

Oxford University Press is a department of the University of Oxford.
It furthers the University's objective of excellence in research, scholarship,
and education by publishing worldwide. Oxford is a registered trademark of
Oxford University Press in the UK and in certain other countries

Published in India by
Oxford University Press
YMCA Library Building, 1 Jai Singh Road, New Delhi 110001, India

First Edition published in 2016

ISBN-13: 978-0-19-946674-0
ISBN-10: 0-19-946674-2

Typeset in Berling LT Std 10/13
by The Graphics Solution, New Delhi 110092
Printed in India by Replika Press Pvt. Ltd

This book is dedicated with much love to my father,
Tariq Habib Mirza, and to Claire Davison-Pégon

Contents

Foreword

Ismat Chughtai wrote 'The Quilt' in 1942,[1] two months before she got married; it was published around the time of her wedding. It is a short story of many layers: the narrator, a grown woman, delves into the 'dark crevasses of the past' to recall the story of a quilt during a winter when she was a small girl, staying with Begum Jan, the wife of an Indian nawab (aristocrat). Scoffing at the reader's expectations of 'romance' from a story that features a 'blanket' or a 'quilt', the narrator then goes on to talk of a complex world of relationships: the jaded conjugal relations between the nawab and Begum Jan, the nawab's attraction to young men in the outside world, and Begum Jan's lesbian relationship with a servant, Rabbo, in the zenana. It is this last relationship that forms the core of the story, witnessed uncomprehendingly by the small girl: the quilt covering the two adult women assumes strange, mobile, animal shapes in the crepuscular gloom of the room that also contains the small girl, supposedly asleep.

I refer to this story not for its lesbian and other themes, which have been noticed by critics. Instead, I refer to it for the subtle relationship that it etches between a mistress and her servant. This might be just as remarkable as its lesbian and other concerns. Chughtai stresses the difference between the classes in material, educational, and physical terms: while Begum Jan is willowy, exceedingly fair, and refined, tending to languish if left on her own, Rabbo is 'lightly marked with smallpox, her body solidly packed; small, dextrous hands, a tight little paunch and full lips, slightly swollen, which were always moist'. A 'strange and bothersome odour' emanates

[1] All references to Ismat Chughtai's 'The Quilt' are from the translation by Syeda S. Hameed. See Chughtai (2004, 7–19).

from Rabbo's body. But along with such differences, there is a strange intimacy between Begum Jan and Rabbo, stretching from the regular massages that Rabbo administers to her mistress during the day to the shape-changing quilt witnessed by the small girl at night.

This mix of difference and intimacy results in a complex circulation of power and, in some ways, it provides, in a few short pages, a subtle and deep exploration of the relationships that existed, at least in certain upper-class families, between masters and servants. One can see a similarly nuanced exploration of servants and 'servant class' characters in other Hindi and Urdu texts from the first half of the twentieth century, for instance by Premchand and Qurratulain Hyder. Nothing comparable exists in South Asian literature in English at least until much later—no, not even in Raja Rao's mythical-realist *Kanthapura* (1938) or the social-realist fiction of Mulk Raj Anand. One can argue that, to some extent, the middle-class realities experienced and drawn upon by the authors of South Asian fiction in English are different. This is partly true, though perhaps only from the 1960s onwards in most cases when middle-class South Asian families, at least professional ones, largely became nuclear families and stopped harbouring live-in servants. Perhaps, in some ways, the most visible South Asian novel that employs a 'servant' to significant effect indicates this change. I have in mind the very physical, 'dung'-lotus, Padma, in Salman Rushdie's *Midnight's Children* (1981).

While it does not seem to have been noticed by postcolonial critics as yet, perhaps because many of them do not read Urdu literature, one can argue that Padma's lineage can be traced back to Chughtai's Rabbo. Knowing Rushdie's intertextuality, one should not be surprised if the derivation is a conscious one. Padma, of course, is presented as the narrator-protagonist Saleem Sinai's caretaker and to-be fiancée. In class and other terms, though, the relationship between Saleem and Padma is reminiscent of that between a master and a servant, especially in the twilight of the aristocratic joint-family system that forms the backdrop for Saleem Sinai. The relationship of power between the narrator-master (Saleem) and the narratee-servant (Padma) in *Midnight's Children* is complex, no doubt, though I will argue that it is far less complex than in Chughtai's story. That is partly because the intimacy is *less*. It is not only because Saleem is impotent; it is also because, to an extent, Padma is less central to Saleem's narrative than most postcolonialists are willing to concede. Growing up in the shadow of reader response theories and feminism, postcolonialists love to portray Padma as the narratee ('reader') without whom Saleem's story would not come into being—quite forgetting (in their excitement at finding good fiction fitting their theories) that Padma leaves Saleem for many pages without Saleem's narrative faltering and that, in any case, Saleem almost entirely ignores Padma's criticism of and demands from his story.

There is a distance between Padma and Saleem, in physical, social, and intellectual terms: Rushdie's exploration of their 'cross-class' relations is consciously restrained by this, despite the claims of the narrator and, following him, postcolonialist critics. The intricate power-laced intimacy of Begum Jan and Rabbo is replaced by redundant discursive claims and physical impotency in *Midnight's Children*. This might well have been purposive on the part of Rushdie, but the difference, as I suggested earlier, also indicates a socio-historical change: the anglophone middle classes rarely live with their servants now. Their servants do not sleep in their beds, and seldom give them body massages. Their servants go away and come back, as Padma does. And yet, as Maryam Mirza notes, servants are essential to middle-class existence in South Asia. This is more so in the case of women, for women still have to manage households even in most professional circles in South Asia. Has South Asian fiction in English used this powerful element, this nuanced relationship—and one that changes from region to region, generation to generation? What has South Asian fiction in English made of its servants? What *can* it make of its servants?

There are, obviously, no fiction narratives in English by servants in South Asia. I would be surprised if there are any English narratives at all by servants in India or Pakistan, for English is the language of a very small section of 'masters'. And yet, despite a relative paucity, South Asian fiction has drawn upon servants, similar 'subalterns', and their relationship to the master-narrators. The matter is deeper than that. The issue of writing about (or not writing about) servants throws up, as Mirza shows, the even more complex matters of genre, representation, agency. After all, can the servant speak—in English? Moreover, to paraphrase Mirza, a focus on the figure of the servant underscores the artificial nature of the divide between the private and public spheres and highlights the construction of gendered, class, and other identities. Of course, Mirza goes beyond the servant per se, examining in the process the politics of friendship and desire across class differences in all the novels. Using domestic servants as a focus, Mirza expands her concerns to examine the poetics and politics of desire in cross-class relations, fully aware of the peculiar paradox of power in any such situation.

A full study of power and desire in cross-class relations in anglophone South Asian fiction has been largely overdue; Maryam Mirza has finally provided it. But she has avoided the pitfalls of doing a meandering survey. Instead, she has selected to focus on women writers: ten significant novels in all. This is a clever choice (given the 'nature' of domestic spaces, alluded to earlier), and it has enabled Mirza to write a coherent and organized study. *Intimate Class Acts* is a necessary book, well-researched and fluently written, which maintains an exquisite balance between text and theory. It is an excellent addition to scholarship on South Asian fiction.

TABISH KHAIR

Acknowledgements

This monograph grew out of my PhD dissertation at Aix-Marseille University and I owe a debt of gratitude to many individuals and several institutions for their support during my doctoral years (2008–12), as well as for their help since the completion of my thesis, making it possible for me to bring this project to a conclusion.

In particular, I would like to offer my heartfelt thanks to Professor Claire Davison-Pégon, my PhD supervisor, mentor, and friend, for her faith in this study and for her extraordinary generosity, invaluable guidance, and continuing support; thank you also to my external examiners, Professors Madelena Gonzalez, Nathalie Vanfasse, and Catherine Pesso-Miquel; the late Professor Chelva Kanaganayakam who was a most generous host to me during my research visit to the Centre for South Asian Studies at the University of Toronto in 2011; the wonderful inter-library loan service at Aix-Marseille University, France; the Solidarité Études Association, France, whose generous financial help facilitated the final year of my PhD; the editors at Oxford University Press India; the University of Liège and the EU for their support in the context of the MSCA-BeIPD-COFUND project; Christian Tikhomiroff for the gift of yoga; Mrs Zareena Saeed and Mr Humair Hashmi for their unstinting support over many years; my friends in Pakistan and France: Geneviève, Ariane, Bernard, Javeria, Emilie, Aleksandra, Faiza, Amir, Giovanni, Mariam, and Christel; Professor Tabish Khair for his *Babu Fictions* and other writings which have been such an important influence on my work: thank you also, Professor Khair, for writing the foreword to this book; Sue Hughes for her enthusiasm for this project and for all her kind help with the editing: I couldn't have done this without you, Sue; my cousin Kashif for seeing me through the dark days of writing with his sense of humour and encouragement; my brother

Vassay; and most of all my father Tariq Habib Mirza for his infinite love, patience, and support.

The following essays have been woven into sections of Chapters 1, 3, and 6 of the book with the kind permission of the publishers: 'Intimacy Across Caste and Class Boundaries in Arundhati Roy's *The God of Small Things*' and 'Female Relationships across Class Boundaries' (see Mirza 2010, 2015).

Introduction
Writing Class, Writing Intimacy

'Have another sandwich. They were made especially.'
'Who made them?'
'The servant who brought them.'
'What servant? I didn't notice.'
—Suniti Namjoshi*

Until recently, subaltern characters in general and domestic servants in particular were often invisible or secondary in Indian and Pakistani anglophone fiction, with few detailed literary depictions of relationships between members of polarized classes. This seems surprising, especially if we consider the omnipresence of economic subalterns within the domestic spaces of the privileged classes to which the vast majority of the exponents and readers of South Asian literature in English belong. Arguably, this relative omission is symptomatic of the societal invisibility and powerlessness of the subaltern classes in the Indian subcontinent, which Namjoshi's fable so eloquently illustrates.

This book is a study of emotional and physical intimacy between the haves and the have-nots as depicted in ten anglophone novels by women writers from India and Pakistan. Rather than from a socio-economic perspective, English-language fiction from the Indian subcontinent has often been read in its historical and political context where hegemony and subalternity are often understood in terms of the colonial encounter. But such an approach, as Tabish Khair (2001, 79–80) warns us, can 'obscure' certain realities, particularly the question of economic inequality. There is also the

* Quoted in Namjoshi (1993 [1981], 38).

danger of fiction by female authors writing in English being seen as representative of the situation of all women, rich and poor, which can elide the dramatic economic differences between them. The rigid class divisions besetting the two countries, which remain deeply patriarchal, have been accentuated by the processes of neo-liberal globalization since the 1980s, while the English language continues to possess a privileged socio-economic positioning in the region. Indeed, an examination of the portrayal of intimacy transgressing class boundaries in English-language fiction by women writers is a pressing concern not only within the field of 'postcolonial' literary criticism, but also within gender studies and cultural studies.

The Anglophone Novel by Women Writers

My study of the depiction of cross-class intimacy draws on ten Indian and Pakistani novels: *Rich Like Us* (1985) by Nayantara Sahgal, *Ice-Candy-Man* (1988) by Bapsi Sidhwa, *The Binding Vine* (1993) by Shashi Deshpande, *The Hope Chest* (1996) by Rukhsana Ahmad, *The God of Small Things* (1997) by Arundhati Roy, *Salt and Saffron* (2000) by Kamila Shamsie, *The Hottest Day of the Year* (2001) by Brinda Charry, *The Space Between Us* (2005) by Thrity Umrigar, *The Inheritance of Loss* (2006) by Kiran Desai, and *The End of Innocence* (2007) by Moni Mohsin. Despite the significant differences between the two countries, in particular the divergent economic paths chosen following Partition, these novels reveal striking similarities in how gendered and classed identities are lived in India and Pakistan, and hence lend themselves to a joint study.

I have focused on the novel, to the exclusion of other genres, partly because of its affinity with an in-depth exploration of class realities. The novel, as Julian Markels (2003, 47) explains, 'is friendly in all its forms to the representation of class as identity site: the Gothic novel and symbolic novel, *Bildungsroman* and *Kunstlerroman*, modern and postcolonial novels, all represent class at various locations that reward a Marxian attention'. Moreover, the novel form has a distinctive position in the literature of the Indian subcontinent. In 'Western' societies, the rise of the novel is often associated with the development of bourgeois capitalism and the growth of the bourgeoisie as a class (Steiner 1969, 328). The development of this genre in the Indian subcontinent cannot be disassociated from the presence of the British. However, as Leela Gandhi (2003, 168) points out, the novel rose to prominence in the 1930s and 1940s when the nationalist, anti-British movement was at its apogee. These divergent origins make it possible for the anglophone novel in the region to encapsulate contrasting 'ideological perspectives and representational strategies' (Jani 2010, 38). Despite the 'elitist' roots of the majority of its exponents, it is an apt choice to examine the literary depiction of intimate cross-class relations.

Furthermore, a focus on the anglophone novel by women writers will allow us to evaluate how the authors have addressed the nuances of economic inequality within societies that are also profoundly patriarchal. Significantly, as Malashri Lal (1995, 21) has pointed out, novels by women are often located in the so-called private, 'female' arena. By focusing on literary works by female authors, I examine not only the reproduction, but also the possible contestation of class and gender identities in spaces that are conventionally deemed 'feminine'. More often than not, South Asian anglophone writers (and their critics), whether male or female, belong to a privileged socio-economic milieu. However, it would be erroneous to contend that a female author benefits from her upper-class positioning in the same way as a male writer. Social power still belongs to men and, as Khair (2001, 179–80) has explained, the woman writer shares 'many of the privileges of the class but does not actually own the power and, to a large extent, the capital'. Therefore, a woman writer in English may be considered at once privileged because of her class (and caste) positioning, and potentially marginalized because of her gendered identity, entailing a complex intersection of various systems of social stratification in her work. By drawing attention to these contrasting identities, I am not suggesting that we simplistically reduce Pakistani and Indian women novelists to their gender, class, or caste, but that we recognize the importance of these systems of social stratification in any literary enterprise. As Edward Said (1994 [1993], xxiv) has argued, while authors are not 'mechanically determined by ideology, class or economic history', they are 'very much in the history of their societies, shaping and shaped by that history and their social experience in different measures'. As we will see in the chapters that follow, the complex interplay of patriarchy and class colours not only male–female relationships, but also emotional ties between women and the political sensibility of the texts is often marked by a negotiation of the female/feminist and elitist identities of the writer.

South Asian female authors writing in English occupy what Rajeswari Sunder Rajan (1993b, 75) has called an 'extremely rarefied field' within literary criticism and are consequently extremely 'visible'. Particularly for a 'Western' readership and critics, they are seen as spokespersons of all Pakistani and Indian women, a perception that does not adequately take into consideration the differences dividing the female population of the region. As Nilufer Bharucha (2001, 94) argues, just as white hegemony within feminism is to be resisted, so too must a 'Third World' hegemony, which also imposes a simplistic sorority on all Indian women. Building on the belief that fiction by female South Asian authors is not necessarily 'a resistant practice' solely because it has been written by women, this book attempts to tease out the various forms that social privilege and subalternity can assume in societies such as India and Pakistan (Rajan 1993b, 75). Indeed, instead of equating subalternity with women (whether writers or characters), my use of the term 'subaltern' subscribes to Guha's (1982, vii) definition of it, according to which the subaltern is 'a name for the general attribute of subordination in South Asian society, whether this is expressed in terms of class, caste, age, gender or any other way'.

In examining how female upper-class authors have depicted subaltern characters and their relationships with members of the upper classes, I am mindful of the possible danger of this sort of literary 're-presentation' becoming an exercise of power (Spivak 1988, 275). But, like Pranav Jani (2010, 43), I do not see subalternity as a discursive space that lies beyond the domain of representation, a view that Spivak's articles 'Subaltern Studies' (1985) and 'Can the Subaltern Speak?' (1988) seem to uphold. Moreover, dictating who has the right to portray whom is arguably another manifestation of the 'cult of authenticity' which Vikram Chandra (2000, n.p.) condemns while responding to critics who deem that only Indian authors residing in India have the right to write about the country.

Such a literary prohibition excludes the possibility of sociocultural dialogue and runs the risk of perpetuating essentialist alterity. As Pranav Jani (2009, 44) affirms, aligning himself with the early Subaltern Studies theorists of the 1980s who sought to recover the voices and histories of the subalterns excluded from elite-centred historiographies (whether colonial or national), 'one can trace and differentiate between various instances of elite representations of subalterns, marking representation as a site of struggle and conflict'.

Class Matters

I use the term 'class' interchangeably with 'socio-economic milieu' and broadly take it to mean 'a large-scale grouping of people who share common economic resources, which strongly influence the type of lifestyle that they are able to lead' (Giddens 2001, 282).

Conventional Marxism focuses on the relations between two classes or 'two great hostile camps' in a capitalist society: the bourgeoisie who own the means of production and the proletariat who are employed (and exploited) by the bourgeoisie with an aim to increase its capital (Marx and Engels 2012 [1888], 35). Notably, domestic servants, as we will see later, have been ignored as a class in classical Marxist thought. For Weber (2009, 405), on the other hand, the 'class-situation' of a group of people depends on the ownership and non-ownership of not only 'material goods', but also of 'definite skills' that can be bought and sold in the labour market. Moreover, Weber (2013, 405), using the caste system in India as an example, sheds light on the importance of the notion of 'status' or 'social honour', as a source of social inequality, based on 'style of life' rather than wealth and income, though class and status 'situations' are often connected in societies.

An important notion within the concept of class is that of social hegemony as it alerts us to the significance of 'ideological domination' in understanding socio-economic inequality (Eagleton 2013 [1994], 134). Hegemony, as Gramsci (1971, 12) explains, is 'the "spontaneous" consent given by the great masses of the population to the general direction imposed on social life by the dominant fundamental group; this consent is "historically" caused by the prestige (and consequent confidence) which the dominant group enjoys because of its position and function in the world of production'. My understanding of class also draws on Bourdieu's (1986) discussion of various kinds of capital, other than economic capital (wealth and revenue). These include social capital (network of human relationships that can be of use to a family or individual), cultural capital (which includes the idea of habitus, cultural goods, and educational qualifications), and, finally, symbolic capital which is tied in to the idea of social prestige.

In South Asia, as elsewhere, any examination of economic stratification needs to take into account other systems of social stratification (whether it is patriarchy or the caste system), as well as the colonial past of the region. As Said (1994 [1993], 269) has observed about the political economy of 'postcolonial' countries at the time of their independence: '[T]he national bourgeoisies and their specialized elites ... in effect tended to replace the colonial force with a new class-based and ultimately exploitative one, which replicated the old colonial structures in new terms.' While this book does bring to the fore similarities in how cross-class relationships are lived in the post-Partition states of India and Pakistan, it is also important to point out that they have not followed identical political and economic trajectories since 1947, nor do they share identical social characteristics. Vicziany (2004, 34), for instance, argues that Pakistani society is less unequal since 'it does not suffer from the extreme socio-economic discrimination of the Indian caste system that continues to prevent dalit and tribal people from rising to their full potential'.

While India adopted 'a semi-planned, semi-socialist economy based on import substitution' after Partition, Pakistan decided to opt for 'a liberal import regime', which explains the limited industrialization in the country (Vicziany 2004, 31). The military has arguably been 'the most important political force in Pakistan' since 1947 and forms a formidable nexus with 'bureaucratic, landed feudal and business elites' (Murphy and Tamana 2010, 48). This nexus has also successfully hindered any meaningful land reforms which would dismantle the feudal (zamindari) system (Kukreja 2005, 139). In India, on the other hand, zamindari abolition acts were passed in several provincial legislatures between 1949 and 1954, however, the legislation was only marginally successful in 'appropriating zamindari lands' and in 'undermining the position of zamindars as economic elites in the countryside' (Sharma 1999, 110).

Economic liberalization in India began in the mid-1980s, becoming official in 1991 with its acceptance, in response to a debt and foreign exchange crisis, of structural adjustment programmes under the aegis of the World Bank and the International Monetary Fund (Deshpande and Sarkar 1995, 3151). Structural adjustment programmes compel 'developing' countries to devalue their domestic currency and remove subsidies from health, education, and social services (Kapoor 2011, 6). The local economies are thus forced to open up to global market forces, which are dominated by the world's 'wealthiest industrial countries' and the benefits of the structural adjustment programmes often go 'disproportionately to the better-off, with those at the bottom sometimes facing even greater poverty' (Stiglitz 2002, xiv–18).

The economic climate in Pakistan since 1947 and the current economic situation in India are informed by neo-liberal policies which not only deepen the chasm separating the rich countries from the poor, but also the gap between the rich and the poor within 'developing' countries. Arundhati Roy (2004, 188), with characteristic eloquence, has highlighted the role that globalization has played in perpetuating age-old inequalities:

> What is globalization? Who is it for? … Is the dismantling and auctioning off of elaborate public sector infrastructure, developed with public money over the past fifty years, really the way forward? Is globalization going to close the gap between the privileged and the underprivileged, between the upper castes and the lower castes, between the educated and the illiterate? Or is it going to give those who already have a centuries-old head start a friendly helping hand?

Javed and Irfan (2012, 20) have noted 'high intergenerational persistence' in Pakistan where 'the rich are rich because they are born rich while the fate of the poor by birth is to stay poor'. And as Sara Dickey (2010, 193) has pointed out, while the liberalization of the Indian economy may have led to an expansion of the middle classes in the 1990s, for the majority of Indians, especially those belonging to the lower classes, vertical mobility remains extremely difficult to achieve. It is worth mentioning that if most class theories consider class as an individual identity, in the Indian subcontinent, without discounting the importance of other identity markers such as gender, perhaps class is best understood as a familial phenomenon. As Dickey (2010, 201) has affirmed:

> Other people judge an individual's class by looking at the individual's family, using signs such as family members' occupations, education, housing and consumer goods. Second, it is primarily the family that provides and decides upon the resources available to each individual.... Finally, each generation passes on cultural and social as well as economic 'capital'—including knowledge, values and social networks—to the next generation.

This approach to conceptualizing class is particularly relevant as several 'upper-class' characters in my study are either children or women who do not participate directly in the economy and thus their socio-economic identities are derived at least in part from what Wright (2000, 23) has called 'mediated class locations' based on 'family ties'.

Most of the literary texts that I examine in this book focus on the relationship between two disparate classes: the Babu elites and domestic servants, a distinct subaltern class. The particularity of the term Babu in the South Asian context needs to be explained: it is, according to Khair (2001, 32), 'a synonym for the upper and privileged, English-educated middle classes, who even when they are profession-based, are particularly rich in cultural and education capital (neither of which is easy to obtain for the lower classes and castes) and sufficiently secure (relative to the poor, illiterate classes) economically'. It is no coincidence then that in seven of the ten novels that I examine, the inter-class relationships are between servants and their employers. There are very few social spaces in India and Pakistan that allow for a prolonged contact between members of divergent classes, leading to intimacy. Bourgeois domestic spaces function, to deploy Mary Louise Pratt's (1992) terminology, as the most significant 'zone of contact' for polarized social classes in the Indian subcontinent.[1] Indeed, domestic service, as Sara Dickey

[1] Ambreen Hai (2014, 40) makes a similar use of Pratt's notion of contact zone in her essay 'Postcolonial Servitude'.

(2000b, 32) points out, 'is an arena in which class is reproduced and challenged on a daily and intimate basis' and 'domestic service interactions constitute the most intense, sustained contact with members of other classes that most of its participants encounter'. Furthermore, for servants who are often women, elite domestic spaces function as a workplace and unlike other kinds of labour, domestic service entails a serious blurring of the 'the conceptual divide between family and work' (Ray and Qayum 2009, 3).

Conventional class theories are fairly deficient in conceptualizing domestic servitude. The menial servant's labour according to Adam Smith (2009 [1779], 270) 'adds to the value of nothing ... does not fix itself or realize itself in any particular subject or vendible commodity. His services generally perish in the very instant of their performance, and seldom leave any trace or value behind them, for which an equal quantity of service could afterwards be procured.' For Karl Marx (1986 [1976], 1044), labour that is 'consumed as services and not in products' which are separable from the worker, and exist as 'commodities independently of him [*sic*]' are of 'microscopic significance when compared with the mass of capitalist production' and should therefore be 'entirely neglected' (Marx 1986 [1976], 1045). As Shah (2000, 89) explains, while in Marxian terms, capital only appropriates labour and not the labourer, this distinction does not apply to servants who are 'appropriated in labour as well as in person ... therefore must be understood as not only standing at the margins of "home," kinship and other belongings but also occupying the interstices of various historical forms of relations that are sedimented and juxtaposed concurrently'.

As elsewhere, in South Asia too, gender and class cannot be understood in isolation from each other. If feminist theorists such as Shulamith Firestone (1970, 1) see all women as belonging to the same, marginalized 'sex class', it is important to recognize, as Sara Ahmed (1996, 75) points out, that gender 'intersects with other social relations such as class and race, such that women's experiences of power and disempowerment are divergent.' Therefore, 'feminist positions' that are 'committed to women as a collective (a structure of social alliance) must accept their status as partial interventions, as limited by the personal/social economies that shape them' (Ahmed 1996, 75). Moreover, by focusing on the depiction of so-called 'female' domestic spaces in this study, I will demonstrate the extent to which domesticity is 'the vehicle as well as the tenor of class identity' with gender being 'crucial to the making of classes as economic determinations' (Dimock and Gilmore 1994, 7).

Intimacies

This book grapples with the 'tense and tender' ties between characters from divergent socio-economic milieus and with the intimate frontiers of class in a profoundly unequal and patriarchal social setting.[2] The 'intimate class acts' of the title refer to ties and 'contacts' of various kinds—romantic, platonic, and sexual. My approach to the question of cross-class intimacy echoes Pratt's (1992, 7) 'contact' perspective within the context of colonial relations, which 'emphasizes how subjects are constituted in and by their relations to each other. It treats the relations among colonizers and colonized, or travelers and "travelees," not in terms of separateness or apartheid, but in terms of copresence, interaction, interlocking understandings and practices, often within radically asymmetrical relations of power.' This asymmetry of class power is essential to my analysis, for in examining cross-class intimacy, I am not discounting the antagonism between divergent classes or the sexes, nor am I attempting to push hierarchical considerations to the background. On the contrary, as Ann Stoler (2006, 13; italics in the original) explains, '*to study the intimate is not to turn away from structures of dominance but to relocate their conditions of possibility and relations and forces of production*'.

I am specifically interested in two types of intimacy: heterosexual romantic love and female friendship. Pierre Bourdieu (2001, 109) has examined the ambiguous possibilities of heterosexual love vis-à-vis patriarchy: 'Is love an exception, the only one, but of first order of magnitude, to the law of masculine domination, a suspension of symbolic violence, or is it the supreme—because the most

[2] I am borrowing here the title of Stoler's 2001 essay 'Tense and Tender Ties: The Politics of Comparison in North American History and (Post) Colonial Studies'.

subtle, the most invisible—form of that violence?' By extension, could inter-class, heterosexual love entail the suspension of at once masculine domination and socio-economic hierarchy? Or, on the contrary, does it dissimulate these inequalities, precluding even the possibility of contesting them? In particular, I am interested in exploring the dynamics of cross-class relationship between upper-class women and subaltern men.

Romantic love has long been the trope par excellence of social transgression and defiance because, as Eva Illouz (1997, 10) explains, 'it reenacts symbolically the rituals of opposition to the social order through inversion of social hierarchies and affirms the supremacy of the individual'. Now, despite the recent and relative 'democratization of intimacy' in urban centres in South Asia, especially in India, marriage in the Indian subcontinent is still primarily a collective, rather than an individual, act implicating the family and the community of the couple (Kapur 2010, 54). Romantic love between individuals belonging to different classes is therefore often perceived as a double threat to the status quo: it breaches both class hierarchies and societal conventions pertaining to marriage and coupling.

Female friendship is the other kind of intimacy examined in this book. While I do use the term 'inter-class/cross-class friendship', my analysis is sensitive to the paradox that it presents. Notably, Aristotle (2014, 1159) has pointed out that 'in friendship equality is primarily equality in quantity and secondarily equality in worth. This is made clear when a great disparity in virtue, vice, resources, or something else comes about, since then the parties are no longer friends and do not even claim that they deserve to be.' I will evaluate the validity of the label 'friend' in the texts examined in this book, especially when it is deployed by an upper-class character to refer to a subaltern character. The use of the term 'friendship' is also complicated by other identitary gaps between the characters, such as that of age.

Social relations between women have always been allowed a certain laxity within society, as much in the 'West' as in the 'East'. As Foucault (1997, 139) explains within the European context, unlike intimacy between men, female intimacy was something that has been accepted and 'tolerated' by society:

Women do each other's hair, help each other with make up, dress each other. Women have had access to the bodies of other women: they put their arms around each other, kiss each other. Man's body has been forbidden to other men in a much more drastic way. If it's true that life between women was tolerated, it's only in certain periods and since the nineteenth century that life between men not only was tolerated but rigorously necessary: very simply, during war.

In the context of the Indian subcontinent, historically, among the elites, domestic (feminine) spaces were further divided into masculine and feminine spaces (referred to in northern India as '*antahpur, andarmahal*, or *zenana*' where women were necessarily in each other's constant company (Chaudhuri 2011, 88; italics in the original). Unlike heterosexual intimacy, the codes of friendship between women are not explicitly dictated by patriarchy. Yet, as we will see, even if female friendship is neither controlled not exposed to surveillance, the way that heterosexual relationships are, it does not exist in a social vacuum. It needs to be understood in the context of various sources of inequality, including the caste system, which is a highly structured mode of social stratification, but also with respect to class hierarchies, which though less institutionalized, are no less important.

According to Louise Bernikow (1980, 119), there is a clear distinction between female and male friendships: in particular, friendship among women is central to the construction of female identity:

Their eyes are forward, like the eyes of men marching to war, fixed not on each other but on what is out there. They are shoulder to shoulder. Female friends are more often eye to eye. It is the creation of 'us' that is important, we two—and in this very different arrangement lie the great depths and the great raptures of our friendship.

Toni Morrison (Tate 1994) too has argued in an interview that the friendship between women is 'extraordinary, different' compared to male friendship, and Elizabeth Abel (1981, 416) contends that 'through the intimacy which is knowledge, friendship becomes a vehicle of self-definition for women, clarifying identity through relation to an other who embodies and reflects an essential aspect of the self'. In my analysis, I will look at whether depiction of female friendship between women from divergent socio-economic backgrounds confirms these claims about the intrinsically 'extraordinary' nature of female friendship and the extent to which it brings in its wake a dissipation of alterity and Otherness.

Outline of the Book

The first chapter is an analysis of the portrayal of the relationship between an elite female child and a maid in three Pakistani novels: *Ice-Candy-Man, The Hope Chest*, and *The End of Innocence*. I examine the extent to which the young age of the bourgeois child allows the relationship to be less tainted and conditioned by class constraints than adult relationships. Equally of interest is how the maid's character is infantilized and how her beauty (and the elite child's relative lack of physical attractiveness) may work to contest or shift social hierarchies. The symbolic use of the servant within the text as a conduit of sexual discovery and class socialization is also explored. Finally, the ramifications of the timing and the events preceding the end of the friendship are examined to evaluate what they reveal about the challenges of maintaining a relationship which breaches class divisions in the Indian subcontinent.

I build on my exploration of female relationships across class in the second chapter by analysing Deshpande's and Umrigar's portrayal of the close emotional bond between adult women from a widely different class positioning. Central to the representation of the cross-class female 'friendship' in these texts is a reflection on traditional 'female' roles and the plight of women in India. As I will show, these novels question, explicitly as well as implicitly, the degree to which the awareness, or indeed the actual experience of patriarchal oppression in its many forms, brings women from disparate socio-economic backgrounds closer together, providing them with a strategy of resistance and survival in a deeply hostile social environment. I examine the spatial setting of the 'friendship' which straddles the public and private spheres, with the geography of the relationship playing a major part in defining it. Also of interest is the constant, often painful, tug between class loyalties and human affection in the texts, particularly in Umrigar's novel. The cross-class relationship between Sera and Bhima in *The Space Between Us* and Shakuntala and Urmila in *The Binding Vine* seems to emerge and exist under an ever-present social gaze, and the reflexive aspect of the relationship, how the protagonists perceive each other and their bond, is examined to better understand the solidarity, or the lack thereof, between them.

The third chapter is an exploration of the depiction of cross-class heterosexual romance in *The God of Small Things* and *Salt and Saffron*. In both novels, the family is portrayed as a powerful private institution, embodying dominant public ideologies which determine the 'forbidden' nature of these relations and revealing how class in the Indian subcontinent is a familial rather than an individual identity marker. The representation of the liminality of the lovers in the two texts, which appears to make them more liable to breaching social coupling norms is analysed. I also consider the doubts of the lovers in *Salt and Saffron* about crossing Pakistan's 'great class divide' (Shamsie 2000, 60) and what this reveals about the politics of the text. Shamsie's novel narrates the story of two cross-class couples, and the insistence in the text on 'transgressive' nature of the relationship between Khaleel and Aliya who arguably share many class markers, is particularly problematic. I also consider the significance of the ending of the cross-class love story and its relation to the class politics of the text.

The fourth chapter focuses on the portrayal of a sexual affair or encounter between lower-class female employees and their male employers as depicted in *The Space Between Us*, *The God of Small Things*, and *The Hottest Day of the Year*. I examine the complex intersection of class hierarchy and patriarchy in the novels and the ambiguity of heterosexual relationships in a deeply hierarchical context, where desire may coexist with coercion, thereby seriously complicating the notion of consent. I look at the depiction of the consequences of this cross-class sexual intimacy for both the subaltern and the elite character, and evaluate the strategies of resistance employed by the subaltern. In Charry's and Umrigar's texts, the liaison results in the subaltern woman becoming pregnant. Her pregnancy and the very different approaches adopted by the two authors to the question of abortion are considered in detail, as they bring to the fore the complex relationship between sexual and economic freedom for subaltern women.

In the fifth chapter, I study the portrayal of romance in *Rich Like Us* and *The Inheritance of Loss* between characters whose class differences are less pronounced than those discussed in the earlier chapters; notably, the lovers, subaltern and elite alike, speak English. The two novels discussed in this chapter, especially Sahgal's *Rich Like Us*, are rare in their preoccupation with the daily, mundane challenges experienced by a cross-class couple over time, moving beyond familial obstacles to the couple's union and happiness. At the same time, the romance takes place within the context of significant political events of Indian history: the Gorkha nationalist movement in Desai's novel and the Partition of India and Emergency rule in Sahgal's text. I will evaluate if and how the cross-class romance becomes subsumed by the question of the nation, in the context of Jameson's (1986, 69) claim that all 'third-world texts' are essentially 'national allegories'.

Through the prism of the ten novels discussed in the previous chapters, the sixth and final chapter of the book examines the complex politics of writing cross-class dialogue in an 'elitist' language. I analyse the linguistic and literary techniques that the writers employ to narrate conversations between elite and subaltern characters, particularly conversations which cannot realistically take place in English. I evaluate whether the authors adopt different 'translation' strategies when narrating in English the speech of an upper-class character that is supposed to have taken place in a 'vernacular' language, and the ideological consequences of such a technique. I also evaluate the ways in which these literary and linguistic techniques may confirm or challenge social hierarchies as well as hierarchies *within* the narrative.

By addressing both the politics and poetics of narrating intimacy across class, my study engages with and builds on a still-nascent body of criticism within South Asian literary studies which underscores the significance of reading postcolonial works of fiction through a socio-economic lens, notably Tabish Khair's *Babu Fictions* (2001) and Pranav Jani's *Decentering Rushdie* (2010). Significantly, this monograph insists on interpreting the subaltern characters in relation rather than in isolation to the Babu characters, so as to arrive at a nuanced understanding of how both subalternity and privilege are constructed and lived in the anglophone Indian and Pakistani novel by women writers.

1

Ayahs and Playmates in *Ice-Candy-Man*, *The Hope Chest*, and *The End of Innocence*

The powerful are stupid … masters are stupid in relation to servants, men in relation to women, adults in relation to children, the rich in relation to the poor….

—Suniti Namjoshi*

Intimate interaction between members of polarized social classes in the Indian subcontinent begins, in many cases, during early childhood for the bourgeois or upper-class child whose primary carer is often a young, lower-class girl. Close encounters across class may also commence early in life for impoverished girls and boys who become the playmates of socio-economically privileged children in whose homes their parents or other adults of the family are employed. If, as Ann Laura Stoler (2002, 119) argues, children embody adult culture only 'in partial and imperfect ways', their socialization into class roles is by definition incomplete, and childhood arguably brings with it greater potential for the transgression of socio-economic boundaries. At the heart of the three Pakistani novels examined in this chapter lies the affective relationship between a young servant girl and an economically privileged female child, inviting a reflection on how age and class identities (which in turn intersect with the gendered norms of a patriarchal society) may inform the complexion as well as the longevity of emotional ties.

* Quoted in Namjoshi (2000, 74).

Class, Age, and 'Friendship'

In *Ice-Candy-Man*, Lenny is about four years old, while her caregiver Ayah is eighteen at the beginning of the text.[1] The age difference in *The End of Innocence* between fifteen-year-old Rani, the granddaughter of a servant, and eight-year-old Laila is not negligible either. This disparity between the characters is of particular relevance as it introduces into the relationship another hierarchy, having to do with seniority in years, which can potentially invert or weaken the status superiority stemming from socio-economic class. In Ahmad's *The Hope Chest*, on the other hand, Reshma, the gatekeeper's thirteen-year-old daughter, is friends with Shehzadi, the daughter of Reshma's father's employer. The lack of a significant age difference between them, as we will see later, underscores the extent to which the life chances of a young girl are dictated by her family's class. Unlike Ayah, Reshma and Rani are not servants themselves, but are nonetheless called upon to perform domestic chores in the upper-class home without being remunerated. In both these cases, the employers belong to the landed aristocracy, reflecting the fact that in a feudal setting the servant's entire family and even future generations are expected to submit to the landowners.

In Sidhwa's novel, Lenny is deeply attached to the young servant girl and one of her first childhood memories is that of Ayah pushing her stroller in pre-Partition Lahore (Sidhwa 1989 [1988], 2). It is important, as Ambreen Hai (2000, 420) explains, not to conflate an ayah in the Indian subcontinent and a nanny in advanced capitalist societies:

> An ayah is very much a servant and a drudge—poor, illiterate, homeless, with no rights or recourse to any higher court of appeal, and vulnerable to all forms of abuse, sexual or otherwise. In reality she would sleep on the floor in the children's room, attend to all their needs, be clothed in cast-offs, and have little time of her own.

[1] The narrative in Sidhwa's novel slows down in the months leading to and following the Partition of India. Lenny's eighth birthday coincides with the Partition of India in August 1947.

As opposed to the prototypical ayah described by Hai, Ayah in *Ice-Candy-Man* is a beautiful young woman, well-nourished, with a voluptuous body, who also possesses a certain degree of independence and spatial mobility. It is precisely this aspect of the characterization that led Hai to criticize Sidhwa for having romanticized Ayah's character. I would argue, however, that Sidhwa *is* conscious that Ayah's situation is not representative of the lot of most lower-class women of the subcontinent. She describes, for instance, the role played by the cook who works at Lenny's house in nurturing Ayah's looks as he plies her with rich, delicious food, without which she would be no different from other 'stringy, half-starved women' of her class (Sidhwa 1989 [1988], 58). Moreover, her spatial freedom can be attributed to Lenny's poliomyelitis which prevents her from attending school, and her need to be entertained serves as a pretext for Ayah to spend time with her friends: 'I gain Ayah's goodwill and complicity by accommodating her need to meet friends and relatives. She takes me to fairs, cheap restaurants and slaughter-houses. I cover up for her and maintain a canny silence about her doings. I learn of human needs, frailties, cruelties and joys' (Sidhwa 1989 [1988], 20).

Given the age difference between them, Ayah can realistically feel only affection and a sense of responsibility towards the little girl, rather than friendship. But there also exists an element of reciprocity, albeit implicit, in their relationship. As we have just seen, it is because of Ayah that Lenny is able to taste the forbidden delights of the adult world; and Ayah, thanks to Lenny, enjoys a degree of freedom and mobility within her own class that would not be available to her otherwise. This complicity between Ayah and Lenny springs from a shared tacit realization: that both of them, in different ways, are subject to the authority of Lenny's parents.

However, Lenny also imagines other affinities between them of which Ayah is oblivious. For example, when Lenny's cousin makes amorous advances towards her and Ayah reprimands him, Lenny interprets Ayah's reaction as a reciprocal gesture in response to her having checked Ice-candy-man as he attempted to slip his toes up Ayah's sari. Lenny's attachment to Ayah also manifests itself in feelings of jealousy, particularly when she learns of Ayah's intention to get married to the masseur. Ayah reacts to Lenny's fit of possessiveness with: 'Silly girl, I won't leave you ... and even if I have to, you'll find another Ayah who will love you just as much' (Sidhwa 1989 [1988], 158). While Ayah indulgently attempts to reassure her, she is under no illusion as to her own role in Lenny's life: she is a servant who can and will be replaced. According to Rollins (1985, 218), 'domestics, indeed, know the Other. And domestics know the meaning of their own lives.' As I will demonstrate later in the chapter, despite Lenny's young age and despite her referring to Ayah as her friend, she too is aware of Ayah's (class) Otherness.

Rani in *The End of Innocence* lives with her grandmother in the servant quarters of the haveli belonging to Sardar Begum (Laila's grandmother) in a village. Laila and her sister Sara, who live in Lahore, visit the village during school holidays, spending most of their time with Rani. Laila is devoted to the young girl, believing that 'Rani alone had the unique ability to make the everyday wondrous and the dull delightful.... She knew how to mend a parrot's broken wing or get a wild squirrel to eat off her hand.... She could do cartwheels, climb to the top of the tallest tree and weave stories' (Mohsin 2006, 11). Rani is aware not only of the age difference between them, but also of the very large socio-economic gap that separates them. When the novel opens, Laila is sent to the countryside to recover from typhoid and hopes to take advantage of Sara's absence to consolidate her relationship with Rani who she knows sees her more like an 'acolyte' than a friend (Mohsin 2006, 12).

Given their similar age, Reshma and Shehzadi's relationship in *The Hope Chest*, in contrast to the other two examined in this chapter, *can* arguably be described as a friendship, even if the 'geography' of their relationship reveals its hierarchical character. As children at the outset of the novel, they play together either in the fields belonging to Shehzadi's family or at her house, but never in the servant quarters where Reshma lives. In the entire narrative, Shehzadi enters the servant quarters on only two occasions: the first time is when Reshma's younger sister is 'declared' dead, and her second visit occurs several years later when Reshma is sent back to her parents' home by her husband. As Beverley (1999, 2) explains, the subaltern 'designates a subordinated *particularity*, and in a world where power relations are spatialized, that means it must have a spatial referent, a form of territoriality'. As we will see later, if Shehzadi's mother Shahana tolerates her presence in the house while she is little, as they approach adolescence, she becomes increasingly vocal in her disapproval of their friendship.

Cross-Class Ties and Divided Loyalties

Laila is shown to constantly find herself in conflict with her grandmother's snobbery. Firmly believing that familiarity breeds contempt, Sardar Begum reprimands her granddaughter for giving, what she deems to be, excessive importance to the servants in general and to Rani in particular: 'You give them ideas above their station' (Mohsin 2006, 182). When Sardar Begum takes a severe tone with Rani, Laila accuses her of being 'mean' (Mohsin 2006, 59); and at the cinema, when Laila discovers that separate rows have been designated for the servants, she pleads with her grandmother to allow Rani to sit next to her. Aware of her strong disapproval of servants eating or drinking in the presence of their masters, it is only upon Laila's insistence that Rani dares to drink tea in Sardar Begum's presence.

However, the text makes a clear distinction between Sardar Begum's attitude towards domestic servants and Laila's parents' treatment of class subalterns. Laila's grandmother's mores are blatantly feudal: she expects complete submission not only from her servants, but also from their children and grandchildren. If in *Ice-Candy-Man* Lenny's family switches to English when discussing the servants in their presence, Sardar Begum does not deem such circumlocution necessary and speaks of them 'as if they were absent. Or perhaps inanimate' (Mohsin 2006, 148). However, Mohsin problematically presents Laila's parents, Fareeda and Tariq, as 'urban' liberals possessing a distinctly different sensibility from Sardar Begum (Mohsin 2006, 58). Therefore, rather than Laila the child clashing with the adults of the family, the text underscores the supposed differences between urban and rural class values and attitudes. While Sardar Begum's servants are overworked and underpaid, Fareeda and Tariq are depicted as being generous towards their help and the peasants cultivating their fields. They are also shown to be averse to the idea of child servants—a testimony to their urban liberalism (Mohsin 2006, 58). Tariq has set up a garments factory which functions as a cooperative providing gainful employment to the young women of the village. In the novel, then, it is the Babu class, embodied by Laila's parents, who collectively voice a discourse that is both socialist *and* feminist—despite the fact that Tariq is a zamindar who continues to protect his feudal heritage, from which he and his family draw full benefit. Moreover, Tariq upholds nationalist, democratic, and anti-imperialist values which he voices at his English neighbour's house, obscuring the pivotal role that the British played in the consolidation of the feudal or zamindari system in India.[2]

Therefore, while the text appears to criticize feudal attitudes and modes of behaviour as embodied in Sardar Begum, it nonetheless does not condemn structural feudalism; neither does it recognize the collusion between urban and rural elites in Pakistan. Furthermore, distinction in the Bourdieusian sense, which is to say the sophisticated gastronomic, literary, and sartorial tastes of the urban, anglicized elites, coincide with moral rectitude in the novel. For instance, it is Tariq who pays for Rani's schooling, and it was upon his insistence that Rani was allowed to attend school against her grandmother's wishes. Thus, the text underscores the humanity of Laila's parents towards Rani, implying that Laila and her parents share the same 'urban' world view and that it is only with adults like Sardar Begum that Laila is in conflict. Laila's egalitarian attitude is portrayed to be a natural attribute of an 'innocent' child who is not contaminated with prejudice against the lower classes, and the novel hermetically preserves Laila's class innocence, discounting the socialization into class roles that begins in early childhood, as has been explored by Sidhwa and Ahmad.

[2] As Barbara Pozzo (2008, 49; italics in the original) explains,

[W]hile feudalism in Europe was slowly declining during the 18th and 19th centuries as a way of structuring social and in particular agricultural relationships, the English rulers consolidated the *zamindari system* as an instrument of land administration that persisted into the 20th century. Under the *zamindari* or *permanent settlement* system, introduced around 1793, lords were declared proprietors of the land on condition of fixed revenue payments to the British regime. Peasants were transformed into tenant farmers, and rents were collected by a range of intermediaries below the level of the *zamindars*.

Moreover, in *The Hope Chest*, Ahmad explicitly grapples with the ways in which a cross-class friendship can pose a challenge to the status quo. Shahana does not object to her daughter spending time with Reshma while she is a little girl; she arguably even uses Reshma as a source of cost-free entertainment for Shehzadi. As her daughter enters her teenage years, however, she seeks to re-establish the 'natural' order of things by putting an end to the relatively 'democratic' interaction that she has allowed so far. As the following extract illustrates, Shahana deploys a number of fencing-off techniques, including the use of the English language, to clearly demarcate class divisions which she fears have become blurred with Reshma's presence inside her house in the capacity of Shehzadi's playmate: '"What was she doing here? Hasn't she gone yet?" She would ask in English. Despite the flimsy cover of English, Reshma always understood the frown and her large frame would shrink visibly in an effort to vanish. Inevitably it embarrassed both girls' (Ahmad 1996, 10). In addressing Shehzadi in English, the language of the elites, Shahana is not attempting to mask her disapproval of Reshma's class inferiority. On the contrary, it is meant to accentuate the class differences between them. As Tolen (2000, 77) explains, employers seek to maintain an upper hand through claiming greater mastery of symbolically valued practices, with English functioning 'as a privileged code, whose monopoly is claimed by the upper class'. By deploying an elite language, Shahana reminds Shehzadi of everything that distinguishes her from her lower-class friend, and seeks to put Reshma 'in her place', lest she forget her inferior social status. Reshma, whose life is characterized by material hardship and deprivation, is fully aware of class divisions and is in no need of a reminder. The few hours that she spends at Shehzadi's house, an air-conditioned domestic space, markedly different from the servant quarters, is perhaps the only time when she can savour physical comfort. As Professor Superb in Mohsin Hamid's (2000, 102–3) *Moth Smoke* observes, access to air-conditioning in the humid, extreme heat of Punjab is an important marker of class privilege.

Upon being humiliated by Shahana, Reshma shortens her visits to Shehzadi's home, but, and it is important to point this out, she never complains to Shehzadi about Shahana's insulting behaviour, indicating once more her awareness of the imbalance in their relationship. Shehzadi tacitly resists her mother's orders, but, while begging Reshma to prolong her stay, does not explicitly apologize for her mother's rudeness. Her pleas aimed at persuading Reshma to extend her visits stem at least partially from selfish reasons—she does not want to lose a playmate. But it also indicates that Shehzadi does not (as yet) see Reshma *only* as a class subaltern and has not completely internalized the class boundaries that dictate human relationships in society. As Stoler (2002, 119) points out, children 'learn certain normative conventions and not others and frequently defy the divisions that adults are wont to draw'. While continuing to spend time with Reshma, and despite her unease with her mother's classist behaviour, Shehzadi does not question the 'logic' of the discriminatory attitude that her elders adopt towards the servants. Recalling that her older sister had played with servants in the fields 'until she grew up', Shehzadi reminds herself: 'I'll *have to* stop soon, too, Nani Ma has been hinting though she hasn't imposed a ban this year' (Ahmad 1996, 67; italics mine).[3] The use of the future tense of the verb 'have to' suggests that Shehzadi has internalized the socially constructed 'inevitability' of this separation.

In *Ice-Candy-Man*, Lenny is never seen to be in conflict with the adults of her family about her relationship with servants in general and Ayah in particular. However, the fact that from a very young age Lenny's care was handed over to ayahs does not indicate her family's complete faith in servants. Lenny hears her mother blaming herself for her deformed leg: 'I'm to blame,' she says, 'I left her to the ayahs' (Sidhwa 1989 [1988], 8). This remark reveals her guilt at neglecting to attend to her own child as well as at choosing to entrust lower-class, and by implication 'unsuitable', women with her care. Indeed, female staff occupies a paradoxical place within bourgeois domestic spaces. As Theresa McBride (1978, 52) explains, in the context of Victorian society, the female servant provided a cushion against the inconveniences of urban life and spared bourgeois parents from the burden of caring for their own children, but her presence was also considered troublesome because she created tensions within the home and evoked fears about the health and well-being of the children. Lenny's mother

[3] Nani Ma (Urdu), refers to maternal grandmother.

faces a similar 'dilemma', but, notwithstanding her feelings of guilt, she never considers dismissing Ayah.

In spite of her very young age, and her love for Ayah, Lenny unquestioningly accepts certain class boundaries in the geography of her own home and thus aligns herself with the class values of the adults in her family. Consider the following passage from the novel: 'Aware of the impropriety of entertaining her guest on the front lawn, Ayah leads us to settle on a bald patch of grass at the back near the servants' quarters' (Sidhwa 1989 [1988], 28). The sentence structure of this seemingly innocuous observation suggests that neither the text nor Lenny considers challenging the supposed 'intrinsic' impropriety of a servant entertaining her lower-class guests on the scrupulously maintained and manicured front lawn, a space which is clearly upper class. This facile acceptance of class norms reveals the ideological socialization of the child. After all, ideology is, as Eagleton (1976, 5) points out, 'that complex structure of social perceptions which ensures that the situation in which one social class has power over the others is either seen by most members of society as "natural" or not seen at all'. On the other hand, Lenny is aware that her family benefits from Ayah's many working-class admirers. For instance, they frequently receive silk and linen household items as gifts from Ayah's Chinese admirer, and it is her Pathan suitor who sharpens all the knives of the house, at no charge (Sidhwa 1989 [1988], 457). If the threshold of the bourgeois household is closely monitored to prevent the entry of socio-economically 'undesirable' visitors, this threshold proves to be remarkably permeable when it is a question of services and goods provided by Ayah's lower-class admirers. However, neither Lenny nor Ayah is shown to be conscious of this paradox, which might indicate that they perceive this contradictory, if not hypocritical, attitude towards class Others as 'normal'.

Moreover, Lenny has already begun to recognize the visible markers of social status. She reads Ice-candy-man's body language in class terms when he takes on 'the cock' posture to seek Ayah's forgiveness, after making innuendo-ridden remarks: 'Ice-candy-man coils forward to squat and, threading his supple arms through his calves from the back, latches on to his ear lobes. It is a punishing posture called "the cock" used in Urdu-medium schools to discipline urchins' (Sidhwa 1989 [1988], 30). Lenny is able to identify this as a 'lower-class' form of apology and already understands that Urdu-medium schools are meant for the lower classes who cannot afford the elite schools where English is the medium of instruction. The English-medium/local-school dichotomy, developed by the British, has become even more accentuated in contemporary Pakistan, where this parallel system of schooling not only reflects, but also reinforces, socio-economic inequalities (Rahman 2005, 25–7).[4]

Lenny is particularly sensitive to the visible markers that distinguish upper-class women from their lower-class counterparts. She is able to tell, for example, that Ayah's saris are made with 'cheap' cloth (Sidhwa 1989 [1988], 3); and that her mother's decision to wear her hair short, as an anglicized, 'westernized' woman, is a sign of independence, whereas a similar haircut worn by a lower-class Muslim woman indicates a coarse upbringing. Lenny's visit to Lahore's red-light area with Godmother in search of Ayah, shows how she positions the women she encounters there on the class hierarchy: 'The bold girls with short, permed hair, showing streaks of stale make-up.... Their crumpled kamizes are too short and the pencha-bottoms of their shalwars too wide. *Even I can see that they are not well brought up*. I have never seen women *of this class* with cropped and frizzed hair; nor using the broad and comfortable gestures of men' (Sidhwa 1989 [1988], 259; italics mine).

Lenny displays her understanding of what is considered to be appropriate behaviour for working-class women; she knows that 'well brought up' women of a lower-class milieu are expected to show reserve in their clothing and body language. What shocks Lenny about these women is not that they do not behave or dress like upper-class women, but that they transgress the specific gendered norms dictating *their own socio-economic milieu*. Notably, despite her young age, she demonstrates a subtle understanding

[4] As Tariq Rahman (2005, 25–7) explains, 'the state has invested heavily in creating a parallel system for the elite, especially the elite that would presumably run elitist state institutions in future. This leads to the conclusion that the state does not trust its own system of education and spends public funds to create and maintain the parallel, elitist system of schooling.'

of how the code of conduct varies not only from one class to another, but also according to other systems of stratification, including gender and age. This understanding is no doubt facilitated by the presence of female servants at her house since 'the relationships between family members and servants form a crucial medium by which the psychological terrain of class and sexist practices is nourished' (Rubbo and Taussig 1983, 14). In fact, the discriminatory treatment of female servants within the bourgeois home 'prepares its children to fulfil their future roles as leaders and perpetuators of a sexist, class-divided society' (Rubbo and Taussig 1983, 14).

Knowing Material Deprivation

Sidhwa's text does not broach the feelings of deprivation that Ayah may experience as a lower-class woman working for an upper-class family or the resentment that she may feel as a result of it. In *The Hope Chest*, however, Ahmad delineates in detail Reshma's poverty-stricken existence before her marriage. The minority status discourse of childhood identified in the writings of James et al. (1998, 210) suggests that all children, by virtue of being powerless and voiceless, are members of a marginalized class. Ahmad's portrayal of lower-class childhood, however, echoes the work of sociologists such as Michael Lavalette (1999, 22) who argue that 'children's lives have been and will continue to be shaped by experiences, restrictions and barriers consequential of the class into which they are born, their gender and their "race"'. Shehzadi and Reshma present an example of 'nurtured' versus 'nurturing' children, respectively: while 'nurtured' children are 'an endless expense' and are 'highly differentiated from older members of society, nurturing children take on the responsibility of adults progressively from a young age' (Hecht 1998, 92). Reshma as the eldest daughter spends most of her time attending to her younger siblings and helping her mother with housework. Apart from the physical comfort afforded by air-conditioning, the time spent with Shehzadi gives Reshma an opportunity to play and thus experience life as a child, indicating the extent to which the very notion of childhood is determined by class.

Ahmad's text also explores hunger as a fundamental and poignant marker of socio-economic class. She describes, for instance, the deprivation experienced by Reshma's family during a period of famine. In a particularly powerful scene, this deprivation is brought into sharp relief against the excess that characterizes Shehzadi life. Reshma, while playing a board game with Shehzadi, is unable to concentrate as she has not had a proper meal in days. Painfully preoccupied by the delectable aromas and sounds emanating from the kitchen, the act of playing becomes an arduous task for Reshma, requiring a monumental effort on her part to suppress the agonizing pangs of hunger:

> As the *pooras* were fished out of the sizzling oil, their enticing smell racked her teeth with longing and filled her mouth with saliva but she concentrated on the game, pretending with great dignity to be indifferent to that luscious smell. For the past two weeks there had not been any oil or butter in their house for Rehmat Bibi to even coat the bread thinly with it. For the whole of the past month they had not eaten anything sweet. (Ahmad 1996, 55–6)

Shehzadi has never experienced such lack and has never known hunger. She sees the snack as an unwanted interruption to the ongoing board game. Moreover, delicacies like *poora*s are a part of her everyday life and she is unable to grasp their significance for Reshma; nor has she any notion of Reshma's physical suffering stemming from starvation, which underscores the limitations of their friendship (Ahmad 1996, 56). Ahmad compels the reader to revisit the conventionally accepted idea of childhood and joy through play within the context of extreme poverty where children go hungry. When struggling with 'nutritional, health and housing problems', play for children inevitably becomes 'secondary' (Roopnarine et al. 1994, 9).

The visit to the cinema in *The End of Innocence* highlights the variety of ways that class differences between Rani and Laila manifest themselves and the deprivation that characterizes Rani's life. This trip has extraordinary significance for Rani who 'never went anywhere': it is the first time that she will enter a cinema hall (Mohsin 2006, 10). Dazzled by the lights and the high ceiling, Rani finds it 'wonderful' (Mohsin 2006, 18). Laila is not impressed by the village cinema which is 'smaller than her auditorium at school' (Mohsin 2006, 17–18). Given her mother's disapproval of the 'vulgar dances with heaving and panting heroines' in mainstream Pakistani cinema, Laila's cinema-going so far had been confined to English-language films (Mohsin 2006, 10). Unlike Bollywood films, whose audience cuts across socio-economic boundaries (Kakar 1990, 25), popular Pakistani cinema caters mainly to working-class men (Qureshi 2010, 185–6), which explains why Rani makes an elaborate effort to convince Laila that the film is worthy of her interest so that she can, in turn, persuade Sardar Begum to allow them to go. Rani draws on numerous Babu-class markers to reassure her that the film would be to her taste. For instance, to alleviate the Otherness of Pakistani cinema and to demonstrate its affinity with Laila and her parents' cultural and aesthetic sensibilities, Rani informs Laila that the lead actors of the film 'is married to that famous singer who has a big house in the best part of Lahore, where [her] Lahore grandmother lives also.... He speaks English and wears jacket suits' (Mohsin 2006, 10). She is seeking to demonstrate to Laila that even though *Heer Ranjha* is not an English-language film, the actors are westernized, urban Babus like Laila and her parents.[5]

However, what convinces Laila to go the cinema is the realization of the importance of this excursion for Rani, which also underscores her deep affection for her. Rather than an impoverished milieu, Laila attributes the lack of diversion in Rani's life to the fact that she lives with her 'dour' grandmother (Mohsin 2006, 10). As discussed, while Laila is shown to be aware of the gaping age difference between them, she is depicted to be unaware of the class differences separating her from Rani. The servant girl, however, is painfully conscious of the importance of money and the world of opportunities that it can open up: 'The things that Laila and Sara spoke of—airports, swimming pools, circuses with Chinese acrobats—were as remote to her as the moon ... she would never see Lahore. Never ride in a train or wear high heels

[5] Masood Pervez's *Heer Ranjha* (1970) is a cinematographic adaptation of a folktale, popularized by Waris Shah in his poem 'Heer' (1766), a tale of two star-crossed lovers who die a tragic death.

or own a suitcase' (Mohsin 2006, 42). According to Rollins (1985, 232), 'domestics do exhibit the extreme consciousness of the Other that is characteristic of those in a subordinate position, and they do express the *ressentiment* of oppressed who do not accept the justness of their oppression'. Of the three subaltern characters explored in this chapter, Rani is the only one who reveals to her friend the reality of their 'friendship' and articulates her feelings of deprivation: 'I matter to you as Rani who lives in Kalanpur. I don't matter to you in school with all your friends who come in cars, or when you go to the cinema in Lahore, or when you're sitting in a hotel eating ice cream. Do I?' (Mohsin 2006, 66). The class markers that Rani evokes include not only material objects, but also a particular lifestyle. However, the question that Rani poses to Laila about her real importance in the little girl's life remains unanswered and becomes rhetorical by default, with Laila (on whose point of view the narrative is largely focused) being excused from having to respond to it because of her age and corresponding 'innocence'.

It is worth noting that in the text Rani is allowed to raise the subject of class differences only with Laila and not with her older sister who is not too young to be unaware of such 'adult' matters. Furthermore, even if Rani does speak to Laila about her marginality, she does not express her resentment vis-à-vis her friend's milieu: Rani indicates her marginal position *in comparison with*, rather than *in opposition to* Laila and her family. The text thus emphasizes the coexistence of disparate classes and its troubling consequences for human relationships; it does not address or acknowledge the exploitation that lies at the heart of any system of social stratification. In particular, the narrative does not recognize that the privileges enjoyed by Laila's feudal family exist *at the expense* of peasant families such as Rani's. While deploring the deprivation suffered by the poorest of the poor, the novel ultimately brings to the fore the sad inevitability of social inequity and avoids examining social structures founded on the systemic exploitation of one group by another.

Indeed, the criticism of 'rural' feudal values in *The End of Innocence*, which are presented as fundamentally different from urban, liberal values, precludes an exploration of how class relationships are lived in a city like Lahore. The narrative, in effect, neatly avoids a collision between Lahore and Kalanpur, the fictitious village where Rani is the only source of entertainment for Sara and Laila. On the one occasion when the sisters do try to organize a trip to Lahore for her, the idea is vetoed by Rani's grandmother. Therefore, the novel maintains a liminal space within the narrative, allowing this relationship across rigid class boundaries to develop and allowing also for it to be perceived as friendship, which is perhaps a tacit recognition of the improbability of this friendship outside a specific spatial and temporal context.

For Laila, her vacations in the countryside are a break from her everyday life in Lahore, but the spatiality of this friendship is anchored in Rani's daily life and is devoid of any exoticism for her. Instead, her interaction with Laila emphasizes her sense of deprivation—both material and emotional. Her father died when she was only a child and after her mother's second marriage, she had to move in with her grandmother, a strict and humourless woman. She feels emotionally neglected and socio-economically marginalized, especially when she compares herself to Laila, who is not only wealthy, but also adored by her parents and grandparents. Rani's affair with the first young man who pays her any attention, and who belongs to a higher socio-economic class than hers, seems to allow her to hope for and imagine a better life for herself (Mohsin 2006, 37). Very aware of the negative perception of domestic work, she is pained by the sad chasm between the meaning of her name ('queen' in Urdu) and her class positioning, a chasm that her lover seems to close by showering her with compliments. As she explains to Laila: 'When I am with him. I'm not Rani, the servant girl. I become someone else. Someone who matters. Like you and Sara' (Mohsin 2006, 66). Despite these explanations, Laila is shown to be unable to understand why the young man is so important to Rani. Therefore, once more, because of its focalization on the elite child's 'innocent' point of the view, the novel avoids engaging in a candid dialogue about the inequality of life chances and its consequences for human relations.

Infantilizing/Sexualizing the Maid

In *Ice-Candy-Man* and *The End of Innocence*, where a fairly large age difference separates the elite child and the servant, the seniority in years does not translate into more developed intellectual capacities. Therefore, age hierarchy is unable to shift socio-economic hierarchies in any tangible way. This portrayal demonstrates that, rather than age, it is an individual's socio-economic class that determines access to cultural capital, specifically the final two 'states' of cultural capital—the 'objectified' state in the form of cultural 'assets' such as books and paintings, and the 'institutionalized' state, which includes educational qualifications (Bourdieu 1986, 243). In particular, when the maid who is older than the elite child turns to her as a source of worldly information, it inverts, to a certain degree, the older-child–younger-child equation. The visit to the cinema in *The End of Innocence* is one such example. Rani understands that Laila's privileged lifestyle includes access to experiences that are denied to her, but she also overestimates the extent of Laila's knowledge when she asks her to explain how the film works. Laila, although a frequent cinema-goer, at the age of eight does 'not understand the mysteries of projection in enough detail to attempt an explanation' (Desai 2007 [2006], 18).

In *Ice-Candy-Man*, Lenny's partial assimilation of the prevailing classist ideology permits her to notice the stereotypical assumptions that dictate the behaviour of adults of her class towards servants, particularly in how they underestimate their intellectual capacities. She notices, for example, that her family members speak to each other in English when discussing Ayah in her presence: 'People spell out the letters thinking Ayah will not understand the alphabet. This occurs so frequently that she'd have to be a nitwit to not catch on' (Sidhwa 1989 [1988], 168). As Rubbo and Taussig (1983, 19) point out, 'servants tend to be reduced to a state of perpetual infantilism'. Lenny is conscious that her family infantilizes Ayah, even while making flattering comments about her (Sidhwa 1989 [1988], 168). However, while the text appears to criticize the condescending attitude of upper-class adults, the depiction of Ayah's intellect within the narrative nonetheless has the troubling effect of infantilizing her. For example, when the division of India becomes imminent, Lenny wonders whether India would be physically 'broken' (Sidhwa 1989 [1988], 92). Ayah's explanation of what Partition would entail echoes the naivety of her eight-year-old charge: 'They'll dig a canal.... This side for Hindustan and this side for Pakistan. If they want two countries, that's what they'll have to do' (Sidhwa 1989 [1988], 92).[6] This explanation does not appear to be an attempt on Ayah's part to present a 'vulgarized' version of the political situation to a child, but rather indicates what she actually believes. Sidhwa's depiction of Ayah's poor grasp of current affairs is particularly unconvincing since politics and current affairs are shown to be a regular topic of detailed discussion in Ayah's wide social circle. Perhaps Ayah's naive response to Lenny's question is an authorial device meant to echo and underscore her innocence and 'in-between' sexuality: she is not yet a woman, but no more a child. Nonetheless, it endows the subaltern with childish ignorance.

Furthermore, this infantilization is coupled with an eroticization of the servant's body. Within the context of the history of domestic servitude in Britain, Lucy Delap (2011, 174) has drawn our attention to the 'close relationship between domestic servants and sex, for instance the sexual insult "slut" was seventeenth-century shorthand for slattern or kitchen maid'. Sidhwa's portrayal of Ayah's sexuality echoes Delap's observation. It is while observing Ayah that, to quote the title of Stoler's (1995) book, the elite child's 'education of desire' begins. Focusing on Ayah's physical beauty and her overwhelming sexual appeal to the detriment of other aspects of her being, and making her the source of the elite child's sexual awakening, has the effect of objectifying the maid and accentuating her subalternity. This portrayal of the maid's sexuality seems to suggest that she is not capable (or qualified?) to impart any other kind of knowledge to the upper-class child. Lenny's erotic imagination is fuelled by the male attention directed at

[6] The infantilization of Ayah's character is even more striking in *Earth* (1998), the filmic adaptation of the book by Deepa Mehta. In the film, instead of Lenny, Ayah addresses Lenny's mother and shares with her fears of what Partition would entail. In response, Lenny's mother scolds her for her unsophisticated reading of the political events: '*Kya bakwas, Shanta*' (What rubbish, Shanta).

Ayah. In fact, even before becoming aware of Ayah's beauty, Lenny discovers the effect it has on men. She remarks at the beginning of the text: 'The covetous glances Ayah draws educate me' (Sidhwa 1989 [1988], 3). Closely monitoring Ayah's interaction with her lovers, her behaviour becomes a yardstick for Lenny to understand her own feelings for the opposite sex (Sidhwa 1989 [1988], 228). Furthermore, Lenny's gaze alighting on Ayah's voluptuous body often mirrors the gaze of her male admirers: 'Up and down, they look at her.... Hawkers, cart-drivers, cooks, coolies, and cyclists turn their heads as she passes ... she has a rolling bouncy walk that agitates the globules of her buttocks ... and the half-spheres beneath her short sari-blouses' (Sidhwa 1989 [1988], 3). Lenny is aware of living vicariously through her ayah, as she attempts to participate in her sexual escapades: '"Massage me!" I demand, kicking the handsome masseur.... They are knowing fingers, very clever and sometimes, late in the evening, when he and Ayah and I are alone, they massage Ayah under her sari' (Sidhwa 1989 [1988], 19). On several occasions, Lenny even seems to confuse herself with Ayah's person. For example, where monitoring Ice-candy-man's toes, which he persistently attempts to slip under the maid's sari, she recounts: 'Sometimes, in the course of an engrossing story, they travel so cautiously that *both* Ayah and I are taken unawares' (Sidhwa 1989 [1988], 37; italics mine).

Lenny's romantic desires are deeply mimetic, informed by Ayah's experiences. But the idea of romance for her is also fraught with anxiety as she is conscious of her physical 'flaws'. Young as she is, Lenny understands that in her society, marriage is the only criterion of success for women and she is often reminded of being at a disadvantage because of her dark skin (Sidhwa 1989 [1988], 85). Interestingly, Lenny does not see a contradiction between the stereotypical conception of beauty and Ayah's visible popularity, despite her dark skin, with men of all classes, religions, and races. While recounting Ayah's beauty, Lenny describes her as being 'chocolate' coloured (Sidhwa 1989 [1988], 3, 18) and evokes the devastating effect of the 'brown gleam' of her belly on her many admirers (Sidhwa 1989 [1988], 100). At no point in the text does Lenny question the validity of the cultural equivalence that is drawn between a fair skin and success in the romantic arena, perhaps because the socio-economic inferiority of the servant and her Hindu religion—Lenny is Parsi—create a clear sense of social alterity. Lenny does not question the aesthetic values of her milieu in the light of the events of Ayah's life and neither Lenny nor the text applies the same criteria of beauty to a domestic servant as to a bourgeois woman.

Sidhwa's novel brings to the fore Ayah's Otherness with respect not only to Lenny, but also to other upper-class women in the text who are spared from sexual violence during India's Partition. If Sidhwa alludes to the domestic violence that Lenny's father inflicts upon his wife, the narrative does not allow itself to address the possibility of the violation of an upper-class female body in public spaces. Rather it is Ayah, a dark-skinned, lower-class Hindu woman, who becomes the victim of public violence and is reduced in the text to a symbol of the conflict between Hindus and Muslims in 1947. The narrative, as Ambreen Hai (2000, 391) points out,

> ends up rendering the class and ethnically inscribed figure of the ayah both expendable and usable for its own purposes.... The border—as limit—then becomes literalized as the body of a female Hindu domestic servant, the only site upon which the unspeakable can be permitted to happen.... In fact the work that this working-class woman does in the narrative is to become the epitome of absolute otherness, the 'other' of the other.

The sexualization of Ayah's body together with the infantilization of her intellectual capacities reduces her to a symbol of an essentially victim sexuality. It also accentuates her class Otherness, even as the text ostensibly condemns such reductionism.

Beauty and Class

The subaltern female characters examined in this chapter share one important characteristic: all three are strikingly beautiful. Arguably, the beauty of the subaltern character works to demystify the stereotypical notion that physical beauty, like moral rectitude, is a 'natural' characteristic of the wealthy. As Namjoshi (2000, 9) comments ironically in *Goja*, 'servants by definition are not supposed to be beautiful. It is not their prerogative.' But if, by endowing the maids with good looks, the authors appear to be subverting classist clichés, ultimately both *Ice-Candy-Man* and *The End of Innocence* bring to the fore the ways in which beauty increases, rather than diminishes, the vulnerability of lower-class females. It exposes them to exploitation and sexual violence at the hands of lower-class men: Ayah becomes a symbol of her Hindu identity and is abducted and raped by her former Muslim admirers, and Rani's beauty draws the attention of a young man who, after seducing and impregnating her, abandons her.

In *The Hope Chest* the implications of the servant's beauty depart from the other two texts, as Ahmad explores how aesthetic hierarchy intersects and complicates social-economic hierarchies. Shehzadi is acutely aware of Reshma's stunning beauty and fair skin. Preference for a light skin colour pervades all strata of South Asian society as it works to improve a young girl's chances in the marriage market. In the region, dark skin along with thinness are '"the most tangible physical expressions of suffering and rejection" and are also associated with the impoverished poor classes who have poor diets and toil in the long hot sun' (Philips 2004, 259). Shahana is dismayed at her daughters' dark colouring, which according to her makes them look like the 'children of the poorest farm workers' who work her family's lands (Ahmad 1996, 19). If dark colouring is associated with socio-economic deprivation, Reshma's lighter skin arguably has the potential to shift class hierarchies. As the following lines demonstrate, Shehzadi compares herself unfavourably to her friend: 'She looked at her own hands, dull and dark in the bright sunlight, and thought how lucky Reshma was to be so fair. She would surely get a good match. Her parents wouldn't be worrying about her the way Shahana had to worry about Rani' (Ahmad 1996, 36–7). Shehzadi's feelings of inferiority are intimately tied in with her future marital prospects. This concern reveals, first of all, that the patriarchal norms that define marriage and motherhood as the ultimate, desirable goal of a woman's life are prevalent across socio-economic classes. However, in the lines quoted earlier, when Shehzadi starts thinking about marriage, she compares Reshma to her elder sister Rani and not to herself: Shehzadi knows that Reshma, who is the same age as Rani, will be married off far earlier. Even though Shahana's primary preoccupation in life is to find suitable husbands for her daughters, unlike Reshma, Shehzadi does experience a 'nurtured' childhood. Reshma, on the other hand, is married off at fourteen to Afsar, a shopkeeper in his thirties with several children, who pays 10,000 rupees for Reshma's hand in marriage. In arranging this marriage, Reshma's father hopes to ensure the survival of his family who have suffered a life of deprivation and lack. As sociological studies show, while cultural preferences are certainly an important factor in explaining the practice of child marriage, poverty and economic deprivation remain the primary causes for this phenomenon.[7] Ahmad, too, underscores the causal link between poverty and child marriage, and highlights the extent to which economic factors can reinforce patriarchal values and seriously limit the choices available to women. Reshma is chosen as a wife by Afsar for her beauty and youth. Without possessing the kind of wealth that Shehzadi's family does, he is financially more secure than Reshma's family. He is, in short, a 'good match' for Rani, as Shehzadi calls it. But Shehzadi knows only too well that the definition of the term 'good match' is not fixed and varies with the bride's class and social positioning. A man who is considered an eligible husband for Reshma, despite her socially constructed 'superior' colouring, would hardly be a good match for an upper-class though dark-skinned girl like Shehzadi's sister.

Unlike the other two texts, in *The Hope Chest* the subaltern's beauty arguably does allow her to be upwardly mobile: since her marriage to Afsar, she no longer belongs to the servant class. But hers is an example of 'marital' mobility as the change in her socio-economic positioning is entirely dependent on her husband, making her ascension a precarious one.[8] As Afsar's wife, she is significantly better fed and better dressed than before, but marriage brings for Reshma another kind of servitude. As a mere child of fourteen, she is made to do housework, attend to her husband's children from his previous marriage, as well as serve her large extended family-in-law. Thus, marriage deprives her even of the few moments of childhood that she enjoyed while living with her parents. More problematically, her husband rapes her on their wedding night and

7 See UNICEF's report 'Early Marriage: Child Spouses' (2001, 6).

8 For a detailed discussion of marital mobility, see Jones (1990, 104–9).

over the following years continues to force himself upon her. By the time she turns eighteen, Reshma has already had three children and is pregnant with her fourth. When he discovers that Reshma had an abortion and underwent a sterilization surgery, Afsar throws her out of the house, forcing her to return to her parents. Therefore, she is deprived not only of the material privileges that came with being his wife, but also of her children.

Unlike Reshma, Shehzadi's sister Rani is better equipped to manage the breakdown of her marriage because of the privileges of her class—not only her parents' money, but also the resulting cultural capital, especially her academic qualifications. Her divorce, then, is not synonymous with a regression in her socio-economic positioning. Ahmad's novel thus compels the reader to examine the intersection of patriarchy and the class system in Pakistan by demonstrating that the two systems of stratification often mutually reinforce each other.

End of the Friendship

In Sidhwa's and Mohsin's novels, the elite child's friendship with her subaltern friend ends under violent and socially 'dishonourable' circumstances for the maid; in fact, the depiction of the end of this cross-class friendship cannot be separated from the problematic portrayal of the subaltern's (social) death. In *The Hope Chest*, however, the narrative, spanning a period of several years, allows the author to explore the changes in Reshma and Shehzadi's relationship once they have transitioned into the adult world.

In *Ice-Candy-Man* and *The End of Innocence*, the child protagonist unwittingly betrays her friend and directly contributes to the ensuing tragedy. This betrayal highlights the dangerous intersection of the childish concerns of the elite character and the profoundly adult anxieties of the young subaltern. Following Partition, a Muslim mob arrives at Lenny's house demanding all Hindu servants to be handed over. Ice-candy-man, reassuring Lenny with promises to protect Ayah, compels her to reveal the location of Ayah's hiding place in the house. He hands Ayah over to the mob, which drags her away. The next time that Lenny sees Ayah is several months later, when she goes to the red-light area with Godmother to help Ayah escape from her forced marriage to the popsicle vendor. Lenny and Ayah's interaction is limited to an embrace. Traumatized and reticent, Ayah turns to Lenny's godmother to voice her desire to return to her family in India, even though she is unsure about the kind of welcome awaiting her.[9] Once she is brought to the 'recovered' women's camp, Ayah does not even seem to fully recognize Lenny: 'And I chant "Ayah! Ayah! Ayah! Ayah!" Until my heart pounds with the chant.... She looks up at us out of glazed and unfeeling eyes for a moment, as if we were strangers, and goes in again' (Sidhwa 1989 [1988], 273–4).

Arguably Ayah is struggling to recognize not only Lenny, but also herself as an ayah—her erstwhile profession. The violence that she was subjected to was not only of a sexual and physical nature, but was also a virulent attack on her identity. Following her abduction, she was violently gangraped by her former Muslim 'admirers' before being forced into prostitution. Moreover, Ice-candy-man compelled her to convert to Islam before marrying her. This multilayered violence is emblematic of his desire to possess and appropriate every aspect of Ayah's being: her body, her beliefs, even her name. If Ice-candy-man is the cause and source of Ayah's suffering, the text does not indicate whether Ayah is aware that it was Lenny who revealed her hiding place to him and effectively betrayed her. While Sidhwa describes at some length Lenny's feelings of guilt, there is no reference to the possible anger that Ayah might feel towards Lenny. The narrative clearly absolves her of all blame because of her young age and does not allow for the possibility that Ayah resents Lenny for her betrayal. Shame is presented as the only reason for her not wanting to see her former employer's family: 'I cannot believe Ayah wouldn't want to see me. See us....' 'No, she is ashamed to face us,' says Godmother.... 'I want to tell her I am her friend ... I don't want her to think she's bad just because she's been kidnapped' (Sidhwa 1989 [1988], 253).

I would contend that this depiction is symptomatic of a conservative approach within the narrative which accentuates the

[9] Women kidnapped and raped during the Partition riots in 1947 were considered 'polluted' and were often rejected by their own families. See Menon and Bhasin (1998).

maternalism of bourgeois women towards lower-class women: the female members of Lenny's upper-class family are endowed with a distinctly protective attitude towards the lower-class female characters. For instance, Lenny's mother rescues Papoo, the daughter of a violent servant, after a particularly brutal beating; and later in the text, Lenny's godmother liberates Ayah from her forced marriage with Ice-candy-man. Her initial feelings of guilt dissipate fairly quickly and are replaced by a condemnation of male violence and a kind of 'triumphalism' about Godmother's role in Ayah's escape (Hai 2000, 430). Moreover, Ayah's departure from Pakistan and return to her family in post-Partition India is arranged by Lenny's mother. Indeed, towards the end of the text, Sidhwa brings to fore female solidarity across class in the face of (lower-class) patriarchal violence, rather than the class conflict between women.

Laila's betrayal of Rani in *The End of Innocence* is also accidental. She is manipulated into revealing Rani's illicit pregnancy to Mashooq, Rani's stepfather, who brutally murders her for her 'shameful' actions. It is years later, upon meeting Mashooq again, that Laila grasps her contribution to the fatal event. This discovery leaves a permanent scar on her conscience and we discover in the epilogue that, even thirty years after Rani's death, Laila is incapable of forgiving herself. However, as in *Ice-Candy-Man*, the text pardons Laila's error, given that she was a young child at the time of Rani's death. The pronounced feelings of guilt experienced by the elite child serves to accentuate the maleficence of the perpetrator who in both the texts is a lower-class man and is additionally of 'lowly' birth. Both Mashooq and Ice-candy-man were born out of wedlock: Ice-candy-man grew up in the red-light district of Lahore, and Mashooq was born into a family that was 'low caste and dirt poor' (Mohsin 2006, 242). Notably, when she confronts him about his inhuman treatment of Ayah, Godmother draws a causal link between his 'low' birth and ignoble conduct, rendering by extension, moral rectitude an innate characteristic of the upper classes: 'You are not a man, *you're a low-born, two-bit evil little mouse! … You're the son of pigs and pimps!* You're not worth the cowries one throws at lepers' (Sidhwa 1989 [1988], 249; italics mine). Thus, in the text, Ice-candy-man's crimes are no longer the crimes of an individual, but those of an entire milieu. While this conflation between the individual and his class is more nuanced in *The End of Innocence*, it nonetheless constructs and maintains class frontiers within the narrative to separate the villains from the heroes.

Mohsin's depiction of Rani's death, in particular when Laila's mother Fareeda attempts to explain to Laila the tragic events leading to the murder, bears the traces of what Victor Li has termed 'necroidealism'. Li (2009, 280) has coined this term to refer to the tendency in literary works, as well as in the writings by Subaltern Studies historians, to idealize the dead subaltern: it is through death that the subaltern becomes a 'heroic symbol of subaltern resistance and utopian difference'. The reader is invited to read Rani's affair as an act of rebellion against patriarchal and religious dogma: 'Your friend was brave, Lailu. Although she had no protector, no support, she went ahead and did what she had to.... Rani's life may have been short—and at the end, brutal—but in that short life, she managed, in very difficult circumstances, to snatch some real happiness' (Mohsin 2006, 348–9). The triumphal tone of the following extract lends further credence to the observation that the dead Rani is constructed as a heroic martyr to patriarchal violence in the text: 'She felt a sudden sense of lightness ... up until that moment she had thought of Rani's life as a tragic waste.... But now she realized with a jolt that for some, the audacity to dream was a feat in itself. Rani's struggle was her achievement' (Mohsin 2006, 349). Amidst this 'celebration' of Rani's struggle against patriarchy, the suffering caused by her socio-economic subordination fades into the background.

Compared with the other two novels, *The Hope Chest* looks more unabashedly at the challenges of cross-class friendship. Shehzadi and Reshma's friendship ends not with the latter's social or physical death, but rather because of their realization, more acute in Reshma's case than Shehzadi's, that the class differences between them forbid the possibility of an egalitarian relationship. Reshma leaves Lahore after her wedding and her next meeting with Shehzadi takes place five years later, by which time Shehzadi is enrolled in medical school and Reshma is pregnant with her fourth child. During these five years, despite the geographical distance, they remained in touch by sending each other gifts: '[G]enerous and expensive ones from Shehzadi to Reshma, and thoughtful, hand-made novelties from Reshma to Shehzadi' (Ahmad 1996, 207). Even if the type of gift offered inevitably reflects the class positioning of the two young women, this simple acts helps to maintain the friendship and creates a sort of equality between the two. Gift-giving, as Iris Young (1997, 355) explains, helps to establish relations of reciprocity since 'there is an equality and mutual recognition in the relation of gift-giving, but of a different order from the equality of contracts and exchange'. Indeed, the dramatic difference between the types of gifts exchanged between the two precludes reductive comparisons and instead accentuates the feelings of reciprocity between them.

Ahmad's portrayal of Reshma's feelings prior to meeting Shehzadi again after an interval of five years merits close examination. It reveals Reshma's continuing doubts about the strength of their friendship as well as her awareness of her new class positioning resulting from her marriage and its relational consequences. Reshma does not want to make the first move not only because she fears a rebuttal from Shehzadi, but also because she does not wish it to be perceived as an admission of social inferiority:

> The old level of intimacy could not be assumed any more. They were no longer friends like they used to be, but she was also a woman with her own place in life, no longer the live-in servant's child, who could be drafted in to do the fetching and the carrying, whose services could be presumed upon. Her husband was a shop owner, independent and proud. (Ahmad 1996, 283)

Shehzadi, however, does not disappoint her. Hugging Reshma warmly, she is genuinely curious about her life as a married woman and tries to fill the gaps created by their long separation. The initial awkwardness dissipates quickly, giving way to a discussion about intimate matters, including Reshma's sex life (Ahmad 1996, 208–9).

The visible markers of class difference between Reshma and Shehzadi, such as clothing, have now become less distinct. Before Shehzadi sees Reshma, she catches sight of her children and is uncertain about their class positioning: while 'too well dressed to belong to any of the servants', their clothing told her that 'they were not children of friends' either (Ahmad 1996, 206–7). But the main difference between the trajectory of their lives, dictated by class, come to the fore when Reshma begins to discuss details of conjugal life, filling Shehzadi with a 'mixture of alarm and dismay' (Ahmad 1996, 209). She is painfully struck by the immense gulf between her own childhood and Reshma's very adult adolescence: 'God, she shuddered as it occurred to her that she would have had the first [child] probably when she was only fourteen. Reshma was merely five months older than her' (Ahmad 1996, 208). Once more, Ahmad's text sheds light on the intersection of patriarchy and the class hierarchies. While visibly Reshma has access to more money than before and is better dressed than her mother, she has paid a heavy price for this social mobility: her economic progression was as much a result of her beautiful body as it was at the *expense* of it. In marrying Afsar, patriarchal logic dictates that her body become his possession: 'They own our bodies, jealously, exclusively' (Ahmad 1996, 286). Exhausted by her multiple pregnancies and the resulting responsibilities, Reshma pleads with Shehzadi to make arrangements for an abortion and sterilization before she returns to her husband in Mardan.[10]

That Reshma, despite her doubts, shares intimate details of her life with Shehzadi is, of course, a reflection of the strength of their friendship, but it also underscores the extent to which Reshma is alone and isolated. Apart from Shehzadi, who she had not met in years, there is no one else on whose discretion and sympathy she can rely. The scene at the hospital draws our attention to both the emotional proximity and the distance between them. Shehzadi has to resort to subterfuge to organize an abortion for her; she does

[10] Till the year 1990, under the Penal Code of 1860 developed by the British for India, abortion in Pakistan 'was a crime unless performed in good faith in order to save the pregnant woman's life'. A new law came permanently into effect in 1997 under which abortion offenses are divided into two categories. Procedures performed before the unborn child's organs have been formed are prohibited except when performed in good faith for saving the life of the woman or for providing necessary treatment. Abortions carried out after some of the unborn child's organs or limbs have formed are prohibited except to save the woman's life. According to Islamic law, the organs and limbs are deemed to be formed by the fourth month of the pregnancy (United Nations Population Division 2001, 20). The old law would have been in place when *The Hope Chest* was published.

not pause at the legal implications of her actions and thinks only of helping her friend and alleviating her pain by whatever means necessary. She invents a medical reason to justify the procedure and provides the hospital administrative staff with a false name and address to ensure Reshma's anonymity. While grateful for Shehzadi's help, Reshma nevertheless feels extremely powerless and vulnerable before the surgery: 'Reshma herself had understood the vagaries of inequality very early in her life. Glancing nervously at Shehzadi now she panicked as she realised she had surrendered herself into this woman's hands' (Ahmad 1996, 213). The risks that Shehzadi takes in organizing the surgery gesture the depth of her affection for Reshma, but they are also indicative of her awareness of her privileged social position as a future doctor and the daughter of an influential judge.

The depth of their bond is highlighted yet again after Reshma is rejected by her husband. As the following lines illustrates, Shehzadi understands Reshma's decision to end the pregnancy and shares with her the pain resulting from that decision: 'Floods of tears poured out of Reshma as she laid her head on her friend's shoulder. For her part, Shehzadi felt deeply responsible for the role she had innocently played in wrecking Reshma's life.... Her eyes welled in sympathy, but, like Reshma, she too did not regret the action—the response it had engendered seemed unfair and unreasonable beyond belief' (Ahmad 1996, 273–4). Despite their socio-economic differences and vast disparity in the formal education to which they have had access, Reshma and Shehzadi share the same feminist conception of the female body, that it belongs to the woman, and are both equally shocked at the husband's behaviour. Reshma's feminist sensibility in the text is shown to have developed naturally as a consequence of her life experiences and not 'learnt' from her educated, upper-class friend. In attributing intellectual agency to Reshma, Ahmad avoids the disturbing class maternalism identified in the mentioned extract from Sidhwa's novel. Reshma is endowed with the ability not only to think, but also to act against patriarchal oppression. If her first reflex after her husband's rejection is to attempt suicide, she quickly rejects this 'solution'. She begins to understand not only the worth of her own life, but also the falseness of patriarchal truths which serve to cultivate guilt and punish women for a socially constructed crime. She also realizes that poverty exacerbates the oppression to which women are subjected. At the end of this formative journey, 'a plan was forming in her head', Reshma comes to see her economic dependence on men as 'a kind of hell from which she had to escape' (Ahmad 1996, 276–7). Up to this point in the narrative, Reshma's gendered and class identities had been defined by the men in her life—first her father and then husband—and their professions. When she begins to train as a midwife and moves into a hostel, for the first time in her life she experiences a modicum of spatial and economic autonomy.

The many hardships that Reshma has to endure rob her of her youth, creating a visible age difference between herself and Shehzadi, and their bond of friendship begins to weaken in the face of growing differences between them (Ahmad 1996, 291). The pre-existing class differences are compounded by a new professional hierarchy at work: at the hospital where they both work, Reshma and Shehzadi occupy distinct positions, and even though they are sharing the same public space, a distance of 'miles' separates them (Ahmad 1996, 291): 'For Reshma this realization was not new. The boundaries between them had been hidden but had always been there, subtle but insurmountable. She had also been attuned to the gap between them which had slowly grown wider since Shehzadi had moved to the college hostel to fulfil her commitment as a house surgeon' (Ahmad 1996, 291). While the goodwill between them is undeniable, it becomes evident that their friendship lasted into adulthood not despite the geographical distance between them, but *because* of it, and at the end of the novel, when they find themselves is close spatial proximity, an end to the old intimacies seems unavoidable.

In the context of nineteenth- and early twentieth-century England, Lucy Delap (2011, 94) observes that 'love and intimacy did exist between servants and children, but it was inevitably shot through with awareness of social chasm, and the ephemerality of the relationship'. In the three novels examined in this chapter too while the young age of the elite child facilitates the development of the cross-class relationship with the maid, it also accentuates the precariousness of their ties, something of which the subaltern characters are far more conscious. As we have seen, the depiction of the end of the friendship is intimately tied in with the gender and class politics of the three texts. However, if the cross-class relationship is a central thematic concern, especially at the beginning of *Ice-Candy-Man* and *The End of Innocence*, Sidhwa and Mohsin later choose to emphasize the devastating consequences of a patriarchal order for lower-class women, while the challenges of maintaining a relationship with class Others are camouflaged within the narrative. Without underestimating the role that patriarchal oppression plays in Reshma's story, Ahmad more candidly explores the ways in which class differences are inimical to long-lasting human bonds. While arguably as pessimistic as the other two novels about the durability of friendship across class, *The Hope Chest* does not make the subaltern's death, either social or physical, a necessary precondition for the demise of the cross-class relationship. It accords considerable agency to the lower-class character by conceiving concrete strategies of survival for women subordinated by both their gender and class in Pakistani society.

◆

2

The (Im)possibility of Female Solidarity Beyond Class?

The Binding Vine and *The Space Between Us*

The sisterhood of women, like the brotherhood of men, is a hollow sham to labor. Behind all its smug hypocrisy and sickly sentimentality look the sinister outlines of the class war.
—Elizabeth Gurley Flynn*

Speaking in 1915, Elizabeth Gurley Flynn declared that 'the "queen in the parlor" has no interest in common with the "maid in the kitchen"', thereby categorically rejecting the possibility of female solidarity across class lines (quoted in Tax 2001 [1980], 181). On the other hand, without underestimating the divisions along class, caste, and ethnic lines in South Asia that situate men and women 'within a variegated life experience', Subhadra Channa (2013, vii–viii) contends that 'as a woman, one can communicate with other women at a level that excludes the male; and this is an experiential interface, a part of the lived experience of women'.

Very few texts within South Asian anglophone fiction grapple in depth with the experience of sustained cross-class communication between women, arguably reflecting the difficulty of imagining and maintaining such a relationship in the adult world. Shashi Deshpande's *A Binding Vine* and Thrity Umrigar's *The Space Between Us* are two notable exceptions. In these novels, both set in Bombay, the female protagonists, elite as well as subaltern, have undergone experiences that have resulted in an acute awareness of

* Quoted in Tax (2001 [1980], 181–2).

male dominance and the marginality of women in society. They are also conscious of how class differences seriously throw into doubt genuine intimacy between women belonging to divergent socio-economic milieus.

Internal Conflict in Cross-Class 'Friendship'

The Hindu maid Bhima and her upper-class Parsi mistress Sera in *The Space Between Us* share an essentially economic relationship whereby one pays for the livelihood of the other. But it is a relationship that has lasted over two decades and appears to entail genuine emotional reciprocity. In *The Binding Vine*, Deshpande depicts the bond between Urmila, a middle-class woman and Shakuntala, who is employed in a menial capacity at a school. The two become acquainted with each other at the beginning of the text when both women are in the throes of emotional turmoil—Urmila is mourning the death of her infant daughter and attempting to come to grips with the conjugal rape of her deceased mother-in-law, and Shakuntala is keeping vigil over her daughter Kalpana, who is in a coma after being brutally raped. These female cross-class relationships emerge and exist under a ubiquitous social gaze, and the reflexive aspect of the relationship, how the protagonists perceive each other *and* their bond, is central to our understanding of it.

Umrigar's novel explores the minutiae of Sera and Bhima's relationship and its lived experience on a quotidian basis. Through the use of analepsis and points of view shifting between Bhima and Sera, Umrigar charts the difficult negotiation of intimacy in a deeply unequal setting over a long period of time. If the title of the text draws our attention to the distance separating Bhima and Sera, the novel itself brings to the fore both the distance *and* the proximity in their relationship. As Umrigar in an interview has explained, what she sought to show in the novel was both 'the connections and the separations … between women of different classes' (Rajan n.d.). Their relationship which has lasted over more than twenty years has resulted in a common past, a shared prospective future and an emotional investment in each other's family. Bhima has known Sera's daughter Dinaz since her birth and cares for her deeply, while Sera paid for the schooling and college education of Maya, Bhima's granddaughter, and is fond of her. Moreover, habit and routine appear to be essential elements of the intimacy between them. After the morning chores, for instance, Bhima and Sera share a cup of tea together in the dining area and talk about matters both trivial and serious, such as Maya's illicit pregnancy at the outset of the novel. So complete seems to be the understanding between the two women that at times they are able to communicate without speaking, without needing words, almost as if they had their own language: 'She raises one eye-brow questioningly, and in answer, Bhima shakes her head slowly from side to side. This is what Sera appreciates most about Bhima, the unspoken language, this intimacy that has developed between them over the years' (Umrigar 2005, 17).

While the text underscores the love and understanding that they share, it never lets the reader forget that theirs is a highly unequal relationship. This inequality is not 'merely' a question of economics—Sera being rich and Bhima poor—but rather reflects the relational and behavioural implications of the two characters' divergent class positionings. To begin with, Bhima calls Sera 'Serabai' (the suffix *bai* meaning madam), while Bhima, who is older than Sera, is called simply by her name. Age hierarchy is still a significant mode of social stratification in South Asia and tends to 'play an important role in structuring interactions between people' (Adams and Dickey 2000, 11). In Umrigar's text, when age and class hierarchies intersect, it is an individual's class positioning that determines her social status: even Dinaz who cares deeply for Bhima, does not add an honorific title to the maid's name when addressing her.

The class discrimination that Bhima experiences in Sera's household is not limited to a lack of respect for her advanced years. Classist attitudes permeate Sera's treatment of Bhima and even the seemingly simple, insouciant act of drinking tea 'together' is fraught with class prejudice and illustrates the hierarchical nature of their relationship: 'They are sitting in the dining room, sipping tea, Sera out of the blue-gray mug Dinaz had bought for her from Cottage Industries, Bhima out of the stainless steel glass that is kept aside for her in the Dubash household. As usual, Sera sits on a chair at the table while Bhima squats on her haunches nearby' (Umrigar

2005, 27). Bhima is not allowed to use the same crockery as Sera, and she sits on the floor, rather than on one of the sofas or a chair. Sera has never needed to explain these rules of eating and sitting to Bhima, and, as a servant, Bhima has never been unaware of their existence. Thus, Umrigar skilfully reveals how these behavioural prescriptions in Indian society, which are deeply embedded in a culture of servitude, are 'at once explicit and unspoken' (Ray and Qayum 2009, 148). The rules dictating how, where, and when the servant may sit, or what Ray and Qayum (2009, 149) have called the 'politics of sitting', are profoundly reflective of class relations, embodying 'hierarchy, inequality and subordination/domination'; therefore, 'even when there is emotional proximity, the physical distance is rarely bridged'.

Umrigar explores at length the upper-class character's awareness of the contradiction between her openly discriminatory behaviour towards Bhima and the emotional closeness that she feels with her. This contradiction is a source of continuing unease for Sera for two main reasons. First, she knows that she can easily put an end to the inconsistency in her behaviour by inviting Bhima to join her at the table; and second, she is convinced that she is incapable of issuing such an invitation. These two unpleasant self-observations give rise to cognitive dissonance within her as she tries, in vain, to formulate a logical justification for her blatant classism. Sera tells herself that if she were to allow Bhima to eat with her at the table, her acquaintances would accuse of 'setting a bad example', making the servants more difficult to manage and effectively encouraging them to demand better work conditions, thereby disturbing the class-based 'natural' order of things (Umrigar 2005, 28). But Sera quickly dismisses social pressure as an explanation for her behaviour, recognizing that the very thought of Bhima sitting on her chair or sofa repulses her intensely. She is particularly embarrassed by her inability to overcome her class prejudice, since her daughter Dinaz does not recoil from physical contact with Bhima and, in fact, often embraces her. The effortlessness with which her daughter touches Bhima fills Sera with mixed feelings which are emblematic of her internal conflict: 'Watching that hug, Sera had been seared by conflicting emotions—pride and awe at the casual ease with which Dinaz had broken an unspoken taboo, but also a feeling of revulsion, so that she had had to suppress the urge to order her daughter to go wash her hands' (Umrigar 2005, 29).

According to Dickey (2000a, 462), stereotypes about the hygiene of servants are at the root of the disgust that employers feel at the mere thought of touching the help: the servants 'represent the dirt, disease, and "rubbish" of a disorderly outside world that employers commonly associate with the lower class and that pointedly contrast with the ideal cleanliness, order, and hygiene of their own homes'. Paradoxically, employers would be incapable of maintaining the cleanliness of their own homes without these supposedly 'unclean' servants. For instance, Sera acknowledges her inability to make the utensils shine the way Bhima does (Umrigar 2005, 18). Furthermore, Sera is aware that Bhima does not conform to the stereotype of the dirty, ill-kempt servant and is in fact 'one of the cleanest people she knows' (Umrigar 2005, 29). However, so deep-rooted is Sera's prejudice that even daily proof of Bhima's exceptional cleanliness does not alter her negative perceptions about the hygiene of servants.

Dinaz, who emerges as the author's spokesperson in the novel, confronted her mother about her hypocritical biases while she was still a teenager: '[You] and Daddy are always talking about those high caste Hindus burning Harijans and how wrong that is. But in your own house, you have these caste differences too' (Umrigar 2005, 27). According to Lau (2010, 45), 'although Dinaz accuses her mother of caste discrimination, her mother is even more guilty of class discrimination against her servant'. I would argue instead that class discrimination needs to be examined in conjunction with, rather than in opposition to, caste discrimination since it mimics prescriptions in orthodox Hinduism which are dictated by a profound anxiety about the ritual pollution of the upper castes by the lower castes. Caste strictures, having to do with ritual contamination, are not restricted to observant Hindu homes alone; instead, 'in virtually all houses, servants eat separately, in the kitchen, often off plates and glasses specially kept aside for them. Therefore, the distinction between employer and servant may be clearly marked by notions of caste contamination' (Ray and Qayum 2009, 153).

If Sera considers Bhima's body a contaminated entity, as a young bride her own body was treated like a source of ritual pollution by her mother-in-law, who humiliated her for entering the prayer room while menstruating:[1] 'Acchut, unclean girl, dirtified the whole room while I was praying' (Umrigar 2005, 75). The pain that these words caused Sera were akin to a physical assault (Umrigar 2005, 78). Yet, the memory of this humiliating experience when her whole being, her very presence, was designated as dirty does not enable her to see parallels with the cruelty in her own behaviour towards Bhima (Ligaya 2006). Bhima too is shown to have prejudices: hers are against Muslims. But, unlike Sera, who is educated, Bhima is able to overcome her groundless biases against another people. Appreciating the kindness of a Muslim man at the hospital where her husband Gopal is admitted, she is able to overcome her religious bigotry and shares a utensil with him (Umrigar 2005, 139).

Umrigar's novel works to demystify 'the rhetoric of love' which characterizes how employers choose to label their relationship with their servants, insisting on the familial and emotional nature of the relationship (Ray and Qayum 2009, 92). As Dinaz points out to her mother, despite telling her friends that Bhima 'is like a family member' and that she 'couldn't live without her', Sera has never asked her to share a meal with her at the dining table (Umrigar 2005, 27). Referring to domestic help as part of the family is a cultural lie, the truth of which is known to both parties and which is meant essentially to camouflage a disturbing reality. This fabrication works to make a profoundly unequal relationship relatively tolerable, not only for the mistress, but also for the maid: for instance, Bhima feels pride at being called 'my Bhima' by Sera (Umrigar 2005, 19). As Bourdieu (1976, 127) has argued, concealment and recourse to euphemisms are essential to maintaining the most 'elementary' forms of domination, of which the master–servant relationship is one example. Nevertheless, the euphemistic expression 'like a family member' highlights the hierarchy and inequality that is inherent in the institution of the family. Employers often have paternalistic/maternalistic relationships with their servants, treating them like dependent children regardless of their age; thus the more 'hidden

[1] As in a large number of religions, the notions of 'purity' and 'pollution' are crucial in Zoroastrianism and menstruation is considered one of the sources of ritual pollution (Choksy 2002).

meaning of "like one of the family" refers to the fact that the servant falls within a familial structure, albeit on the lowest rungs' (Ray and Qayum 2009, 96).

The cross-class friendship in *The Space Between Us* is a source of internal conflict not only for Sera, as we just saw, but also for Bhima, who at times vacillates between feelings of resentment and gratitude. In one scene, Sera's son-in-law Viraf offers to buy a dishwasher to lighten Bhima's workload, but Sera quickly rejects this offer, advising Viraf to save his money, while also ostensibly complimenting Bhima's dishwashing skills: 'My Bhima can put your fancy dishwashers to shame. Not even a foreign-made machine can leave dishes as clean as Bhima can' (Umrigar 2005, 19). Bhima, however, does not appreciate this gratuitous compliment, which she reads as a dismissal of her physical pain (she suffers from arthritis) and a way for Sera to safeguard her son-in-law's interests, as opposed to Bhima's. She is also angered at Sera's impatience at her tardiness, which is a result of having to wait in line to use the communal 'toilet' in the slum, but immediately feels guilty for resenting her mistress (Umrigar 2005, 20). Reminding herself of Sera's many acts of generosity over the years, she chides herself: 'And who looked after you when you had malaria? Was it your ghost of a husband? Who gave you money just yesterday, so that you could take a cab to Maya's college.... *It was this same woman whose salt you eat, who you are thinking ugly thoughts about. Shame on you*' (Umrigar 2005; italics in the original).

For the most part, Bhima does not question Sera's discriminatory treatment of her, finding solace in hegemonic ideology which informs socially admissible behaviour for both classes. Sera too finds comfort in attributing her prejudices to class ideology, convincing herself that she is a defenceless victim of her upbringing: 'Try as she might, she cannot transcend her middle-class skin' (Umrigar 2005, 116). Perhaps in telling herself that Sera's discriminatory behaviour is a consequence of her class positioning, Bhima wishes to avoid interpreting it as a personal insult. With a few exceptions, Bhima is shown to feel nothing but gratitude and loyalty towards her mistress; she is a *namak halal* servant, true to her mistress's salt and is obedient, grateful, and submissive. As the following passage illustrates, she is committed to protecting Sera's interests, even in her absence: 'Unlike most of the servants who shop for their mistresses, Bhima tries never to waste a paisa of Serabai's money. To Bhima, it is a matter of trust. Serabai trusts her enough to send her grocery shopping on her own. So it is right to protect Serabai's finances as zealously as if she were spending her own money' (Umrigar 2005, 99). If Sera's generosity exceeds what is strictly expected of her as an employer, Bhima too is deeply concerned about Sera's well-being, both material and emotional. For example, she informs Dinaz about her mother's loneliness after her father's death, and it is in response to Bhima's expression of concern that Dinaz and her husband move into Sera's apartment to keep her company (Umrigar 2005, 293).

Umrigar's novel not only focuses on the challenges faced by Bhima as a lower-class woman living in Bombay, but also brings to the fore her many qualities; one critic even finds her character to be a caricature of virtue, who is 'too good to be true' (Ligaya 2006, n.p). Bhima, for instance, makes an enormous emotional sacrifice by swallowing her anger and deciding not to tell Sera that her son-in-law impregnated Maya. Her decision is informed by her desire to not cause pain to Sera and Dinaz, 'the only two people who have ever treated her like a human being, who have been steadfast and true to her, who have never despised her for being ignorant or weak' (Umrigar 2005, 288). As this excerpt illustrates, Bhima is prone to romanticizing her relationship with Sera, perhaps not wanting to recognize that Sera's treatment of her, despite her generosity, has been in many ways inhumane and deeply discriminatory. Bhima perceives her mistress as a superior being and her sacrifices make the maid's character reminiscent of the Mammy figure in American culture and literature, especially since, as I will discuss later, Bhima is in awe of Sera's Parsi identity. The Mammy figure, as bell hooks (1981, 84–5) explains, 'was portrayed with affection by whites because it epitomized the ultimate sexist-racist vision of ideal black womanhood.... They saw her as the embodiment of woman as passive nurturer, a mother figure who gave all without expectation of return, who not only acknowledged her inferiority to whites but who loved them.' At the end of the novel, when Bhima is forced to reveal the truth to Sera, she refuses to listen to Bhima and dismisses her from her position. Despite this unjust treatment of her, Bhima is shown to feel pity and compassion for her mistress. But I would argue that rather than rendering her a subcontinental Mammy figure, in emphasizing Bhima's loyalty and devotion, Umrigar's novel echoes the depiction of servants in the works of Tagore and his didactic intentions. Umrigar has even dedicated her book to 'the real Bhima and the millions like her'. Tagore's purpose in making 'servants into markers of loyalty, submissiveness, and sacrifice was to awaken the consciousness of their employers … by deliberately capturing the suffering of a subordinated class, the actual effort was to amend the wrongs that the dominant class perpetrated on the subalterns' (Banerjee 2004, 149).

But if Umrigar accentuates Bhima's integrity and suffering in the novel, the servant is not portrayed as a consistently pity-inducing martyr. Unlike Sera, Bhima for many years had a happy, egalitarian marriage and a fulfilling sex life. Moreover, Bhima does not remain a passive victim of class ideology; at the end of the narrative, with the help of her granddaughter, she arrives at a much clearer understanding of the reality of her relationship with Sera. It is also worth noting that the prologue of Umrigar's novel is narrated entirely from Bhima's point of view, as is the opening chapter. This poetic device works to counter Bhima's subordination in the extra-literary world and results in a prioritization in the novel of 'the consciousness of its subaltern protagonist to whom the story belongs as a whole' (Varma 2012, 152). Through its formal aspects, 'the novel seeks to undo the class asymmetry of the archetypal servant/mistress story' (Varma 2012, 152).

Unlike *The Space Between Us*, Deshpande's novel is narrated entirely from the middle-class protagonist's point of view, and the reader does not have access to Shakuntala's thoughts and feelings about her cross-class friendship with Urmila. The nature of the cognitive dissonance that Urmila experiences with regards to this relationship is substantially different from Sera's internal conflict: Urmila is philosophically torn between the supposed universality of the experiences of women and the realization that there is much that separates them from each other. Sera's concerns are more of a practical nature as to how she should conduct her cross-class friendship with Bhima, a question which does not appear to be, at least initially, problematic for Urmila. She asks Shakuntala to call her by her first name without adding the suffix *tai* for respect. In fact, it is Urmila who chooses to call her Shakutai to show respect for her advanced years. Urmila invites her to her house and also visits her on several occasions. She touches her and is touched by her, without her considering the politics of touching a class Other. Urmila's grief over her daughter's death seems to create a liminal emotional space, allowing her to disregard the tacit strictures that govern cross-class relationships under 'normal' circumstances. Her grief arguably makes her more 'sensitive' to the Other's despair and leads her to befriend Shakuntala, the mother of a rape victim (Sharma 2005, 47). But, as I will discuss later, her reaching out to Shakuntala does not imply that Urmila is oblivious of class strictures.

The socio-economic differences between Shakuntala and Urmila are not as stark as those separating Bhima and Sera. Shakuntala is employed at a school in what appears to be a custodial position, which is arguably less socially 'degrading' than domestic servitude. According to Shah (2000, 91), there are several reasons for the socially constructed inferiority of domestic workers: to begin with, 'both the work and station of domestics are historically associated with certain aspects of slavery and indentured labor'. This 'devaluation of domestics' is further exacerbated since, in most cultures, servants are employed to perform the tasks that are in themselves inferior functions in the gendered division of household labour (Shah 2000, 91–2). Moreover, unlike Bhima, Shakuntala lives in a chawl, a one-room tenement, and not in the abject poverty of a slum. Sera's and Urmila's class positionings too are not identical. Urmila's family is not as wealthy as Sera's; Urmila recalls, for instance, the false splendour of her grandparents' house and the meagreness of her father's bank balance at the time of his death. Unlike Sera, Urmila does not own a car and uses public transport where she comes across people of all classes. Also, Urmila's milieu is less anglicized than Sera's—her family speaks several 'vernacular' languages alongside English, including Marathi, Kannada, and Hindi. As Maria Couto has pointed out, Deshpande's work, unlike most Indian novels in English, introduces the reader 'to the ambience of lower middle class life in homes without an English veneer and without the hybridity of the urban upper classes' (quoted in Bhalla

2006, 61). Arguably, Urmila's lower-middle-class positioning, like that of the protagonists of other novels by Deshpande, aids the relative ease with which she is able to cross-class boundaries in her interaction with Shakuntala. Paradoxically, if the class differences and consequent internal conflicts besetting Urmila and Shakuntala's relationship are less pronounced, the emotional intimacy between them is also not as intense as that between Sera and Bhima; a paradox that is rooted in the ambiguous nature of domestic service as a profession. As Judith Rollins (1985, 156) explains, what makes it 'an occupation more profoundly exploitative than any other comparable occupation grows out of the precise element that makes it unique: the personal relationship between employer and employee'.

Spatial Aspects of Class Identities

The upper-middle-class spatial context of Bhima and Sera's relationship gives rise to a 'peculiar intimacy' (Ehrenreich 2003, 87). As Adams and Dickey (2000, 2) explain, echoing Rollins's observation discussed earlier, in domestic service, 'unlike most other types of labour, the work takes place at the employer's home, and relationships between domestic workers and employers is developed at close-range, creating a more intense dynamic of self-other contrast than is found in most work setting'. Bhima is aware that her employer is a victim of domestic violence, a fact of which Sera is terribly ashamed, and which she does her best to hide even from her 'closest' friend who belongs to the same socio-economic milieu as her. However, Bhima's knowledge of Sera's secret cannot be read as a sign of emotional closeness. Sera does not voluntarily share this information with Bhima: she simply makes no effort to conceal the truth from her. This, I argue, can be seen as an example of deceptive sharing and false intimacy stemming from Sera's indifference towards Bhima's opinion, and it ultimately underscores, rather than eliminates, the hierarchical differences between them. Socially, the servant is almost invisible to Sera and she does not consider Bhima significant enough to make an effort to keep up appearances in her presence.

Unlike Sera, Bhima actively and consciously shares her secrets with her mistress, secrets that she would go great lengths to hide from her neighbours in the slum. But this act of sharing too is indicative of the two women's distinctive social positionings, rather than of the strength of their feelings for each other. Bhima is aware of Sera's regard for her and shares her problems because she is seeking both financial help and practical advice. Sharing of this kind does not lead to greater knowledge of the Other. At the end of the text, when Bhima is dismissed by Sera, she realizes how little she really knows her mistress. This realization highlights once more the emotionally confusing nature of domestic servitude: Bhima is aware of the minutiae of Sera's preferences, how she likes her tea, for example, and that she doesn't like starch on her laundered clothes, but has 'no idea what she thinks' (Umrigar 2005, 307–9).

In Umrigar's novel, bourgeois spaces and the proximity between polarized classes that they entail, function as a microcosm of India's metropolitan cities where excess and abject deprivation exist side by side. As Nath and Aggarwal (2007, 223–4) have noted, 'there are slums in every suburb of middle income people' in Bombay,[2] with the slum dwellers often working as domestic servants for the residents of the suburb. Sera's apartment is less than a fifteen-minute walk from the slum where Bhima lives. However, the first time that Sera visits the slum and is confronted with the terrifying filth and foetid smells, she feels as if she has 'entered another universe' (Umrigar 2005, 112). It is an aspect of the city's reality against which the wealthy denizens immunize and blind themselves, until, under exceptional circumstances, they are made to enter these spaces of extreme poverty:

> It was one thing to drive past the slums that had sprung up all around the city. It was another thing to walk the narrow byways that led into the sprawling slum colony—to watch your patent leather shoes get splashed with the murky, muddy waters that gathered in still pools on the ground, to gag at the ghastly smell of shit and God knows what else, to look away as grown men urinated in the open ditches that flowed past their homes. (Umrigar 2005, 113)

[2] In all the literary texts that I have examined in this book, the city is referred to as Bombay, not Mumbai.

Sera's sole visit to the slum takes place when she goes there to enquire about a gravely ill Bhima. The visit works to underscore the behavioural differences between the two women: the warm welcome that Sera receives at the slum accentuates the daily discrimination to which she subjects Bhima in her flat. Despite her illness, Bhima asks for her granddaughter to serve Sera her favourite drink and, with her neighbour's help, finds a chair so that Sera will not have to sit on the floor. Therefore, even in her own intimate, private sphere, Bhima does not challenge class codes, but reproduces them. Sera is discomfited by the sharp contrast between Bhima's behaviour and her own: 'The generosity of the poor, Sera marveled to herself. It puts us middle-class people to shame. They should hate our guts, really. Instead they treat us like royalty. The thought of how she herself treated Bhima … filled her with guilt' (Umrigar 2005, 114–15). Sera's thoughts, though not spoken aloud, are reminiscent of Foucault's concept of 'the speaker's benefit' in the context of sexual repression, where 'the mere fact that one is speaking about it has the appearance of a deliberate transgression' and gives the illusion that the person 'who holds forth in such language places himself to a certain extent outside the reach of power; he upsets established law' (Foucault 1978, 6).

In a similar vein, Sera limits herself to articulating the injustice of class inequality and feeling remorse over her discriminatory treatment of Bhima, without making any effort to change her behaviour, as if the mere speaking to herself about it obviates the need to make any real changes. In fact, after this visit to the slum, more than ever before, Sera sets out to spatially demarcate her relationship with Bhima, while remaining generous towards her with both her time and money. She brings Bhima to her home, feeds her, and pays all her medical bills—but does not allow her to sleep inside the flat and instead makes her sleep on the balcony. It is almost as though, having transgressed the ideological boundary that allows her to recognize the extent to which her behaviour towards Bhima has been unjust, Sera regresses in practical terms by re-establishing the spatial boundaries separating her from Bhima. Thus, paradoxically, Sera's generosity towards Bhima during the illness, instead of attenuating their differences, has the effect of accentuating them.

In making Bhima sleep on the balcony, Sera is seeking to create an 'inside' within her flat to maintain the distinction between the filth of the outside world (in particular the slum where Bhima lives) and the cleanliness of bourgeois domesticity (Umrigar 2005, 115). As I discussed earlier, despite evidence to the contrary, Sera has always associated filth with Bhima, and now having visited the slum, finds a spatial justification for her prejudice. She attributes a fixed, geographical identity to her, reducing her to the insalubrious slum where she is forced to live: 'Each time she thought of the slum she recoiled from Bhima's presence, as if the woman had come to embody everything that was repulsive about the place' (Umrigar 2005, 115). Sera also seems to understand how spaces are intimately tied in with the social hierarchies and is concerned about the 'permeability of household boundaries' (Dickey 2000a, 463), which can sap an employer's authority. Therefore, notwithstanding Bhima's exemplary honesty, Sera closely monitors the entry and exit of her flat and does not trust her with the keys to the front door.

Two scenes in the text, which take place outside the confines of bourgeois domestic spaces, further accentuate the socio-economic differences between Bhima and Sera. When trying to have her granddaughter enrolled in a university, Bhima speaks to the registrar in Hindi only to be rudely rebuffed by him. However, when Sera addresses him 'in her best clipped, convent school English accent', the clerk becomes apologetic and 'under her haughty, upper-class gaze' hastens to comply with her orders (Umrigar 2005, 23). Bhima is in awe of Sera's haughtiness in the public arena, temporarily forgetting the terrified woman who is beaten by her husband in her own home. Bhima attributes to her an almost god-like omnipotence which her history of domestic violence easily throws into doubt. Her perception of Sera's supposedly innate superiority also has to do with Sera's Parsi identity and her light-coloured skin, which sets the community apart from other ethnicities in India (Singh 2008, 30). Indeed, in these moments of powerlessness in the public sphere, Bhima embodies a racially servile attitude that places Sera above not only herself, but the majority of the other inhabitants of Bombay as well.

The second encounter between Bhima and Sera in a public arena takes place in a hospital where Bhima's husband is admitted after a serious work injury which worsens with the development of an infection caused by medical negligence. Bhima's pleas for help are met with indifference, with the staff not even deigning to discuss her husband's condition with her (Umrigar 2005, 211). Knowing that her presence would inspire greater competence, Sera visits Bhima at the hospital with her husband Feroz. The bright and shiny presence of Sera and her husband contrasts sharply with the squalor of the government hospital which is meant for the least-privileged stratum of society: 'To Bhima it seemed the two of them in their good clothes and their clean glowing faces, were a splash of color against the black and white background of the dark, dingy room. They looked like film stars compared to the rest of us, she thought, like gods dropped from the sky onto this mortal earth' (Umrigar 2005, 212). Once again, we see Bhima attributing divine powers to Sera which reflects Bhima ideological acceptance of hegemonic values; as Eagleton (1991, xiii) points out, it is ideology that 'persuades men and women to mistake each other from time to time for gods or vermin'.

Bhima's muteness at the hospital and the university, her inability to make herself heard or even to be perceived as a worthy interlocutor, and her mispronunciation of English words (turning 'infection' into 'inflexion') echo John Beverley's binary concept of 'verbal fluency-power versus mutism-subalternity' (1999, 28). Her social inferiority and illiteracy render her speechless, while Sera and Feroz are endowed with verbal fluency in public spaces. Bhima is fascinated by the influence that they wield at the hospital and this episode triggers a reflection on the nature of power. She initially concludes that social power is a result of one's academic credentials: 'Watching how Feroz Seth has completely dominated the conversation with the doctor had sealed her belief in the power of education' (Umrigar 2005, 217). But then almost immediately, she is struck by contradictory evidence: after all, the doctor too is educated. So she wonders about 'the missing part' that explains social supremacy (Umrigar 2005, 218). I find Umrigar's characterization of the maid in this scene lacking in credibility, since Bhima does not even consider the importance of wealth in social interaction, something of which she is shown to be profoundly aware elsewhere in the text. While this portrayal of Bhima's thought process does not fully subscribe to the stereotypical representation of the masses in Indian anglophone literature and their 'childish lack of comprehensibility', her contemplations in this scene nevertheless belie the intelligence that she exhibits otherwise, especially if we consider her reaction to Sera's violent marriage, which will be discussed later (Khair 2001, 343).

The 'sites of interaction' as Sonita Sarker (2001, 225) calls them, between Urmila and Shakuntala encompass two classes of domestic spaces (Shakutai's room in a chawl and Urmila's house), but most of their interaction takes place at the government hospital where Shakuntala's daughter is lying in a coma. These spaces symbolize 'institutions of modernization that define women's place in both the public and private spheres' (Sarker 2001, 225). If the doctors and the hospital staff in Deshpande's novel appear to be more accessible and less apathetic to the underprivileged than in *The Space Between Us*, the hospital still serves as a microcosm for class relations in a wider societal context, reflecting the challenges faced by the lower classes in their daily dealings with the upper classes. The first time that Urmila sees Shakuntala, she is crying uncontrollably, having just learnt that her daughter was raped. She is unable to communicate with the doctor since he does not speak Marathi, Shakuntala's mother tongue, leading Urmila, who also speaks English, to act as an interpreter. Their first in-depth conversation takes place in the chawl where Shakuntala lives, and Urmila cannot help but notice the transformation of Shakuntala's body language in her own home: the moment they enter her room, 'she becomes confident, authoritative' (Deshpande 2001 [1993], 61). Deshpande thus highlights the spatial nature of class identities: in her own home, as a single mother, Shakuntala is not only able to speak, but also seems to possess a modicum of agency.

The hospital is both a classed and a gendered space in the text, allowing Deshpande to explore the relationship that women of different classes have with public and private social environments. Mira, Urmila's stepmother-in-law, was a victim of conjugal rape, but was not robbed of her privacy or forced to share intimate details about her marital life; Kalpana, on the other hand, because of her socio-economic inferiority, is admitted to a government hospital where her story will become public. Moreover, in the hope of being able to keep Kalpana's hospital bed that Shakuntala is being told persistently to vacate, she will have to (on Urmila's advice) disclose further details of her daughter's tragedy to a journalist. As Sarker (2001, 234) explains, 'because of Shakutai's class background and situation (placed in the hospital rather than in the home), Kalpana's plight is already made public through hospital and police records ... there seems to be no way for Kalpana's experience to be dealt with privately, as Shakutai pleads that it should be'. Indeed, both texts highlight the fact that spatial privacy is a luxury that only women of means can afford. Bhima, for instance, dreams of having her own private bathroom so that she would not have to queue up to use the filthy communal 'facilities' at the slum which has no plumbing. Shakuntala describes to Urmila how, as a young bride living in the corridor of a chawl with her husband who refused to work, even sex had become a public act performed in the presence of strangers (Deshpande 2001 [1993], 110–11).

Shakuntala's visit to Urmila's house also works to reveal several kinds of gendered class differences between them. Shakuntala is clearly ill at ease in bourgeois domesticity and 'perches herself awkwardly on the edge of a chair in the living room', as if she is attempting to take up as little space as possible—to sit without sitting (Deshpande 2001 [1993], 109). She cannot help but notice the relatively modern conveniences with which Urmila's kitchen is equipped. Within the domestic sphere, the kitchen is an important area where women's class differences manifest themselves. In an essay Deshpande (1992, 18) has described in vivid detail how for Indian women the kitchen was, for the longest time, a place of suffering and drudgery, a place where women 'were chained to endless, tedious labour, crouching for hours before a smoking fire'. But if life in the kitchen for middle- and upper-class women has substantially improved and is in any case facilitated by servants, for women living in the chawls and slums, it remains extremely difficult. As Shakuntala remarks, glancing enviously at Urmila's gas stove: 'This was one of my dreams; to have gas to cook on. It makes cooking very easy, doesn't it?' (Deshpande 2001 [1993], 110). Urmila appears to conduct her relationship with Shakuntala unselfconsciously, sharing her private space, serving her tea in the same crockery that she herself uses, and even touching her.

While Urmila anticipates her mother's negative reaction to Shakuntala's presence in her home, she does not articulate her own feelings on the matter. Given their discordant history, Urmila wants to set herself apart from her mother's snobbery. But the oblique reference to her expected reaction belies the ease and unselfconsciousness of this interaction and reveals instead Urmila's awareness of the unusual nature of her budding friendship with a lower-class woman.

While Urmila does recount the envy and the unease that Shakuntala experiences in upper-class domestic spaces, she does not share her own impressions of the chawl. Barbara Korte (2010/2011, 295), in her study of the literary representation of abject poverty, warns that there is a risk of it becoming the literary equivalent of slum tourism. Urmila's impressions of Shakuntala's place are devoid of a description of olfactory and auditory sensations and contain only a few visual details. It is almost as though Urmila is forcing herself to remain neutral to an environment which we know is very different from her own home. Perhaps this can be read as a poetic choice that Deshpande has made to avoid the pitfalls of a voyeuristic approach to poverty.

However, if the text avoids elitist or classist voyeurism, it gives way to another kind of voyeurism. While Urmila feels guilty about staring at Kalpana's listless, battered body, she nonetheless describes it in detail: 'Her face is discoloured in patches, the lips dark and swollen, parted as she breathes. Her arms, symmetrically arranged outside the covers, one strapped down for the IV tube, are pathetically thin, the wrists as small as a child's' (Deshpande 2001 [1993], 89). The passage, intended to provoke the reader's pathos, arguably works to emphasize patriarchal violence and oppression over class injustice: a tendency that I have noted in Chapter 1 as well.

Female/Feminist Solidarity

Both *The Space Between Us* and *A Binding Vine* question, implicitly as well as explicitly, the extent to which the shared experience of patriarchal violence and specifically 'female' sorrow brings together women from polarized classes. Besides their shared experience of maternal suffering, Urmila finds another affinity with Shakuntala when she discovers that 'what has happened to Kalpana happened to Mira also' (Deshpande 2001 [1993], 63). The first intimate conversation between Bhima and Sera takes place after Sera is subjected to a particularly violent beating by her husband. Bhima has already been working for Sera and her husband for several years, but has, so far, only been a silent witness of the violence endured by her mistress. But now, seeing her bedridden for days, Bhima allows herself to comment on her mistress's private life. She begins by offering to give her a massage. Sera finds it difficult to not only understand, but also articulate her hesitation at the thought of Bhima touching her: 'She tried to muster some resistance but found that she couldn't come up with one good reason for why Bhima's hands should not touch her' (Umrigar 2005, 108). Sera is Parsi, while Bhima is a non-brahmin Hindu; thus the laws of untouchability are not applicable in this situation, yet, inter-class physical intimacy, as we saw earlier, is often informed by notions of ritual pollution. However, the rules of cross-class physical touch are not as clearly spelt-out as religious ideology, which explains why Sera is unable to articulate them.

Once Bhima begins the massage, the softness of her skilled hands comforts Sera's bruised body and her words soothe her anguished mind. The two women share a moment of extraordinary complicity and Sera experiences an almost mystical closeness to the maid. She is struck by the difference between the innate selfishness of the sexual act with her husband and the generosity of the consolation that Bhima is able to give her. The following passage depicts the first instance of Sera seeing and feeling Bhima as she would another human being, and not just a servant:

> She had long accepted that Bhima was the only person who knew that Feroz's fist occasionally flew like black vultures over the desert of her body, that Bhima knew more about the strangeness of her marriage than any friend or family member. But now Sera felt as if Bhima had an eyeglass to her soul, she had penetrated her body deeper than Feroz ever had. (Umrigar 2005, 110)

Bhima too is aware of this new closeness and takes the liberty of giving advice to her mistress on a subject as deeply private as her marriage. At the end of the text, Bhima will recall how Sera, in reading extracts from books and the newspaper to her, sought to 'unshackle her mind' of ignorance (Umrigar 2005, 308). Sera tried to show Bhima, for example, how groundless her fear was that the Muslims would conquer India and chase out all the Hindus: she explained to her that this fear was cultivated by self-serving politicians who 'played each group against each other' (Umrigar 2005, 308). However, now it is Bhima, an illiterate woman, who reminds Sera that she should defend herself and instead of hiding her husband's brutality, should seek her family's and friends' help to escape from her abusive marriage (Umrigar 2005, 111). While Sera cannot bring herself to follow Bhima's advice, her words produce a feeling of immense relief and gratitude as they represent the acknowledgement of her suffering by another human being.

The maternalistic overtones in upper-class women's relationship with their lower-class counterparts that I identified in Sidhwa's *Ice-Candy-Man* can also be found to a certain degree in Deshpande's novel, since it is Urmila who instructs Shakuntala on how to conduct herself and sheds feminist light on Kalpana's rape. When Shakuntala bemoans her fate for having given birth to a daughter, whom she sees as a burden, she provokes Urmila's angry indignation (Deshpande 2001 [1993], 60). It is the lower-class woman who repeats and perpetuates patriarchal discourse, notably in holding her daughter responsible for the rape. Urmila, the upper-class woman, then takes it upon herself to 'educate' her:

> 'Shakutai, for God's sake, stop blaming her. Why do you blame her, how is it her fault?' She looks at me in amazement…. 'Whose fault is it then? Who do I blame?' 'The man, the man who did this to her. Don't you see, can't you see he's the wrongdoer?' She looks at me in silence, eyes wide and startled, as if the thought of the man has never occurred to her (Deshpande 2001 [1993], 147–8).

In *The Space Between Us*, however, as we saw, it is the servant who takes a feminist stance on domestic abuse, rather than her mistress who has been educated in the best schools of Bombay. In portraying the maid as the 'enlightened' one of the two, Umrigar is not underestimating the importance of education for women, but rather challenging the myth that formal schooling and a university education automatically and inevitably produce a keener understanding of the destructive workings of a patriarchal society.

Since she was born into a wealthy family, Sera's reasons for staying in the marriage appear to be social, rather than economic. At the beginning of her marriage, Sera had once returned to her parents' house, with the intention of ending the marriage. But she decided to go back to the marital home, primarily because she feared living the life of a single mother and felt that she needed the 'protection and safety' that Feroz gave her in the 'ugly' city of Bombay (Umrigar 2005, 196). It is, of course, paradoxical that in public spaces Sera should feel secure in the presence of the very man who continually terrorizes her in the privacy of their bedroom (Umrigar 2005, 196). Sera has arguably internalized patriarchal 'truths' that make a clear distinction between the safety of the marital home and the physical and sexual dangers of the outside world. Ideologically, she is living in what Helena Michie (1991, 58) has termed a 'domestic carceral'—despite the sad reality of her relationship with her husband, Sera holds on to the myth of marriage as a shield against the ugliness of the world. She sees it a 'benign' alternative to the life of a single woman, and cannot see that she 'is more likely to be physically attacked by her husband than by a stranger (Michie 1991, 58). Indeed, it is ironic, as Sunita Reddy (2001, 95) points out, that 'to avoid brutalisation of one kind, women willingly submit themselves to the brutality of another kind in the institution of marriage'. Through their depiction of the violence borne by upper-class female characters, both Umrigar and Deshpande demystify classist clichés that designate only lower-class, impoverished women as the victims of conjugal violence. According to Akhila Sivadas, such violence has 'nothing to do with class' and is 'prevalent amongst both rural and privileged class [*sic*]' (quoted in Bhattacharya 2004, 23).

Unlike Sera, Bhima did experience conjugal bliss, albeit for a few years, so that when Sera asks her whether Gopal beats her too, she can confidently reply in the negative (Umrigar 2005, 111). However, Bhima's marriage ultimately fails as well, once Gopal becomes an alcoholic and abandons his family. For Sera, this is another example of their similar fates as women: 'They were alike, Bhima and she. Despite the different trajectories of their lives—circumstances, she now thinks, dictated by the accidents of their births—they had both known the pain of watching the bloom fade from their marriages' (Umrigar 2005, 111). In fact, several times in the text, Sera uses the expression 'we women', to ally herself with Bhima: 'We women, we live for so much more than ourselves' (Umrigar 2005, 296). Here, the use of the collective pronoun 'we' suggests that the classist *Us* versus *Them* dichotomy occasionally gives way to the notion of a shared identity based on gendered experiences. According to Sara Dickey (2000a, 480), if employers are keen to distinguish themselves from their servants, they also look for similarities, primarily for selfish reasons: they wish to transform servants into less threatening members of the lower class. For sociologists such as Susan Ostrander (1987, 51), domestic service is by definition incompatible with the idea of female solidarity, since the 'privileged women's use of other women is personally exploitative, divisive among women, and inherently conservative'. However, I would contend that the bond that Sera feels with Bhima does not appear to be a cognitive strategy that is meant to render Bhima's presence less threatening in the bourgeois household. After all, Bhima too draws parallels between her life as a woman and Sera's. For instance, when Feroz dies, Sera is overcome by feelings of guilt and blames herself for having been 'such a poor wife' to him (Umrigar 2005, 260). These words resonate with Bhima because they remind her of the guilt she felt when Gopal left her: 'Every time the men leave, the women are the ones who ask for forgiveness' (Umrigar 2005, 261). Notably, the solidarity that Sera feels with Bhima is sometimes in opposition to the men of her own class. For example, when Sera's son-in-law insists on a speedy abortion for Maya ('I'm surprised that we've waited all this time, actually'), Sera bristles at his proprietorial use of the pronoun 'we' and his 'casual' tone when discussing the operation: 'Just like a man, she thinks. As if getting rid of a child is as easy as taking a shit' (Umrigar 2005, 69).

In stark contrast to Bhima, Shakuntala in *The Binding Vine* explicitly denies the possibility of having experiences and perceptions in common with an upper-class woman like Urmila. Shakuntala repeats the refrain 'you cannot understand' when she is sharing her problems with her. For example, she recalls her attempt to end her first pregnancy at a juncture in her life when she had only just begun to become relatively financially independent. Shakuntala finds it impossible that Urmila, who is free of financial constraints, could ever understand why she wanted an abortion: 'You can't understand, you won't understand, how will you?' (Deshpande 2001 [1993], 111). Shakuntala insists on her alterity with respect to Urmila and describes female emancipation as a luxury that only upper-class women can afford: 'Women like you will never understand what it is like for us. We have to keep to our places, we can never step out' (Deshpande 2001 [1993], 148). She even rejects the possibility that a bourgeois woman can know the fear of a sexual attack the way a lower-class woman does (Deshpande 2001 [1993], 149). But for Urmila, the fear of rape knows no class boundaries and she recalls being aware of the sexual threat posed by men from a very young age: 'I was only a child when a boy, crazed by his adolescent desires, accosted me on a lonely path in Ranidurg.... It is the same look I see mirrored on the face of a colleague when he looks at me, even in the midst of a crowd, I feel sexually threatened' (Deshpande 2001 [1993], 149).

Indeed, rape and its social consequences for women lie at the heart of the novel and it works to depict the universality of certain female experiences. As Rajeswari Sunder Rajan (1993, 77) explains, 'rape as the forcible penetration of the female body by the male sexual organ is the expression of male sexual domination and hence of patriarchy itself. Opposition to rape viewed thus has served as one of the planks of a global feminist movement.' Deshpande appears to have consciously highlighted that neither the victims nor the perpetrators of sexual crimes belong to the lowest socio-economic stratum of society, and that often the rapist is known to the victim. Kalpana was raped by her uncle, a working-class man, and Mira's rapist was her own husband, a bourgeois male. But if Urmila insists on the universality of the experience of rape, she treats her stepmother-in-law's marital rape as fundamentally different from Kalpana's attack. When her friend Priti expresses her desire to develop Mira's story into a screenplay, Urmila immediately rejects the idea: 'She's not a symbol. She's Mira who wrote *This book is mine as all can tell, if you steal it you will go to hell,* the girl who wrote *"Strictly private and confidential"* on her books' (Deshpande 2001 [1993], 40; italics in the original). Urmila is conscious of the dangers of a rape victim being reduced to an emblem of patriarchal oppression, robbing her of her individuality. The raped woman's new identity as a social cause can become 'an emotional war-cry and the prelude to the virtual disappearance of the concerns of the woman herself' (Rajan 1993, 72). But, as Sonita Sarker (2000, 232) has also noted, Urmila's vehement opposition to the possibility of Mira being reduced to a symbol contrasts jarringly with her active role in making the lower-class woman's rape public: it is at Urmila's request that her journalist friend writes an article about Kalpana. From the very beginning Shakuntala is categorically against making Kalpana's rape public, fearing loss of face within her community which would make it impossible for her or her sister to find a husband. But she acquiesces to Urmila's advice, in the hope that the hospital will not force them to vacate Kalpana's bed once the media attention is focused on her. Shakuntala's acceptance of Urmila's advice arguably has its roots not only in Shakuntala's despair, but also in her class conditioning which makes her see the hegemony of the upper-classes as a consequence of their 'natural' intellectual superiority.

Urmila perceives herself as fundamentally different from Priti, who she feels is a parasite feeding on the problems of other women as source material for her film projects. Indeed, critics such as Sathupati Sree (2003, 89) perceive Urmila as a 'crusader' when referring to her quest to help other women. But Urmila's involvement in Kalpana's affair is not entirely devoid of selfishness: her attempts to help Shakuntala, and by extension 'underprivileged' women as a category, function to reassure Urmila of her own virtuousness, and perhaps also of her agency. In coming to Shakuntala's rescue, she deprives her of the ability to make a decision about Kalpana's story. Even within the narrative, Urmila's maternalistic attitude is criticized by her friend Vanaa, who accuses her of using Shakuntala for the purposes of self-glorification: "'I asked her before we spoke to Malcolm, it was her decision." "Hers! What does she understand? You know what she thinks of you, she thinks you're … oh, God Himself. You've taken advantage of that. It's not fair"' (Deshpande 2001 [1993], 171).

But if Vanaa questions the supposed altruism underlying Urmila's actions, she underestimates Shakuntala's intellectual capacities, judging her to be an ignorant and inexperienced woman. Therefore, while Vanaa and Urmila may appear to have ideologically opposing points of view, both infantilize the subaltern. The maternalist overtones of Urmila's attitude towards Shakuntala are particularly striking in the following passage, where it seems that Shakuntala is filling the void created by the death of Urmila's daughter: 'I sit and listen. I murmur soothingly. I hold the rough hand in my own, I pat it comfortingly. Perhaps it helps, I tell myself, for someone to listen to her. And perhaps it answers, to a small extent, the question I keep asking myself: "Why do I come here?"' (Deshpande 2001 [1993], 93). Significantly, the text reveals the unequal nature of the relationship by excluding any possibility of conscious reciprocity on Shakuntala's part: spending time with Shakuntala helps Urmila to overcome, however momentarily, her sorrow over her daughter's death, but Shakuntala is not even aware of Urmila's recent loss. Moreover, if Shakuntala shares intimate details of her life with Urmila, Urmila does not proffer any information about herself. Therefore, I contend that the text does not allow for the possibility of the subaltern *consciously* offering any kind of moral support to the upper-class character. As illustrated earlier in my discussion of *The Space Between Us*, sharing of secrets and confiding in another human being is a class act, informed by socio-economic differences between individuals. It is with a man, Bhaskar—a doctor belonging to the same milieu as herself—that Urmila shares her pain (Deshpande 2001 [1993], 187). If her refusal to confide in Shakuntala can imply that a poor, illiterate woman cannot provide any kind of emotional support to an upper-class woman, it can also be read as a rejection within the text of a natural or instinctive affinity between women.

At the beginning of the novel, when Urmila advises her to report the crime to the police, Shakuntala voices her fears of being harassed by them—fears that Urmila is quick to dismiss (Deshpande 2001 [1993], 62). The reaction of the policeman, however, lends credence to Shakuntala's doubts. His attitude is both misogynistic and classist, declaring that all lower-class women are promiscuous and suggesting that Kalpana might be a prostitute (Deshpande 2001 [1993], 88). Towards the end of the text, Urmila begins to question her earlier decision to get the press involved: 'The worst had happened when Kalpana was raped, I had told myself. But to Shakutai the exposure had been just as bad. Now, to see Kalpana become an issue, to see it become a game in which charges and counter charges are exchanged, I realise, is much worse' (Deshpande 2001 [1993], 179). However, even if Urmila appears to become conscious of the limitations of her powers of judgement, the text continues to assign her the role of a social activist, making her responsible for women like Shakuntala and Kalpana. As Deshpande has maintained elsewhere:

> The disgrace is not the girl's, the disgrace is the criminal's. But that is not how it is—because [the mother] thinks that it will hurt her family. It's really the dilemma which Urmi, the narrator, faces because, if she makes it public, it's possible the family is going to be affected, and if she does not, you know it's like saying the woman is the one who is in disgrace, who has done wrong.[3]

It seems that for Deshpande, the decision about whether or not Kalpana's rape should be made public is a dilemma faced by Urmila and *not* by Shakuntala and her family. Moreover, Kalpana, the rape victim, is in a coma and hence mute with 'no chance of survival', while the upper-class rape victim, Mira, even in death can be heard and read through her writings (Deshpande 2001 [1993], 86). Indeed, the depiction of subaltern speech, and its absence thereof, is quite problematic in this novel, as it is repeatedly rendered secondary to that of the bourgeois character's. This narratival subordination is compounded by designating the upper-class character as the first-person narrator of the novel. Shakuntala is often shown to be sobbing uncontrollably, her words 'incoherent' and 'garbled' (Deshpande 2001 [1993], 166). In contrast, Urmila is in control of her grief, which is shown to have a dignified quality about it, steering clear of hysteria:

> I can feel grief welling up in me. I must be calm, I must not give way. I remove my glasses, wipe them, noticing with detachment that my hands are trembling. I put them down gently on the table, as if the small click is a signal, my grief gushes out of me with a frightening violence. I slip down to the floor, put my head on the table and give way. In a while it is over. (Deshpande 2001 [1993], 86)

[3] Deshpande's comments about her novel *The Binding Vine* appear on the BBC webpage, http://www.bbc.co.uk/worldservice/arts/features/womenwriters/deshpande_works.html (accessed 8 March 2015).

Anne Carson (1995, 126) notes that the male characters in classical European literature are endowed with coherent speech, while their female counterparts are susceptible to chaotic emotions taking the form of uncontrollable outflows of sounds, including 'shrieking, wailing, sobbing, shrill lament, loud laughter, screams of pain or of pleasure and eruptions of raw emotion in general'. At times, Deshpande's portrayal of Shakuntala appears to subscribe to this model, but with a classist configuration: the upper-class character Urmila is able to reason even when she is overcome with grief and is capable of coherent speech, while the subaltern woman is doomed to incoherence in public spaces. When Shakuntala does speak, it is often either to call upon Urmila to help her ('Urmila, help me, they're sending Kalpana away') or a renunciation of speech whereby Shakuntala confesses to her verbal incompetence and asks Urmila to speak for her (Deshpande 2001 [1993], 166). Their interaction with Malcolm, the journalist, is one such instance:

> 'You tell him, Urmila.' Shakutai pleads with me.
> 'What shall I tell him?'
> She is silent for a moment. 'Whatever you think you should—to help Kalpana.' The words seem to be forced out of her.
> I hesitate, then turn away from her. 'She was raped,' I tell Malcolm. I have spoken in English but Shakutai's face tells me she knows what I've said. (Deshpande 2001 [1993], 169)

In this passage, it is not Shakuntala's linguistic incompetence that prevents her from communicating with the journalist (Malcolm does appear to speak Marathi), but rather her inability to speak at all. If initially Urmila hesitates from speaking for Shakuntala, she then fully embraces the role of her spokesperson. More problematically, because Urmila communicates with Malcolm in English, Shakuntala cannot intervene or correct her if she does not get the facts right. Thus, paradoxically, in insisting on shattering the silence surrounding rape, both Urmila and the text impose a class-based silence on Shakuntala by rendering her incapable of participating in the conversation.

Urmila appears to adopt two contrasting feminist positions within the text in the context of her 'friendship' with Shakuntala. On the one hand, she insists that female experiences are independent of class positioning, especially their common experience of sexual violence and motherhood: 'Sometimes I think it's women who take parenthood seriously, men don't, not to the same extent, anyway' (Deshpande 2001 [1993], 76). On the other hand, she dismisses the notion outright that two human beings would share the same perceptions merely by virtue of their common gender: 'I thought it ridiculous that two persons should share a vision only because they belong to the same sex' (Deshpande 2001 [1993], 125). Her perception of Shakuntala as the Other is evoked several times in the text. The following conversation with Kalpana's doctor is but one example: '"Tell me, is getting married so important to a woman?" I have to think. "Yes." I say finally. "For women like her, definitely"' (Deshpande 2001 [1993], 87). Urmila then goes on to explain that for women 'like' Shakuntala, marriage is synonymous with security and protection from the outside world. However, Urmila's childhood friend Vanaa, a middle-class woman, submits completely to her husband's will and does not question the validity of the institution of marriage. Therefore, it seems that when Urmila refers to women 'like' Shakuntala, she could well be referring to a particular mindset rather than (solely) to a woman's socio-economic positioning. Indeed, Urmila is well aware of her ideological differences with Vanaa, their visions 'as different as the views [their] houses, facing opposite directions, had' (Deshpande 2001 [1993], 125). Moreover, Shakuntala's fears concerning her daughters remind Urmila of her own mother's fears about her safety as a child; she recalls, for instance, 'the hysteria' with which her mother greeted her once when she came home unusually late (Deshpande 2001 [1993], 150). Urmila's ambivalent engagement with feminist thought and her problematic interaction with other women, including her own mother, hints at how female solidarity even within the same class cannot be considered a given. She is highly suspicious of mainstream feminist theories; in a scene that borders on the absurd, Urmila is dismissive of her friend's film project primarily because she quotes Virginia Woolf while discussing it. But she also fights to establish her feminist credentials within her marriage by refusing to partake of her husband's salary. Indeed, Urmila vacillates psychologically between feelings of closeness with and serious ideological distance from women, and this ambivalence remains unresolved at the end of the text.

The ending of *The Space Between Us* also explicitly invites a reflection on female solidarity across class. Bhima is dismissed from her job as soon as she is compelled to inform Sera that it was Viraf who seduced and impregnated her granddaughter. While recognizing Sera's many acts of kindness, with Maya's help (as we will see in Chapter 4), Bhima is at last compelled to face up to Sera's betrayal and ceases to idealize her relationship with her. The rhetorical questions that Bhima asks herself at the end of the text work to dispel any remaining illusions of solidarity that she shared with Sera:

> What do these people mean to you, after all? Discarded you like an old, stale slice of bread when the time came, didn't they? Didn't Serabai choose her son-in-law's obvious lie over your obvious truth? Didn't she hide behind the folds of family when she had to choose? And did she slap his face when he called you a thief? Did she ask him to get out of the house when you told her what he had done? No, instead she asked you to leave. (Umrigar 2005, 311)

As Elora Chowdhury (n.d.) has observed, Umrigar's novel 'enables a discussion of circumstances where women's loyalty to family, class and community specific structures ostensibly trump an alliance based on a "common" gender based oppression'. Bhima realizes that Sera's support of her son-in-law stems from the desire to protect her daughter's feelings, but also from class loyalty and a shared ethnicity: Sera and Viraf possess 'the same fair skin, the same confidence when talking to strangers, the same educated way of speaking' (Umrigar 2005, 312). This realization of the insurmountable distance between them leads her to declare at the end of the novel: 'I have no mistress' (Umrigar 2005, 317). Of course, Bhima's liberation from servitude is ideological, not economic: the very next day, she will have to look for employment entailing menial labour, in all probability as a domestic servant in another upper-class woman's home.

Rather than sustained female solidarity between women belonging to polarized classes, the ending of the two texts underscores the female protagonists' instinct for survival. Bhima, who is initially devastated at being dismissed by Sera, musters the courage to face the daily challenges that are the lot of lower-class women in a city like Bombay. Shakuntala and Urmila too are able to overcome their debilitating emotional pain, but without the possibility of a future together. Thus, both novels, while shedding light on the commonality of the experiences of the female characters, nevertheless present class as an ultimately insurmountable barrier that condemns women to fight their shared battles separately.

◆

3

Loving Class Others in *The God of Small Things* and *Salt and Saffron*

Love marriages … are widely viewed as a most unholy union. They challenge 'natural' (that which qudrat, *nature, has created) caste hierarchy, and social considerations of class, status and standing.*

—Perveez Mody*

South Asian anglophone fiction provides us with far more examples of heterosexual romantic relationships that defy ethnic, religious, or racial differences rather than class boundaries, a frequently recurring theme in popular Hindi cinema. This pattern can arguably be traced back to the secular origins of the contemporary anglophone novel in the region and the much larger, socio-economically diverse audience of commercial Hindi films.[1] Cross-class romance in Bollywood films is endowed with 'the "transcendent" power flouting strict endogamous codes that ensure social distance across class and caste boundaries' (Virdi 2003, 73). A romantic relationship across class can be seen as an act of contestation for two reasons: in addition to breaching class boundaries, it flouts social taboos that are still associated with romantic love in the Indian subcontinent. Mixed-class love implies not only the sexual act, but also potentially the 'legitimate' institution of marriage—homogamy and endogamy playing a crucial role in the reproduction

* Quoted in Mody (2007, 333).

[1] For an examination of the relationship between Nehruvian nationalist secularism and the Indian English novel, see Srivastava (2007, 19–47). Also see George (1996, 131) for a discussion of the difference between the readership of Indian English novels and Hindi cinema audiences.

and perpetuation of socio-economic inequalities (Driver and Driver 1987, 125). Social sanctions concerning exogamous marriage apply in particular to women who, according to patriarchal logic, are the repositories of familial and communitarian honour. Cross-class love and marriage, then, present a formidable challenge not only to patriarchy, but also to socio-economic stratification.

Both the texts examined in this chapter depict romantic relationships between elite women and lower-class males. In *The God of Small Things* by Arundhati Roy, Ammu, an upper-caste, upper-class Syrian Christian falls in love with Velutha, an untouchable carpenter. In Kamila Shamsie's *Salt and Saffron*, Aliya is a young Pakistani woman from an aristocratic family who falls in love with Khaleel, an American of Pakistani descent, whose parents are from Liaquatabad, one of the more modest neighbourhoods of Karachi. Four years before the beginning of the narrative, Aliya's aunt Mariam elopes with Masood, a cook employed by Aliya's family.

Liminality and Transgression

The two authors emphasize the ambiguous positioning of the lovers, well before the romantic transgression occurs: their 'liminality' appears to make them particularly susceptible to breaching social boundaries (Turner 1974, 232). Even before they begin the affair, Ammu and Velutha can be characterized as 'liminal entities' as they seem to 'elude or slip through the network of classifications that normally locate states and positions' in society (Turner 1969, 95). Ammu's unorthodox choices in life as a woman (her 'love marriage' to a Hindu, subsequent divorce, and return to the parental house with two children in tow) have made her something of a social outcast. After her divorce, Ammu resists pressure to resign herself to a sexless, desireless life, which her family sees her fit to live (Roy 1997, 45). Her liminality is compounded by her 'untamed' personality, living 'in the penumbral shadows between two worlds' (Roy 1997, 44). The text accentuates the innate, natural quality of her non-conformist behaviour, almost as if she has been only *partially* socialized by her milieu and her family: 'Ammu had not had the kind of education, not read the sort of books, not met the kind of people, that might have influenced her to think the way she did. She was just that sort of animal' (Roy 1997, 180). But the text also indicates that Ammu is not a complete outsider to her socio-economic milieu: she is very much a product of her class. As the following extract shows, she strongly believes in a hierarchy of social manners and is unforgiving towards her children if she deems them to have behaved in a 'vulgar' manner: 'Ammu hated them blowing spit-bubbles. She said that it reminded her of Baba. Their father. She said that he used to blow spit-bubbles and shiver his leg. According to Ammu, only clerks behaved like that, not aristocrats' (Roy 1997, 84). As Anuradha Needham (2005, 378) has also pointed out, Ammu's 'out-of-placeness' which fuels her love for Velutha does not 'exempt her from the contradictions that flow from her simultaneous investment in some class-marked values'.

If Ammu's (relatively) independent thinking is a cause for much suspicion among her family members, Velutha too does not subscribe to the culturally designated code of conduct for a young man of his caste and class. Velutha rejects the prevailing ideology that defines him as an innately inferior being, leading his father Vellya Paapen to fear for him: 'He couldn't say what it was that frightened him. It was nothing that he had said. Or done. It was not *what* he said, but the *way* he said it. Not *what* he did, but the *way* he did it. Perhaps it was just a lack of hesitation. An unwarranted assurance' (Roy 1997, 76; italics in the original). It is not only Velutha's quiet self-confidence that sets him apart from other men in his social position, but also his skills and ability: in addition to his talent for carpentry, he has 'a way with machines' (Roy 1997, 75). He is hired by Mammachi as a carpenter and is put 'in charge of general maintenance' of the family-owned pickles and preserves factory. Velutha has to bear the brunt of his 'touchable' colleagues, according to whom Paravans were not meant to be carpenters (Roy 1997, 17). They resent him for not practising a profession befitting a Dalit: one of the several occupations often associated with death and filth, which have historically been the lot of the lowest castes in India.

Roy's text thus reveals the tension between caste and class identities: Velutha's profession and corresponding salary would seem to accord him a higher working-class position than what would be compatible with his Dalit status. While caste and class are certainly two distinct systems of social stratification and should not be collapsed into each other, it is important to note that there exists a 'broad congruence' between the two (Chakravarti 2003, 13). Caste, as Gail Omvedt (1982, 14–15) has pointed out, 'still is a material reality with a material base' and it 'continues to have crucial economic implications today'. *The God of Small Things* reveals the measures taken by the upper-caste, upper-class elite to consciously align class and caste categories, thereby severely limiting social mobility. For instance, in an attempt to restore the 'natural' order of things which Velutha's talent and expertise have disrupted, Mammachi pays him a salary that is lower than what would be commensurate with his job description.

Velutha's political convictions are also crucial to our understanding of the liminality of his character. In particular, his membership of the communist party and active participation in the workers' march is an expression of his discontent with the status quo. It is his presence at the march that leads Ammu to realize that the two might share a common sensibility and an aversion to the established order, be it socio-economic or patriarchal: 'She hoped it had been him that had raised his flag and knotted arm in anger. She hoped that under his careful cloak of cheerfulness, he housed a living, breathing, anger against the smug, ordered world that she so raged against' (Roy 1997, 175–6).

Mariam in *Salt and Saffron* is also a liminal being, although the nature of her liminality is different from Ammu's. Her father Taimur renounced the privileges of his family upon coming down from Oxford. He decided to accept his 'historical role' by becoming the valet of an English army officer instead of taking up a preordained position in the Indian Civil Service or an English-run company, where his social/racial inferiority would have been camouflaged (Shamsie 2000, 24). During her fifteen-year stay at Aliya's parents' home, Mariam spoke only Urdu to address Masood, the family cook, and then only about the menu for the day. Her communication with everyone else was limited to elaborate gesticulations. Mariam's father's extraordinary decision to choose to become a subaltern, the possibility that her mother belonged to a lower-class background, and her eccentric mutism, all contribute to her ambiguous positioning within the Dard-e-Dil family. Aliya wonders whether this ambiguity made it possible for Mariam to 'acknowledge possibilities more unlikely than ghosts' and to fall in love with a servant, an unimaginable event for the other members of the family (Shamsie 2000, 221). Aliya and her cousin perceive Mariam's silence to be a sort of political statement, 'a protest against the prejudice built into language' and they wonder if her speaking to Masood 'in questions not in imperatives' was her way of 'undercutting the whole employer-servant paradigm' (Shamsie 2000, 214). It can be argued that the almost compulsive intellectualization by the Dard-e-Dil family of Mariam and Masood's love story is indicative of the elite characters' disbelief over such a union. It also keeps the discussion firmly away from the profoundly discomforting thought that one of their own willingly shared her body, the most intimate of spaces, with a servant. While emphasizing Mariam's alterity, the text also brings to the fore her unmistakeably aristocratic mannerisms which, it is implied, can be neither simulated nor learnt. For instance, even though no one in the family knew or recognized her when she first arrived at Aliya's parents' house, the servants showed her into the drawing room reserved for the most distinguished guests, indicating her 'obvious' social superiority (Shamsie 2000, 54). Mariam's arrival coincided with Aliya's birth and the text constructs Aliya as sharing Mariam's liminality: she and Mariam are referred to as 'not-quite twins', two individuals who are spiritually entwined without being biological twins: 'Everyone grew more garrulous than normal around Mariam Apa, except for me. I've heard that twins communicate in the womb before tongue and throat and larynx form, so they know how to speak to each other without speech' (Shamsie 2000, 57). Aliya's alterity is expressed primarily in her awareness of her own snobbery and in her desire to overcome it, a quality that is lacking in her other relatives.

Masood's behaviour too sets him apart from his own class. Like Velutha, he has an air of self-assurance, absent among other servants and his skills and professional capabilities appear to be the source of his self-confidence: 'Oh, he was never anything but polite, but you always knew that he knew he could leave and get a job anywhere else if we crossed certain lines' (Shamsie 2000, 152). Thus, in accentuating the identitary ambivalence of the protagonists, both texts gesture to the preconditions necessary for not only living, but also *imagining* love that transcends the boundaries of class and caste.

Class Ideology and the Family

In both novels, the family acts as a repository of class ideology, whose members articulate the social unacceptability of cross-class romance in often vehement terms; it is the family that is the primary obstacle in the way of the lovers' happiness. As discussed in the Introduction, class in the Indian subcontinent is a familial rather than an individual identity and the practice of arranged marriages works to accentuate the immense influence of the family on an individual's life choices. Therefore, heterosexual cross-class romance should be read not only as an act of social transgression, but also, specifically, as transgression against the institution of the family.

Roy's novel highlights how the family and institutionalized powers (the police and the communist party) work together to reinforce social hierarchies. Once Mammachi learns of Ammu's affair with Velutha, she is filled with 'unmanageable fury' at her daughter who, according to her, has 'brought the family to its knees' (Roy 1997, 258). When Baby Kochamma denounces Velutha to the police, she claims that he not only attempted to rape Ammu, but also kidnapped Estha and Rahel. In transforming their love affair into rape, Baby Kochamma is seeking to 'contain the scandal and salvage the family reputation in Inspector Thomas Mathew's eyes' (Roy 1997, 259). It is clearly the bourgeois family that is the primary architect of the couple's tragedy.

It is important to note that it is not only the bourgeois family, but also the subaltern's father, who is scandalized and shaken into destructive action upon discovering the affair. Vellya Paapen betrays his son and is even ready to kill him for his transgressions (Roy 1997, 78, 256). However, despite this depiction of a tyrannical and perverse familial structure, Roy's text also envisions a different kind of family, one that is harmonious and nurturing. It is no coincidence that the first time that Ammu recognizes Velutha as a sexual being and a potential lover is when she sees him playing with her daughter: 'The man standing in the shade of the rubber trees with coins of sunshine dancing on his body, holding her daughter in his arms, glanced up and caught Ammu's gaze' (Roy 1997, 175). She will eventually 'love by night the man her children loved by day' (Roy 1997, 44). Indeed, Ammu, Estha, Rahel, and Velutha form, what Jani (2010, 209) has called, a 'virtual' family that is unable to unite in real life, but is linked both bodily and spiritually. Therefore, notwithstanding the profoundly transgressive nature of the affair, there is an almost conventional complexion to Velutha and Ammu's relationship. If Ammu rages furiously against the status quo, her affair with Velutha does not indicate a desire for anarchy, but rather the hope to find another kind of order, a 'more enabling family and form of community', as Needham (2005, 385) has noted.

Shamsie in *Salt and Saffron* also underscores the threat that inter-class love poses to the notion of familial honour and reputation. The Dard-e-Dils believe that in marrying Masood, Mariam has 'blemished the family name' (Shamsie 2000, 129). They seek to deny any consanguinity with Mariam to protect the 'honour' of the young women in the family who are of a 'marriageable' age: 'Family reputation is the most precious jewel in a young bride's *jahez*' (Shamsie 2000, 129).[2] Having met him on a flight, Aliya encounters Khaleel for a second time in the London Underground when she is accompanied by her cousin Samia. Samia takes on the role of the family's spokesperson and forces Aliya to leave the train as soon as Khaleel mentions Liaquatabad, the name of the neighbourhood in Karachi where his parents came from and where his extended family still lives. Samia spells out the inappropriateness of starting a romantic relationship with Khaleel in the following words: 'The poor live in Liaquatabad. The poor, the lower classes, the not-us' (Shamsie 2000, 31). And then to dissuade her cousin even more persuasively, Samia reminds her of Mariam's elopement, an event that remains a source of profound shame for the family.

After Aliya's return to Karachi, it is Samia who has an opportunity to see Khaleel again and writes to her cousin to spell out all that makes him an exceedingly ineligible bachelor: 'I've gathered enough info from him to know that his Karachi relatives'

[2] Jahez, in Urdu, means dowry.

English is weak, they've never left the country, and they believe in the joint-family system (the horror, the horror, imagine living in a house teeming with your own relatives, never mind someone else's)' (Shamsie 2000, 190–1). These criteria that Samia enumerates construct Khaleel's Otherness in terms of cultural, rather than material differences. Specifically, Samia seems to subscribe to the stereotypical dichotomy between 'tradition' and 'modernity': being able to speak English (well), having a familial structure that resembles the nuclear family, and thus privileging the individual instead of the collectivity, all for her are synonymous with being 'modern' which in turn is equivalent to intellectual superiority and open-mindedness. The 'traditional' joint-family system, which provokes Samia's horror in the text, often entails the cohabitation of several generations of the family under the same roof. But a family, as Qadeer (2006, 191) points out, 'can be "joint" in many ways and under different norms, such as living under one roof, living near each other, or even in far-off places but maintaining a single ceremonial head or common property. Alternately, the jointness could only be for specific functions or rituals, such as taking care of the elderly or widowed or religious worship.' While Samia condemns Khaleel for having relatives who 'believe' in the joint-family system, she fails to recognize that the Dard-e-Dil clan is a deeply traditional family which exercises a great degree of influence on its (young) members, constraining their choices; as a female relative, who is aware of Aliya's growing feelings for Khaleel, pointedly remarks: 'Of course you don't marry an individual. You marry a family' (Shamsie 2000, 190). Moreover, the flat in London where Aliya stays is co-owned by several members of the family. Aliya's world, despite her travels abroad, is seriously bounded and her social life is centred on her extended family.

In order to further accentuate Khaleel's ineligibility, Samia reminds Aliya that given his economic background, it is likely that his parents have arranged a marriage for him, yet another proof of their backwardness. Ironically, the direct interaction between Khaleel and Aliya is limited to only two meetings and all further communication between them is mediated by Aliya's family in London, giving their 'relationship' a distinct 'arranged' quality. Indeed, Khaleel appears to be far more independent than Aliya, despite his 'backward' social milieu: but this contradiction does not seem to be recognized within the text.

Unlike *The God of Small Things*, Shamsie's novel makes a clear distinction between the crass snobbery of Aliya's extended clan and the open-mindedness of her immediate family: Aliya discovers at the end of the novel that her grandmother, who she thought despised Mariam for having married a servant, was actually hostile towards Mariam because she had been in love with her father and was in fact jealous of Mariam's mother. Aliya also realizes that her father's silence about the marriage did not stem from shame, but rather from pain at Mariam's sudden departure. Exculpating Aliya's immediate family, as I will show later in the chapter, allows Aliya and Khaleel's love story to have a happy ending, but one that is firmly located within an upper-class spatial setting.

Desiring the Other

The lovers in both these texts, in addition to facing the disapproval of their families, themselves have doubts about their cross-class romance, recognizing that they are venturing into forbidden territory. In Roy's novel, Velutha attempts to stem his growing attraction to Ammu, by reminding himself that she belongs to the elites who have oppressed men like him for centuries: 'He tried to hate her. *She's one of them*, he told himself. *Just another one of them*. He couldn't' (Roy 1997, 214, italics in the original).

When Ammu realizes that the armless man that she sees in her dreams, and who makes her so happy, can only be Velutha, she tries to stop her children from visiting him. But unlike Aliya, Ammu does not fight her desire for the lower-class character, even while she ostensibly forbids her daughter Rahel from spending time with him: 'By not mentioning his name, she sensed that a pact had been forged between her Dream and the World.... She knew who he was—the God of Loss, the God of Small Things' (Roy 1997, 220; italics in the original).

That very evening, she meets Velutha outside the dilapidated History House for their first night of love. Rather than Ammu, it is Velutha who is filled with terror, aware of the significance of such a meeting: '*I could lose everything. My job. My family. My livelihood.*

Everything' (Roy 1997, 334; italics in the original). Desire trumps fear, however, and they commence a passionate liaison that lasts only thirteen nights. Aijaz Ahmad (2007, 116) has criticized Roy's portrayal of the love affair, arguing that it is essentially the exercise of a 'libidinous drive'. He contends that Ammu and Velutha are propelled by an irresistible passion, becoming 'pure embodiments of desire' who are cut off from the socio-economic complexity that foregrounds their relationship (Ahmad 2007, 116). I would argue that this criticism does not adequately consider the distance separating Ammu and Velutha from the status quo; neither does it take into account the terror that fills Velutha before and after making love to Ammu. Moreover, Ahmad disregards the lovers' painful awareness of the social significance of their relationship. As Kalpana Wilson (1998, n.p.) points out, 'even Velutha's first word "Ammukutty" ("Little Ammu"), when they finally meet on the riverbank, takes us back to the time when Velutha, though several years younger, used this pet-name while offering his hand-made gifts on his outstretched palm, as he had been taught, so Ammu would not have to touch him'. That Ammu and Velutha decide to flout the 'love laws' does not indicate their blindness to social divisions. On the contrary, they are very aware of the social and historical obstacles in the way of their love and also of the price that they will have to pay for it: 'They knew there was nowhere for them to go. They had nothing. No future.... They knew things could change in a day' (Roy 1997, 338–9).

In Shamsie's novel the narrative focuses almost entirely on Aliya, the upper-class character (who is also the first-person narrator), and her doubts and misgivings about the transgressive relationship. She has to battle with her family's disapproval as well as her own snobbery. When they meet at a café in London, Aliya is filled with horror at the sight of Khaleel pouring tea into the saucer before drinking it—the preferred manner of consuming hot beverages among the lower classes of Pakistan. This gesture for Aliya becomes symbolic of the insurmountable distance between them. Once back in Karachi and unable to forget him, she tries to convince herself that she is not like her other family members and is capable of overcoming her class arrogance: 'I've deconstructed it, analysed it, and I have refused to take on the attitude of my relatives with their centuries of in-bred snobbery' (Shamsie 2000, 32). She tries to reassure herself by invoking the possibility that Khaleel's lower-class manner of drinking tea was actually designed to test her arrogance (Shamsie 2000, 185). Moreover, the text appears to celebrate any confession of snobbery as proof of honesty and seems to cast the discriminatory attitudes that result from social inequality as inevitable: '"Why can't we roll with it; see where time and tide take us?" "Because Liaquatabad." I couldn't believe I'd said it out loud. But instead of looking offended he smiled at me, as though grateful for the truth' (Shamsie 2000, 65). Therefore, when faced with Aliya's class prejudice and discriminatory attitude, instead of anger or indignation, Khaleel is shown to feel gratitude. Moreover, this confession does not lead him to re-evaluate his affection for the young woman: he continues to pursue her and, more oddly perhaps, continues to socialize with her extended family even after she has left for Karachi. This is not to say that the text does not underscore Aliya's feelings of being imprisoned by her family's snobbery or her unease at their reaction to Mariam's marriage to Masood, making her feel 'so sick, so trapped' (Shamsie 2000, 71). But the novel seems to subscribe to a conservative hierarchy of 'flaws': if Khaleel is deemed an unsuitable suitor by Aliya because of how he drinks his tea, her professed snobbery in no way alters Khaleel's positive perception of her.

Moreover, Khaleel often voluntarily lets Aliya monopolize the conversation, it is implied, in deference to her talents as a storyteller. Tellingly, their conversations are punctuated by his requests for her to speak or to continue speaking (Shamsie 2000, 61–6). Thus, the text provides a logical and aesthetic justification to explain Aliya's monopoly of speech with respect to the subaltern character. Khaleel's desire to know more about Aliya contrasts sharply with Aliya's lack of curiosity about Khaleel and his past. She does not ask him any questions about his family, maintaining, as she sees him pour tea into a saucer, that she knew 'right then everything [her] family would need to know about Khaleel's parents' (Shamsie 2000, 63–4). As Iris Young reminds us, the act of asking a question suggests respect for the Other and a recognition of one's own ignorance. Moreover, without 'a moment of *wonder*, of an openness to the newness and mystery of the other person, the creative energy of desire dissolves into indifference' (Young 1997, 357; italics in the original). The reconstruction of Khaleel's life by Aliya, based on two facts (the modest Liaquatabad origins of his parents and the way he drinks his tea on one occasion), is marked with reductionism. Khaleel's call against Aliya 'pigeonholing' him and his family in Liaquatabad is largely ignored not only by Aliya, but also by the text (Shamsie 2000, 63). Furthermore, in *Salt and Saffron*, only the elite characters are endowed with a clear genealogy and history, while the lower-class characters are condemned to a timeless state, living in an eternal, unchanging present. Lacking individuality, they become marginal voices within the narrative. This essentialist aspect of the text becomes even more striking when the narrator weaves the Dard-e-Dil clan's story into important 'real' events of South Asian history, such as Akbar's reign and the Partition of India, while Khaleel's family's past is devoid of any socio-historical markers. Even more tellingly, apart from a brief reference to his father and brother, Masood's family is not discussed in the text.

It is important to note that Velutha's is not the central perspective in Roy's novel, a large part of which is narrated from the point of view of Rahel, an upper-class character. Moreover, it is only after Roy has already evoked the trauma of the upper-class non-Dalit family that she reveals to the reader the price that Velutha had to pay for his 'transgressions'. And yet, Velutha remains resolutely central to the novel. The structure of the text and the gradual unfolding of Velutha's tragedy compel readers to reconsider and revise their understanding of the relationship between the characters and the agency that they actually possess. Rather than conceal it, the text recognizes the chasm between Velutha (and by extension his caste and class) and the implied reader. As Jani (2010, 199) explains:

> The narrative constructs an implied audience that is unable to approach Velutha's story except from a distance, slowly working through the trauma of Ammu's family and discerning the various, overlapping sites of violence and brutality. Rather than producing an elite-centered narrative, however, this progression allows for a complex rendering of power relations in postcolonial society and a lesson in how subalternity is produced through the selective processes of storytelling.

In employing Rahel's perspective and binding the reader to her moral sensibilities, Roy creates a discursive space that is rare in anglophone literature from the Indian subcontinent: she allows for the possibility of elite characters to reflect on the status quo and acknowledge their own complicity (Jani 2010, 208). They are able to feel genuine empathy for and solidarity with the subaltern. Instead of usurping Velutha's voice, these characters become 'vehicles for the recovery of subaltern stories' (Jani 2010, 208).

Transgressive Bodies

The transgressive quality of cross-class, cross-caste relationships can be attributed, to a large extent, to the breach that they entail of social laws governing physical contact with the Other. These laws are explicit within the caste system and while tacit, the laws dictating cross-class physical interaction can be equally prescriptive.

Aliya is shocked to learn from her mother that Mariam hugged Masood goodbye before he left Karachi: 'A hug! I wouldn't have, and Masood carried me piggy-back style as a child' (Shamsie 2000, 79). The shock turns to revulsion when she discovers that the couple later eloped: 'I felt disgust. *She's having sex with a servant*. Those words exactly flashed through my mind. Not Masood, just a servant' (Shamsie 2000, 113; italics in the original). Aliya's reaction underscores the stereotypical association of servants with dirt and filth among the upper classes. The irony of this stereotype is particularly stark in Masood's case, since he was responsible for preparing sumptuous meals with his bare hands, which the Dard-e-Dils were more than happy to consume. Earlier in the novel, while her cousin Samia gives her a massage, Aliya observes that when abroad what she missed about Karachi 'was the intimacy of bodies' (Shamsie 2000, 14). However, as we have just seen, this 'intimacy of bodies' is far from all-encompassing and universal; it is, in fact, dictated and severely checked by class and gender divisions.

Aliya's disgust at the thought of her aunt having sex with a servant echoes Baby Kochamma and Mammachi's reaction to Ammu's affair with Velutha. The similarity of their attitudes gestures to the extent to which class differences mimic the discriminatory attitudes cultivated by the caste system. Baby Kochamma wonders disbelievingly: '*How can she stand the smell? Haven't you noticed, they have a particular smell, these Paravans?*' (Roy 1997, 78; italics in the original). Ammu's mother too is filled with extreme disgust: 'She thought of her naked, coupling in the mud with a man who was nothing but a filthy *coolie*.... Like animals, Mammachi thought and nearly vomited. Like a dog with a bitch on heat' (Roy 1997, 257–8, italics in the original). In these cited passages the categories of class and caste inferiority mutually reinforce Velutha's subalternity. Mammachi perceives (or insists on perceiving) Velutha as a 'coolie': a deeply pejorative term employed to refer to unskilled labourers. Roy thus reveals the rigidity of caste and class boundaries: despite his training and skill as a carpenter, Velutha remains a 'coolie' and is deprived of social mobility. Furthermore, the sexual act between Velutha and Ammu is perceived as something 'unnatural', akin to bestiality—as though, in flouting caste and class codes, the lovers had lost their *humanness*, and thus their place in human society.

In these two texts, the body is a frontier that both signals, and is itself marked by, social inequalities. The subaltern's body, and its eroticization, then, take on considerable political significance.

Eroticized Male Subaltern

While the narrator in *Salt and Saffron* makes no reference to Masood's looks, the other lower-class character, Khaleel, is shown to be a young, good-looking man. Aliya's aunt in England, for instance, writes to say that she finds Khaleel 'delicious' (Shamsie 2000, 135). When Aliya's parents meet him for the first time, they at first conclude that their daughter's feelings for Khaleel stem only from his physical attractiveness (Shamsie 2000, 239). The depiction of Velutha's beauty in Roy's novel is more complex and merits closer attention, especially since Ammu and Velutha's is a sexual relationship. While his physical beauty is central to the affair and to the final lovemaking scene, it is important to recall that for (other) elite women like Mammachi and Baby Kochamma, the very sight and smell of Velutha inspire profound disgust.

Roy's text includes several detailed descriptions of Velutha's physical beauty, as perceived by Ammu: 'She saw ridges of muscle on Velutha's stomach grow taught and rise under his skin like the divisions on a slab of chocolate.... Contoured and hard. A swimmer's body. A swimmer-carpenter's body. Polished with high-wax body polish' (Roy 1997, 175). Sujala Singh (2006, 190) finds that Velutha's body in the novel is 'described obsessively'. Indeed, the focus on Velutha's body has invited a number of criticisms, especially in the context of the observation that he is often bare-chested, dressed only in a mundu. As Bhatnagar (2001, 96) explains, 'men and women of the lowest castes were not allowed to wear clothing above the waist'. This historical fact, according to Victor Li (2009, 287), seriously problematizes Roy's portrayal of the subaltern body: 'It is one thing, for example, to have our gaze directed at the eroticized beauty of Velutha's subaltern body (an eroticization not unlike that visited on the punka-wallah's body in *A Passage to India*); it is another to learn that the author's gaze ignores the fact that subaltern nakedness is a mark of social humiliation.'

In a similar vein, Roy's characterization of Velutha could also perhaps lend itself to criticisms of gratuitous eroticization of the working-class male body. As the following passage clearly demonstrates, Ammu attributes her lover's muscular beauty to his occupation as a carpenter: 'As she watched him she understood the quality of his beauty. How his labour had shaped him. How the wood he fashioned had fashioned him. Each plank he planed, each nail he drove, each thing he made, had moulded him. Had left its stamp on him. Had given him his strength, his supple grace' (Roy 1997, 334). In his article on the eroticization of the working class in gay literature and pornography, Stephen Donaldson (1990, 1405) contends that the psychological source of the attraction that the working classes exert on the elite comes from the perception that the upper classes have lost their masculine vitality. Men from the leisured classes are seen to be 'removed from the exercise of physical power, while the (young) males of the lower class are more robust, earthy, grounded, more in touch with their sexuality, more physically aggressive, in short, more macho' (Donaldson 1990, 1405). While it is difficult to deny that the subaltern's body in the text bears the stamp of his physical labour, it is worth noting that the portrayal of Velutha's masculinity does not conform to stereotypical notions of a working-class masculinity that is overtly aggressive and macho. On the contrary, in the final scene, it is Ammu who initiates physical intimacy with him: 'She went to him and laid the length of her body against his. He just stood there. He didn't touch her.... She unbuttoned her shirt.... She pulled his head towards her and kissed his mouth.... A kiss that demanded a kiss-back' (Roy 1997, 335). Far from ascribing him a clichéd 'working-class' virility, the text accentuates Velutha's gentleness: 'He stroked her back. Very gently.... He was careful not to hurt her' (Roy 1997, 335). Velutha's manner with Ammu's children does not subscribe to conventional notions of masculinity either and his paternal attitude is not based on authority or distance. Remarkably at ease with the children, Velutha's multiple talents defy traditional masculine/feminine divisions: he not only cooks for them, but also teaches them to use a planer and to fish (Roy 1997, 79). Note also that when Velutha is arrested, the policemen remark that his nails have been painted red, resulting in cruel jokes about his sexual orientation (Roy 1997, 310–11). Velutha had allowed Rahel to decorate his hands, which is a poignant reminder of not only his indulgent affection for the twins, but also his relaxed attitude towards his masculinity.

Velutha's body is stamped also by nature. Particularly, in the final scene of the novel, when he meets Ammu on the banks of the Meenachal river, Velutha appears to be an organic part of his natural surroundings: 'As he rose from the dark river and walked up the stone steps, she saw that the world they stood in was his. That he belonged to it. That it belonged to him. The water. The mud. The trees. The fish. The stars. He moved so easily through it' (Roy 1997, 334). Divya Anand (2005, 97) finds a description such as this reduces Velutha to the figure of the 'noble savage'. However, I would argue that this portrayal takes on an entirely different meaning when we read Velutha's affinity with nature as part of Roy's critique of rampant capitalist development and the environmental devastation that it brings in its wake. In fact, Velutha's violent death underscores the degradation of the Meenachal river which the adult Rahel cannot but notice upon her return to Ayemenem. As Jani (2010, 216) has also remarked, 'the critique of capitalist modernity in Roy's novel often develops through representations of a deteriorating nature; the possibility of transforming that modernity, likewise, is projected through (lost scenes of) lush, natural beauty that are crucially, linked to (the loss of) Velutha himself'.

Furthermore, it is important to note that the focus on Velutha's body and his near-nudity instead of objectifying him, allows the text to uphold a specific kind of beauty. The repetitive references to Velutha's 'black' body are particularly worthy of analysis. In India, and more generally in South Asia, the concept of skin colour 'embraces much more than chromatic qualities, for the semantics of colour include cultural perceptions and judgments about associated moral and behavioural qualities, health and appearance, and individual and collective identities' (Philips 2004, 253). More specifically, a cultural association exists between dark skin and a lower-caste status. As Tickell (2007, 25) explains, this identification of dark skin with the lowest castes may well be the result of the work of some 'European scholars who "racialized" caste in their widespread assumption that caste divisions had developed after advanced Aryan races had invaded northern India in the pre-Vedic period and subjugated darker-skinned native Dravidian peoples, excluding them from "twice-born" caste status'.[3] The social perception of the 'inferiority' of dark skin is reinforced by its association with the lower classes in the region, as we saw in Chapter 1. Furthermore, as Priya Menon (2010, 135) has remarked, 'whiteness is spectacularized, played out aloud, encoded and articulated, in every walk of life in contemporary Kerala. It's no secret that Kerala's touchstone for its standards of beauty is largely governed by whiteness.' Physical beauty, then, is closely tied in with social hierarchies, and in this cultural context, is very much colour-coded. Ammu's lover's skin is 'so black' that his parents named him 'Velutha', meaning 'white' in Malayalam (Roy 1997, 73). Indeed, Roy appears to make a conscious effort to insist on the beauty of Velutha's blackness, of his 'dark legs' and 'smooth ebony chest' (Roy 1997, 334–5). The novel seems thus to echo the political sentiment encapsulated by the slogan 'black is beautiful' through which the black community in the United States sought to modify established notions of beauty. According

[3] This biased view of Indian history was in keeping with 'nineteenth-century European theories about racial evolution and made the further conquest of India by the British seem inevitable and beneficial' (Tickell 2007, 25).

to bell hooks (1996, 120), this slogan 'worked to intervene in and alter those racist stereotypes that had always insisted black was ugly, monstrous, undesirable'. While Dirk Wiemann (2008, 291) concedes the anti-racist element in the portrayal of Velutha's body, he nonetheless insists that the Dalit character's 'desirable athleticism' is marked by a facile, normative idealization which depends on 'readily available, overdetermined images of bodily perfection'. On the contrary, Velutha's physical attractiveness is far from conformist or conventional: in fact so unconventional is his beauty that it is *invisible* to most members of the elite who have been schooled for centuries to see only ugliness in the members of the lowest castes. Velutha's body—indeed his entire 'Dalit' being—produces a feeling of deep-seated disgust among Ammu's family, as we saw earlier.

Ammu's awareness of Velutha's beauty and her response to it are a testament to her liminality and her refusal to subscribe to dominant ideologies. The focus on Velutha's physique, particularly during his intense sexual encounters with Ammu, works to reclaim culturally acceptable notions of beauty and male/female sexual desire. Indeed, as Kancha Ilaiah, asserts 'beauty and ugliness are both culturally constructed notions that gradually transform our consciousness', and thus 'it is important that these notions be recast to change the hegemonic relations that have been brought into force in the process' (quoted in Amin and Chakrabarty 1997, 169). Therefore, the depiction of Velutha's beauty is neither gratuitous nor is it fetishized. It is, in fact, intimately tied in with the subaltern-centred sensibility of the novel.

The depiction of Khaleel's beauty, on the other hand, is in keeping with his cultural sophistication and conforms to the aesthetic standards of the Dard-e-Dils, aiding the happy ending of the romance.

Transgressions: Imagined and Real

Salt and Saffron seems to invite us to read the two cross-class love stories in conjunction with each other. In fact, it is Aliya's meeting with Khaleel that works as a narrative device compelling Aliya to remember her aunt's story which the rest of her family is determined to forget. However, such a parallel reading necessitates an exaggeration of the transgressive nature of Aliya and Khaleel's romance. The importance of Khaleel's geographical origins is amplified in the text, by insisting on the importance of his distant ties with Liaquatabad, a neighbourhood in a city that he has never visited. After meeting with Khaleel and acknowledging her growing fondness for him, Aliya thinks to herself: 'I'm fated to bring ruin to my family. Me and Mariam' (Shamsie 2000, 71). This observation which conflates Mariam and Aliya, conflates also Khaleel and Masood and simplifies the vast disparity in the material realities of the two men. Masood was a servant, born in a village, who did not appear to have had access to any form of formal schooling. On the other hand, 'polished and urbane' Khaleel grew up in the United States where he completed his undergraduate education and has had the opportunity to travel to Europe (Shamsie 2000, 52). While Masood and Mariam are certainly separated by immense social, cultural, and material differences, the distance between Khaleel and Aliya is far less pronounced, as Rehana Ahmed (2002, 16) has also observed.

But while the text consistently highlights the transgressive nature of Aliya and Khaleel's encounter, paradoxically, it also accentuates Khaleel's highbrow predilections which align him with the Dard-e-Dils. When we first meet him, he is carrying a copy of John Ashbery's selected poems and repeatedly quotes canonical poetry in the English language. The narrative seems to imply that while Khaleel is an inferior in material terms, as far as his cultural capital, and in particular his literary tastes are concerned, he is not just Aliya's equal, but is *more* than her equal because of the improbability of his achievements, given his lower-class origins. As Bourdieu (2010 [1984], xxv) points out, 'to the socially recognized hierarchy of the arts, and within each of them, of genres, of schools or periods, corresponds a social hierarchy of the consumers. This predisposes tastes to function as markers of "class".' The text ensures that Khaleel's tastes conform to Aliya's definition of sophistication and cultural distinction, winning him the admiration of her extended family, which further erodes the supposedly transgressive nature of the relationship. Aliya and Khaleel's story is constructed to accentuate the challenges faced by Mariam and Masood and, by extension, inter-class romantic couples in Pakistan. However, in highlighting their common tastes, while simultaneously overestimating Khaleel's cultural alterity (for example, the mediocre English spoken by his distant relatives), the narrative pushes material considerations that underpin class culture to the background.

Velutha and Ammu's affair lasts only thirteen nights with 'few representations of the two interacting' (Azzam 2007, 158). I would contend that the limited textual space given to the interaction between the lovers is a testimony to the transgressive nature of their relationship. It suggests that a romantic relationship such as theirs, which violates the laws of caste and class as well as patriarchy, can take place only in a temporally and spatially defined context. The lack of any in-depth interaction between Masood and Mariam, on the other hand, is worthy of closer attention. Their romance lasted, in all probability, over fifteen years, while they were both living in Aliya's parents' house. However, Aliya can recall only an extremely limited number of occasions that could have hinted at any affinity between the two. Aliya insists to her incredulous American friend that Masood and Mariam's relationship was a platonic one (Shamsie 2000, 99). It is only in conversation with her former ayah that she realizes that while the Dard-e-Dil family were completely blind to the love between her aunt and the cook, it was obvious to the other servants. Aliya then acknowledges that this blindness sprang from the deep-seated belief in the impossibility of any romantic inclinations between two individuals from such disparate socio-economic positionings (Shamsie 2000, 211). Thus, the text attributes the absence of any descriptions of the interaction between Masood and Mariam to the elite family's inability to imagine the presence of any romantic feelings between them.

However, the occasional use of magical realist elements in the novel, notably in the depiction of Mariam's fantastical mutism, has problematic consequences for the class politics of the text. Mariam's refusal to speak bars the possibility of exploring her relationship with Masood, an omission which continues with the couple's departure from Pakistan (and the narrative). We are not told how the couple found the financial wherewithal to migrate to Turkey and set up a flourishing restaurant. Furthermore, the narrative does not concern itself with the intricacies of their daily life in Turkey, where one partner does not speak the local language and the other is mute by choice. How did a woman so accustomed to a life of leisure and material comforts adjust to her new socio-economic positioning? How did Masood find success in a setting that is so different, culturally and materially, from the life that he had known previously? As pointed out earlier, Masood does not appear to have had any formal schooling, while Mariam reads Virginia Woolf and Mirza Ghalib, and is very fond of Cocteau's *Orphée* (Shamsie 2000, 189). In this context, it is useful also to recall Masood's angry reaction when, many years earlier, Aliya's father suggested that he accompany the family on their holiday in Europe: 'It was the only time I saw Masood exhibit anything approaching anger. He stood up straight and said that of course, he was just a servant, he would cook in whichever kitchen he wanted him to cook in, even if it was a country where he knew no one and couldn't speak the language' (Shamsie 2000, 133). Given this reaction, it would have been interesting to see how he managed to make a life for himself in Turkey, where he knew no one and couldn't speak the language. Neither does the text give us any indication as to how Aliya and Khaleel's relationship will be lived on a daily basis. In fact, their 'relationship' consists of three meetings in London and a reunion of sorts in Karachi at the close of the novel, which is constructed as a happy ending.

Ending of the Love Story

In fiction, transgressive love stories that defy the boundaries of class, race, or heterosexuality tend to either have a happy ending or a tragic one. According to Aijaz Ahmad (2007, 114), twentieth-century novels privilege an optimistic ending, and both Hollywood and Bollywood have echoed this inclination to have love triumphing over all. The other conventional ending, common in the nineteenth century novel, but of which examples can also be found in contemporary literature, is the tragic one, where the lovers pay the price of death for their transgressive desires, and are essentially helpless under the weight of social oppression.

Salt and Saffron is a case of 'love triumphant and permanent, overcoming all obstacles and difficulties' with a happy ending for both the cross-class couples (Cawelti 1976, 41–2). While we learn of Masood and Mariam's marriage early on in the novel, the reader and Aliya are in the dark as to what happened to them after the elopement. It is only towards the end of the text that we discover that they are settled in Istanbul where they run a now world-famous restaurant. The couple's lifestyle, it is implied, is more than comfortable. It is also at the end of the novel that Khaleel comes to see Aliya in Karachi where the two voice their plans to travel to the United States together. Indeed, the text interweaves the endings of the two love stories: Khaleel's arrival brings with it an intimation of Mariam's happiness. Khaleel and Aliya's reunion is orchestrated through what Rehana Ahmed (2002, 26) has referred to as 'an improbable chain of events': Aliya's family in London takes charge of Khaleel's ticket and organizes a layover in Istanbul where her great-aunt hands him a package of food from Masood's restaurant. A cousin of hers collects him from the airport and escorts him to Aliya's parents' house in Karachi. Thus, the spatial setting of Khaleel and Aliya's happy reunion is her parental home located in a wealthy area of the city and Khaleel's troublesome ties to Liaquatabad are forgotten. The question that he had asked Aliya at the beginning of the novel, 'If I come to Karachi, will you visit me in Liaquatabad?' remains unanswered (Shamsie 2000, 64).

When savouring the food brought by Khaleel from Istanbul, Aliya is finally able to picture her aunt happy and content. This imagined happiness too has an affluent setting, without the narrative delving into how it became economically and materially possible: 'When I tasted the food I saw Mariam in a kitchen, *a vast glorious kitchen*, brushing saffron off her husband's neck and dusting it on to her own lips.… When I tasted that food, I saw Mariam older and happier' (Shamsie 2000, 241–2; italics mine). For Khaleel and Aliya too the happy ending takes place 'offstage', in terms of geography (away from Pakistan) and narrative space (the reunion occurs at the end of the novel). While Khaleel is welcomed by the Dard-e-Dils because of his sophisticated literary tastes and good looks, the novel's conclusion excludes any possibility of Masood and Mariam's return to Karachi. Earlier in the text, Aliya's cousin Samir confesses that if he were to come across Masood, he would not invite him to his home, but would, however, inform him that 'his palate misses him' (Shamsie

2000, 185). The novel's denouement echoes Samir's sentiments: it is only Masood's *cooking* that is allowed narratological re-entry into the novel, while Masood and Mariam's return to Pakistan is deemed impossible. Although a reunion is hinted at, it can be imagined only in Istanbul, and not in Karachi. The 'happy' ending of the novel is effectively mitigated by its refusal to adequately address material questions and by the upper-class setting of the lovers' happiness. As Rehana Ahmed (2002, 26) has also pointed out, 'their eventual home remains a space of mystery and fantasy where the social hierarchies that divide them in Karachi are dissolved'. The ending of both the cross-class love stories, entailing a departure from Pakistan, glosses over the socio-economic inequalities besetting Turkey and the United States—the lovers' destinations. Moreover, as Sara Ahmed (2000, 86) warns us, 'the assumption that to leave home, to migrate or to travel, is to suspend the boundaries in which identity comes to be liveable, conceals the complex and contingent relations of antagonism which grant some subjects the ability to move freely at the expense of others'. Geographical mobility, which is essential to the two couples' shared future, is constructed to resolve the problems posed by class differences, but the narrative does not address the material aspect of this mobility in any detail.

Unlike *Salt and Saffron*, in *The God of Small Things* the lovers' lives come to a tragic end. After being falsely accused not only of raping Ammu, but also of killing Sophie Mol and kidnapping the twins, Velutha is brutally beaten and murdered by the police. A grief-stricken and socially ostracized Ammu falls ill and dies a few months later, leaving the twins emotionally rudderless. The tragic ending to their love story is indicated fairly early on in the novel, but given the non-chronological, non-linear quality of the narrative, it is only as we approach the end that we are able to reconstruct the chronological sequence of events. The closing passage is a detailed description of Velutha and Ammu's lovemaking and the novel ends when they take leave of each other, promising to return the following night.

The final scene has been perceived by some critics as an alternative, utopic ending to the novel's tragic conclusion. Aijaz Ahmad (2007, 116) has criticized Roy's emphasis on sexual desire, maintaining that the author depicts the erotic as a 'sufficient mode for overcoming real social oppressions'. While finding the portrayal of Velutha's murder 'entirely credible', Ahmad (2007, 116) contends that Ammu's death is 'contrived' and contradicts the construction of her life as a woman of 'great grit'. For him, Ammu's demise is largely devoid of political significance; it subscribes to a clichéd convention in fiction that dictates that 'women who live impermissibly must also die horribly', and is a case of a character dying quickly because the author does not know 'how to let them go on living' (Ahmad 2007, 116). But Ahmad's reading of Ammu's tragic demise gestures to a privileging of Velutha's 'public' transgression in the form of his participation in Naxalite politics, over Ammu's sexual, therefore 'personal', transgression, by implication making Velutha a worthier martyr (Bose 2007, 125).

Bose draws our attention to the arbitrariness of this reading which designates Ammu's personalized challenge to the 'caste/class/gender/sexuality nexus' through the sexual act as 'soft politics', while Velutha's intervention in communist ideology acquires a higher political status (Bose 2007, 125). Furthermore, Ahmad's analysis neglects to take into account the lovers' painful awareness of the limitations of their liaison. Indeed, in regarding the lovemaking scene as a happy ending to the text, Ahmad not only overestimates the emancipatory power attributed to the erotic in the novel, but also undervalues the political significance of desire in general. It is difficult to deny the political ramifications of the sexual act, if we recall Mammachi's uncontrollable rage at her daughter for having 'defiled generations of breeding' (Roy 1997, 258). In her eyes, Ammu has not just contravened the 'sacred' laws of untouchability, but has also flouted patriarchal and class strictures. Therefore, as Armstrong and Tennenhouse (2014 [1987], 2) insist, 'we must see representations of desire, neither as reflections nor as consequences of political power but as a form of political power in their own right'. However, while it is important to acknowledge the politics of erotic touch, it is also crucial not to exaggerate its emancipating force in the novel, as Bose (2007, 223–5) appears to do. Sexual intercourse is certainly constructed as an act of resistance against social oppression in Roy's text, but it is also ultimately an inadequate form of rebellion. Lévinas reminds us that 'the caress consists in seizing upon nothing, in soliciting what ceaselessly escapes its form toward a future never future enough, in soliciting what slips away as though it *were not yet*. It *searches*. It forages' (1971, 257; italics in the original). Despite the lyricism of the closing passages, the reader is never lulled into forgetting the tragic destiny of the lovers. In particular, the non-linear chronology of the novel never allows the reader to lose sight of the obstacles that stand in the way of a love this transgressive or of the price that will have to be paid for it. As Jani has also pointed out, 'the novel succeeds in its project precisely *because* it portrays the inability of sexuality to smooth over oppression of the subaltern' (2010, 210; italics in the original).

Both novels examined in this chapter deftly illustrate the profoundly subversive nature of cross-class romantic relationships in a society riddled by rigid class divisions. However, the happily-ever-after for the two couples in *Salt and Saffron* is firmly located in elite spaces. The subaltern characters' perspectives are secondary to Aliya's and by choosing not to address pressing material aspects of the 'happy' ending, rather than the liberating power of love and romance, the novel underscores the invincibility of class prejudice within Pakistan. On the other hand, *The God of Small Things* locates a lower-class Dalit at the heart of its narrative, making him the centre of the emotional universe of Ammu and her twins. Thus, in Roy's novel, despite its unequivocally tragic ending, human intimacy can and does shift oppressive hierarchies, even if such a victory is short-lived and the punishment meted out for it, breathtakingly brutal.

◆

4

Domestic/Employee Seduction in *The Hottest Day of the Year*, *The Space Between Us*, and *The God of Small Things*

[T]he most common form of corruption: the abuse of authority exercised by the boss or the foreman over a woman working in his shop, by the master over his servant, in a word, domestic seduction or employee seduction.

—Louis Martin*

Lennard J. Davis (1987, 123) has argued that in the classic novel, well through the nineteenth century, convention demands a physically attractive hero or heroine. And physical beauty among the poor, particularly 'poor virgins', often signals their future social ascension and indicates that they 'can or should transcend class lines', as Richardson's Pamela does (Davis 1987, 123–4). In the works that I examine in this chapter, however, the physical attractiveness of the lower-class female makes her particularly vulnerable to abuse of power, and her socio-economic class positioning certainly does not improve as a result of her association with an upper-class male. The three texts considered here illustrate the potential for exploitation in a sexual relationship between a Babu male and a subaltern woman who is either directly (as in *The Hottest Day of the Year* and *The God of Small Things*) or indirectly (as in *The Space Between Us*) dependent on him for her livelihood. This abuse of power has its roots in a culture of male authority, which is a hallmark of patriarchy, as well as in the socio-economic privilege conferred upon the male by a highly unequal society.

* Martin quoted in Jean Elisabeth Pederson (1998, 50).

Consent, Coercion, and Desire

Even without the added dimension of class differences, defining and ascertaining consent in heterosexual relationships within the context of male dominance can be problematic. As Geneviève Fraisse (2007, 86) points out, historically, when a man consents he seems to 'decide', to 'declare', whereas a 'consenting woman' makes a choice, but 'within a space of dependence towards an authority'. Moreover, the word 'consent' carries two sets of connotations: its positive meaning evokes 'accepting' or 'subscribing', while its negative meaning suggests 'tolerating' or 'being subjected' to the Other (Fraisse 2007, 87). Pointing to the inequality between the sexes, Catharine MacKinnon (1989, 172) takes a more radical stance and has called heterosexuality 'male supremacy's paradigm of sex'. When the relationship takes place under the conditions of gender as well as economic inequality, identifying a woman's consent and determining whether or not she was subjected to coercion becomes even more challenging. The notion of consent is further complicated by the desire that she may feel for the upper-class male and the possibility that this desire may itself be informed by patriarchal discourse as well as class ideology.

In Roy's novel, the upper-class, upper-caste male Chacko has sexual relations with a number of women working for him at his factory. In *The Hottest Day of the Year*, Charry depicts the affair between Sundar and his live-in servant Sudha which lasts several weeks and results in her becoming pregnant. In *The Space Between Us*, rather than an affair, an isolated sexual encounter takes place between Viraf, Sera's son-in-law, and her servant Bhima's granddaughter Maya. Like Sudha, Maya finds herself pregnant following the encounter. While sexual relations between master and maid can work to reproduce and reinforce gender and economic hierarchies, they may also lead to a blurring of social borders and boundaries. When the liaison results in a pregnancy, it opens up the prospect of a biological connection between the two classes and concrete proof of the crossing-over. It can also lead to calls to legitimize the relationship through marriage. Moreover, these relations across class can conjure up, as Mammachi so dreads, 'Feelings' as opposed to 'Needs' and thus the possibility that the affair may in fact be or become a bond of love (Roy 1997, 169).

Roy's novel underscores not only Chacko's gender- and class-based exploitation of his employees, but also his abuse of ideological power. He turns his attention to the most attractive of his female workers and uses Marxism and its egalitarian edicts as a means to neutralize the power of cultural mores that prescribe distance between disparate classes as well as between men and women:

> He would call them Comrade, and insist they call him Comrade back (which made them giggle). Much to their embarrassment and Mammachi's dismay, he forced them to sit at the table with him and drink tea. Once he even took a group of them to attend Trade Union classes that were held in Alleppey. They went by bus and returned by boat. They came back happy with glass bangles and flowers in their hair. (Roy 1997, 65)

If, at first glance, Chacko's actions seem hypocritical but essentially harmless, the reader quickly learns that his workers are also made to satisfy his libido. Chacko's behaviour does not invoke the disapproval of his family; Ammu is the only one who perceives her brother's conduct towards his female employees as abuse of power, leaving no room for consent: 'An Oxford avatar of the old zamindar mentality—a landlord forcing his attentions on women who depended on him for their livelihood' (Roy 1997, 65). Perhaps Ammu is particularly sensitive to this kind of exploitation, having herself been targeted by her ex-husband's English employer. But given her marginalized position within Keralite society as well as within her family, and her financial dependence on her bother, her condemnation of his behaviour carries little social weight. Mammachi and Baby Kochamma's indulgent attitude towards Chacko's transgressions is in stark contrast to the shock and outrage that Ammu's liaison with Velutha provokes and reveals upper-class women's complicity in promoting sexual double standards: '"He can't help having a Man's Needs", she said primly. Neither Mammachi nor Baby Kochamma saw any contradiction between Chacko's Marxist mind and feudal libido' (Roy 1997, 26). Mammachi even has a separate entrance constructed to Chacko's room so that the 'chosen' female workers need not enter the house, thereby maintaining the illusion of bourgeois respectability.

Furthermore, she gives financial handouts to these women, using this 'transactional device' to keep at bay any confusion about the nature of Chacko's relationship with them (Bahri 2003, 203): 'She secretly slipped them money to keep them happy. They took it because they needed it.... The arrangement suited Mammachi because in her mind a fee *clarified* things. Disjuncted sex from love' (Roy 1997, 169; italics in the original).

Mammachi's actions echo the attitude of nineteenth-century British colonialists with respect to interracial sexual relationships. According to Lucy Bland, while 'interracial *sex* between white men and black women was seen as meeting men's "natural" sexual urges, actual marriage was strongly disapproved of' (2005, 31; italics in the original). Moreover, as Tirthankar Chanda (1997, 40) explains, in facilitating her son's exploitation of lower-class women, Mammachi is demonstrating her acceptance of the tenets of patriarchal society where women are the marginalized Other, and 'the eternal victims of an unfavourable *rapport de force*'. Mammachi's actions reinforce not only patriarchal codes, but also the ideology of socio-economic stratification. She deprives these subaltern women of dignity in order to cement her own sense of bourgeois decorum and to underscore the economic superiority of her son and his family. Indeed, in paying the women, whom she clearly deems unworthy of her son's affections, Mammachi is attempting to reassure herself (with some success, it seems) that her son is using them to satisfy his purely physical needs without any emotional involvement. She wants to see them as prostitutes because the status of a lover would imply shared desires and a degree of equality between the two parties. In a later scene, which is not devoid of humour, Mammachi also tries to 'remunerate' Chacko's English ex-wife during her visit to India, who she refers to pejoratively as a 'shopkeeper's daughter' (Roy 1997, 168). In 'paying' Margaret, her objective is the same as when she slips money to Chacko's female workers: to reinforce and maintain the frontiers of class that can so easily become blurred by sexual intimacy.

The depiction of cross-class carnal relations in Charry's novel is more complex and detailed, not only because the affair lasts about three months, but especially because Sudha appears to be infatuated with her employer, imagining that theirs is a romantic relationship.

It is important to note that Sundar, and not Sudha, initiates the affair. Charry, like Roy and Umrigar, seems to consciously subvert bourgeois clichés according to which maids and lower-class women are the 'initiators of debauchery' and bourgeois males the passive victims of their iniquitous machinations (Stoler 1995, 144). Early on in the text, Nithya, the young narrator, catches her uncle Sundar surreptitiously eyeing Sudha (Charry 2003 [2001], 40). The text compares him to a menacing tiger, 'lean, hard-eyed and muscled' (Charry 2003 [2001], 21) and accentuates the voyeuristic, predatory nature of his gaze: 'Sudha flitted in and out busy with her usual morning chores, and I watched Sundar watch her from behind *The Hindu*—Sudha's just visible ankles. Sudha's waist, back and neck, the clear, smooth untouched skin of her cheeks and forehead' (Charry 2003 [2001], 74). This extract draws the reader's attention to Sudha's beauty and innocence by evoking her 'virgin' skin, as well as emphasizes Sundar's duplicity, as he leers at her behind the *Hindu*, an English-language Indian newspaper that symbolizes his Babu position in Indian society. Despite belonging to the same Brahmin caste, Sundar's milieu contrasts sharply with the poverty in which Sudha's family lives. For instance, Nithya wonders privately if Sudha 'got enough to eat when she was at home' (Charry 2003 [2001], 32–3).

At first Sundar initiates bland, apparently innocuous, conversations with her, but within days something resembling a bond seems to develop between the two. Nithya notices a new sense of excitement in Sudha, but her uncle appears to her to be in perfect control of his emotions and as detached as always: '[W]hen he spoke to Sudha his voice was as it always was—steady, low and unexcited' (Charry 2003 [2001], 84). Soon afterwards, one evening, Nithya catches her uncle entering the maid's room (Charry 2003 [2001], 40). In her analysis of Hardy's *Tess of the d'Urbervilles*, Christine DeVine (2005, 158) argues that if 'a man has a power advantage over a woman when he seduces her (in addition to the gender advantage society bestows on him) then one might easily consider that seduction is the equivalent of rape'. Nithya does not witness the sexual encounters between Sudha and Sundar and thus we, as readers, do not know whether Sundar deployed physical force or verbal threats to compel her to submit to his advances (and therefore effectively raped her), or seduced her with words, gifts, and caresses. Moreover, how should we address the possibility of consensual sex and shared desires between master and maid? MacKinnon (1989, 177) has questioned the very validity of heterosexual desire expressed by a woman and perceives it as an unhealthy eroticization of male dominance. For the most part, in male–female relationships, MacKinnon (1989, 177) contends, 'women are socialized to passive receptivity: may have or perceive no alternative to acquiescence; may prefer it to the escalated risk of injury and the humiliation of a lost fight; submit to survive'.

However, Sudha's behaviour following her first night with Sundar does not allow us to easily conclude that she was raped or that she submitted passively to her employer's advances. Sudha becomes 'more beautiful' (Charry 2003 [2001], 116) once the affair begins and, indeed, behaves more like a woman who desired, rather than reluctantly acquiesced to, sex: 'She went about her work humming songs.... But she was also restless sometimes. She would then come looking for me and want to talk. I could sense excitement in her, and fear, and something else I didn't have a name for' (Charry 2003 [2001], 85). Given the 'ideology of premarital chastity' still prevalent in the Indian subcontinent, it also appears that in becoming Sundar's lover, Sudha is conscious of transgressing age-old social taboos, a realization that provokes both excitement and trepidation in her (Puri 1999, 115). It seems possible, if not probable, that her perception of her relationship with Sundar is coloured by a degree of what Puri (1999, 126) calls the 'fusion of love and sex, or the romanticization of sex and the eroticization of love'. Perhaps Sudha feels the need to romanticize the sex, or to see it as eroticized love, after the act, so as to appease her guilt over the transgression. She also appears to be flattered that a wealthy and educated man is taking an interest in her. As Nithya wonders:

> Maybe she liked him because he made her feel pretty and desirable even though she was a servant ... and because he was handsome and had been to college. And because Sudha liked big things, adventure.... *Maybe* that's how the high-school girls at St Mary's—the sports captains and house leaders—really were. Beneath their smart jackets and skirts and swinging hair. (Charry 2003 [2001], 123; italics mine)

The use of 'maybe' when comparing a servant with the well-to-do older girls at her school highlights Nithya's understanding of class as a defining personal trait. Although, she is able to see beyond adult hypocrisy and is not duped by her elders' warnings about calling Sudha a servant, Nithya, like Lenny in *Ice-Candy-Man* and Shehzadi in *The Hope Chest*, has inevitably internalized class stereotypes, seeing servants as Others, inherently different from her and other members of her own class even when they share the same gender and caste. But Nithya does not appear to be the only one who has internalized class stereotypes. Sudha's perceptions of privilege at being associated with an upper-class man mirror Maya's feelings of pride in *The Space Between Us* when she has sex with Viraf, and suggest that the subaltern woman's desire for the upper-class male can also be informed by not only patriarchal discourse, but also hegemony in Gramscian terms, which lead her to conceive of men of wealth as intrinsically superior to subaltern men. However, Sudha's character does grow to see the error in her logic which caused her to equate a high socio-economic positioning with moral rectitude. When Sundar deserts her upon learning of her pregnancy, she confesses to him bitterly her naiveté at believing him to be a 'big' man only to find him completely lacking in moral courage (Charry 2003 [2001], 145). Thus, in Charry's novel the development of the subaltern's class and gender consciousness comes about through a process of painful disillusionment with, as we will see now, fatal consequences.

The sexual relations between Viraf and Maya are limited to one single episode and, unlike Sundar and Chacko, Viraf's conduct, at least until after he has had sex with Maya, does not seem be a case of calculated exploitation. While in *The Hottest Day of the Year* and *The God of Small Things* the reader is left speculating about the exact nature of the relations between the subaltern and the upper-class male, in *The Space Between Us* Maya relates the incident in detail to her grandmother and it is worth analysing this episode in depth as it tellingly reveals the blurred boundaries of desire, consent, and coercion. Significantly, it also constitutes a 'testimonial narrative' (Tagore 2009, 9) within the text, marking the subaltern's 'desire not to be silenced' (Beverley 2004, 34). Chapter 21 of the novel closes with the words 'So Maya tells', in response to Bhima's gentle exhortation: 'Tell me the whole story.' The following chapter is entirely devoted to Maya's story, which is narrated in the third person. I would argue that the poetic device of rendering Maya's first-person account to her grandmother in the third person effectively 'authenticates' Maya's word and presents a direct challenge to Viraf's dismissal of Maya's testimony.

As Maya recounts to Bhima, when Viraf arrived at Sera's mother-in-law's flat where she occasionally works as a maid, he was tired and irritable following an argument with his wife. Maya attempted to cheer him up by offering to make him tea, and the text clearly indicates that she had no intention of seducing him. Maya had always been fond of Viraf, but her affection for him was platonic and can almost be described as sisterly (Umrigar 2005, 272). Viraf too did not appear to have considered Maya an object of erotic desire, but rather 'a cute little puppy' (Umrigar 2005, 272). At his request, she began massaging his neck. This massage, however, quickly turned erotic. Maya found herself fascinated by his physical beauty and personal hygiene, which in her mind set him manifestly apart from the men she encounters in her slum. More importantly, she interpreted his physical assets as proof of his innocuousness: '[C]ompared with the louts who strolled around the slums in their plaid lungis, with backs that looked as hairy as the bears in the circus, Viraf's back looked as unthreatening as a loaf of bread' (Umrigar 2005, 275). When she realized that Viraf is aroused by her touch, conflicting feelings invaded her, including pride at being desired by a man like him:

> And her awe turning to pride and then pride turning to panic, as Viraf half-rose from the bed and gently but firmly pushed her back on it.... Her stomach dropped and then, as Viraf lowered his lips to her bosom came a flood of other feelings, a flood that rushed into her thighs, breaking down the dam of resistance, making her legs feel heavy and weak. (Umrigar 2005, 277)

Maya's desire for Viraf was undeniable even if it was tempered by some hesitation: 'She protested; she did not protest. It did not matter, because it was inevitable what was about to happen, what was happening and they both knew it; they were like swimmers caught in the same current' (Umrigar 2005, 278). She felt the physical pain that comes with the loss of virginity, but also clearly derived pleasure from the act (Umrigar 2005, 277).

In this scene, Viraf does not resort to violence to sleep with Maya; but what about coercion through other means? Can the incident be defined as a case of seduction—'weakness induced by another' (Conly 2004, 112)? Can we, or rather should we, dismiss the desire that Maya felt for Viraf, or that Sudha may have felt for Sundar before he abandoned her, as a mere product of gender and class ideology and the subaltern woman as nothing but an inert embodiment of it? While recognizing the coercive power of class superiority and male dominance, I would argue that such an interpretation can deprive the female subaltern of all agency and deny her ownership of her body and its longings. As Moore and Reynolds (2004, 30) contend in their critique of the writings of Jeffreys and MacKinnon, which throw into doubt the possibility of genuine female desire for men and hence a woman's capacity to give real consent: '[I]f feminism is to offer women an agenda for greater ownership, control and enjoyment of their sexuality, it has to offer an agenda that accepts the pleasure in and desire of women for heterosexual sex.' To take this argument further, we cannot preclude, without reducing the subaltern to a puppet, the possibility of her pleasure in and desire for heterosexual sex, even when the liaison takes place under conditions of patriarchy and economic inequality.

Moreover, Umrigar seems to imply that what happens between Viraf and Maya *following* the sexual act is more important than the act itself, and in doing so turns it into what can perhaps be called post-sex rape. As soon as Viraf's libido is satisfied, realizing that he has put his marriage in jeopardy, he tries to manipulate Maya by using both moral and emotional arguments and attempts to cultivate guilt in her by accusing her of seducing him: '[T]hat was a bad thing you did, tempting me like that, taking advantage of me while I was in a weak mood' (Umrigar 2005, 279). Viraf also reminds Maya of the debt that she and her grandmother owe Sera. Maya, however, responds angrily to this unsubtle emotional blackmail, refusing to be cast as the unscrupulous perpetrator of adultery: '"I didn't do anything," she said loudly. "That is … you were the one who jumped on me like a rabid dog"' (Umrigar 2005,

279). Faced with her lack of submission, Viraf tries a different tactic: he threatens her with the loss of her grandmother's job and informs her that as a servant her word is of no consequence (Umrigar 2005, 279).

Viraf's observation about the scant social value of Maya's testimony underscores the extent to which the chances of a social group's word being taken at face value (even by its own members) is informed by patriarchal as well as class ideologies and he uses this double advantage to coerce Maya into silence. Indeed, when Bhima first discovers that Maya had sex with Viraf, she almost instinctively blames Maya and hastens to point out her moral shortcomings:

> First, you tempted a decent married man, and then you lied to me to throw me off the scent of your shame. Pissing in the pot you have been eating out of. Betraying the trust that the whole Dubash family had in you … Namak haram,[1] every letter that you know to read, every stitch of clothing that you wear, every grain of salt in your mouth comes from Serabai's generosity. (Umrigar 2005, 269)

In choosing to relate the incident, Maya not only succeeds in breaking the coercive silence imposed on her by Viraf, but also, as we will see later, compels an ideological shift in Bhima's thinking.

Umrigar's novel accentuates the gap between Viraf's physical beauty and the ugliness of his behaviour towards the subaltern. Moreover, in the light of this incident, his bonhomie, constant attempts at humour and good manners acquire an almost artificial quality. He speaks, what Bourdieu (2010 [1984], 172) has called, the 'highly censored language of the bourgeois'. In Maya's presence, however, Viraf lets the mask drop, shocking her with his use of crude language and reminding her of the uncouth male residents of the slum (Umrigar 2005, 272). Umrigar's text invites a reflection on the superficiality of bourgeois sophistication, which may work to conceal a 'cynical, corrupt nature' (Umrigar 2005, 282). When Viraf learns of Maya's pregnancy he resorts to yet another kind of manipulation and coercion—without confessing his role in the

[1] *Namak haram* in Urdu/Hindi means a traitor to one's master's salt, ingrate.

proceedings, and feigning to defend Maya's best interests, he forces Bhima and Sera to compel Maya to have an abortion. Like Roy and Charry, Umrigar also appears to consciously emphasize the male characters' Babu identity to explode more effectively the myth of their intrinsic moral superiority to lower-class men: Chacko is a Rhodes Scholar and a self-professed Marxist—Ammu bitingly calls him a 'a spoiled princeling playing Comrade, Comrade' (Roy 1997, 65); Viraf is highly 'Westernized', listening to British and American music instead of Hindi songs; Sundar too is anglicized and university-educated. The characterization of upper-class men in these three texts diverges sharply with the conservative depiction of lower-class (and lower-caste) men and their supposed inherent depravity in Sidhwa's *Ice-Candy-Man* and Moni Mohsin's *The End of Innocence,* as we saw in Chapter 1.

Illicit Pregnancy: A Challenge to Bourgeois Respectability

Roy, Charry, and Umrigar highlight the threat that the subaltern woman's pregnancy by an elite man presents to bourgeois respectability and the hypocritical reactions that such an event elicits, providing insight into the workings of interlocking gender and class privilege.

While Mammachi and Baby Kochamma respond to Chacko's 'libertine' activities with indulgence (Roy 1997, 168), they are deeply concerned that these encounters may result in an illicit pregnancy, which in turn would lead to demands to legitimize the sexual relationship: 'They only worried about the Naxalites, who had been known to force men from Good Families to marry servant girls whom they had made pregnant' (Roy 1997, 256). The capitalizing of 'Good Families', as Deepika Bahri (2003, 230) points out, 'reveals the narrator's contempt for their alleged goodness while also typifying the conventionality of these habits among young men from "Good Families" who can entertain their libidinal needs without sacrificing bourgeois respectability'. As we know, the fears of the two women about the consequences of Chacko's affairs do not materialize. Instead, it is Ammu who, in loving Velutha, becomes the biggest threat to the family's reputation and 'honour'.

In *The Hottest Day of the Year* and *The Space Between Us*, however, the subaltern does become pregnant by her male employer, which proves to be a crucial element of the narrative. Fearing the dishonour of her family, particularly her father who is a priest, Sudha tries to obtain an abortion, but fails because of lack of money and support from her lover. Sundar, behaving with flagrant hypocrisy, accuses her of having loose morals and condemns her for having succumbed to his advances, conveniently forgetting that Sudha was a virgin before the affair began. When he finds her conversing with a young priest, he uses that incident as an example and as proof of her libertine character. It is worth noting that Sundar arms himself with conventional religious as well as patriarchal discourse to denigrate Sudha, and cites her supposed depraved character as a moral justification for abdicating all responsibility for the pregnancy: '"You know that no respectable brahmin girl would go up to a strange man and begin talking to him." "I know that." "You do? And of course someone like you wouldn't care." Sundar turned and left the room' (Charry 2003 [2001], 122).

In Richardson's *Pamela*, 'a shared moral culture' between master and servant works to allow for the possibility of conjugal, rather than merely sexual, intimacy between the two characters (Straub 2009, 156). No doubt aware of the importance of (perceived) shared morals and the obligations that this may imply, especially since Sudha is also a Brahmin, Sundar hastens to distinguish himself from her, thereby precluding any demands on her part to legitimize their relationship through marriage. He also points out to the maid her Otherness and moral inferiority vis-à-vis 'respectable' middle-class women and girls: 'I also have my widowed sister's reputation to think of … and Padma's daughter is under my care now' (Charry 2003 [2001], 147). This sudden concern for his sister highlights Sundar's hypocrisy, since he has been misappropriating her money for years, and effectively robbing her of agency. It also presents an example of patriarchy and class hierarchy reinforcing each other to create divisions amongst women, thereby seriously complicating the possibility of female solidarity across class lines.[2]

[2] In contrast to the work of socialist feminists which underscores the compatibility and 'partnership between patriarchy and capital' (Hartmann

Sundar forbids Sudha from having an abortion in Thiruninravur which would jeopardize his reputation and instead orders her to return to her parents' house. When Sudha insists on his help and asks him to accompany her to Madras to see a doctor, he rejects her request: '"Why can't you come?" … when he spoke again it was with an air of finality. "I will not"' (Charry 2003 [2001], 147).

According to Spivak (1996, 292), '[even] when the subaltern makes an effort to the death to speak, she is not able to be heard, and speaking and hearing complete the speech act'. I would argue instead that, even when the subaltern is perfectly capable of speaking and is able to be heard, she is met with a *deliberate* refusal to hear, because what she has to say is a call directed at the elites, compelling them to take responsibility for the subaltern's plight. The quoted extract from the novel indicates that Sundar can hear Sudha only too well. He understands perfectly what her words imply for him and his social status, and wilfully decides to not respond to her plea. As Goja's character in Namjoshi's text observes: 'The reason the voices of the poor go unheard is that what the poor have to say isn't acceptable' (Namjoshi 2000, 137).

Initially, unlike Sidhwa's in *Ice-Candy-Man*, Charry's depiction of female relationships seems to avoid the perils of a somewhat naive feminism according to which female solidarity can easily overcome the barriers posed by class. Janaki, Nithya's aunt, considers Sudha to be a corrupting influence and expressly forbids Nithya from spending any time with the maid. As Ann Stoler (1995, 141) points out, referring to the preconceived notions of European colonizers about the sexuality of indigenous servants, '[children] must be protected against exposure to the dangerous sexuality of the racial and class others, not because their sexuality is different but because it is savage, unrestrained and very much the same'. If Sudha is exploited and deserted by her upper-class lover, Janaki does nothing to help the young woman. In fact, she condemns her in brutal terms, showing complete insensitivity to the maid's plight. Moreover, a

2013 [1981], 196), some feminists have argued that the two systems are not necessarily mutually reinforcing, and in fact contradict each other. See, for instance, Johnson (1996) and Gordon (1996).

latent rivalry between the two women manifests itself in their final verbal exchange. Sudha expresses her contempt for Janaki, accusing her of jealousy: '"You never liked me," Sudha said very softly, and she sat down on her bed, "because I'm different from you. I have things you'll never have. You can't bear to see anyone happy … you want us all to be as lonely as you…. Even now, in spite of everything that's happened, I'm grateful I'm not you"' (Charry 2003 [2001], 164).

Janaki, as a widow, has a severely marginalized status within the Brahmin community of the small town of Thiruninravur. Her neighbours exhort her to learn to live, at thirty-four years of age, 'without desire' and to resign herself to a solitary, monotonous existence, precluding any possibility of remarriage (Charry 2003 [2001], 53). But while both Sudha and Janaki experience social exclusion in a deeply patriarchal society, it does not bring them closer together; on the contrary, they turn viciously on each other. Charry has thus depicted the devastating consequences of a patriarchal social order not only for male–female relationships, but also for the relationships that women have with each other. It seems possible that Janaki fears that her finances (which are controlled by her brother) will completely slip out of her hands with the arrival of the baby. As a childless widow, she is aware of her socially weak position within the Brahmin community and her family, and perhaps feels that Sundar and Sudha's affair will only increase her marginality. During their final confrontation, when Sudha asks Janaki whether or not she agreed that her brother 'should do something' about the pregnancy, Janaki responds with a shrug, declaring the matter closed for further discussion (Charry 2003 [2001], 163). Like her brother, Janaki resorts to Othering to clearly differentiate her middle-class sexuality from the maid's and suggests that for 'a woman like' Sudha prostitution may be a suitable profession (Charry 2003 [2001], 164). The pitiless words that Janaki directs at Sudha are clearly designed to humiliate and cause pain: 'You are a disgrace to everything … to your parents, to your caste, especially to your poor parents…. If I were you … I'd kill myself, that's what I'd do. Why don't you do that' (Charry 2003 [2001], 164). Abandoned by Sundar, unable to find a doctor willing to carry out an abortion, and following this ugly confrontation with Janaki, Sudha kills herself. I will examine the importance and consequences of her suicide later in the chapter.

At the beginning of *The Space Between Us*, before learning of what happened between Maya and Viraf, Sera is shown to resent Maya for her illicit pregnancy, especially since it coincides with Sera's daughter's (and Viraf's wife's) 'respectable' gestation. 'The unwanted pregnancy had cast a pall on the Dubash household, so that the baby growing like a weed inside of Maya was smothering the happiness that they should be feeling at the thought of the child flowering within Dinaz's belly' (Umrigar 2005, 119). Umrigar skilfully deploys dramatic irony to expose the falseness of the distinction that Sera makes between the two pregnancies, and by extension, reveals the fiction of bourgeois sexual restraint. Upon discovering the truth, Sera invokes bourgeois and patriarchal clichés about the amorality of lower-class women to reject Viraf's implication in the affair. In depicting Sera's open hostility towards Maya, Umrigar underscores not only the depth of the mistress's gendered class prejudice, but also the inextricable link between the myth of bourgeois moral rectitude and the supposed innate licentiousness of the working classes: '"I can excuse you stealing from me, but to challenge my son-in-law's honor, that I can never forgive you for.... What your Maya did is her business." Sera screams. "She can be a whore with fifty men for all I care. Just don't involve my family in her sickness"' (Umrigar 2005, 303).

However, Sera's violent reaction is an attempt not just to silence Bhima, but also to quell her own doubts. If, by dismissing Bhima, Sera is attempting to restore her son-in-law's dignity and save her daughter's marriage, the text makes it clear that Sera's world as she knew it has been 'shattered' (Umrigar 2005, 320).

The Politics of Abortion

The right to abortion is a central trope of Leftist women's movements and is intimately tied to questions of individual choice and control over a woman's reproductive life. In particular, as bell hooks (2000, 28) points out, economically underprivileged women who are deprived of 'class power' lose 'all control over their own bodies' when denied access to 'safe, inexpensive and free abortions'.

Charry's novel appears to echo this observation: it is very likely that Sudha commits suicide not because of disappointment at her lover's rejection, but because she was unable to get an abortion and hence avoid dishonouring her family.

Umrigar's treatment of the theme of abortion diverges from Charry's: Maya initially refuses to reveal the identity of the man who impregnated her and unlike Sudha seems to accept her pregnancy despite the unpleasant circumstances that led to it. When Bhima questions her about the identity of the father of the child she is carrying, her response is as follows: 'What does it matter who the father is, Ma-ma? The fact is that the baby is growing in my stomach, not his. That makes it my curse and my blessing, no one else's …' (Umrigar 2005, 41). Maya's words are reminiscent of the feminist slogan 'My body belongs to me', and her desire to keep the baby hints at her struggle to regain control of own destiny and her own body (of which she feels the baby is now a part).[3] Bhima and Sera believe that abortion is the only solution to this predicament which would allow Maya to complete her studies, find a suitable job (one that does not involve domestic servitude) and thus escape a life of crippling poverty. It is only upon Bhima and Sera's insistence (who themselves are being pushed by Viraf) that Maya consents to having an abortion while clearly perceiving it as an intrusion and indeed, a violation of her body.

Viraf's motives in forcing Maya to have an abortion are of course quite different from Sera and Bhima's. He wants to eliminate all proof of his indiscretion, realizing fully that an 'illegitimate' child resulting from a sexual transgression with a servant would threaten his reputation and his marriage: 'Look, we have to be practical about this. Maya has gone and gotten herself pregnant. And if we sit by and do nothing, we're just prolonging her misery. Seems to me an abortion is the only practical thing to do' (Umrigar 2005, 69). It is Viraf who asks a doctor friend of his to 'take care' of Maya, and all the medical expenses are borne by Sera who, at that point in the narrative, is completely unaware of her son-in-law's involvement and wishes only to help Bhima. The abortion brings no emotional

[3] My use of the word 'baby' in this chapter echoes Maya and Bhima's use of it in the novel.

relief to Maya and only heightens her hatred towards the Dubash family (Umrigar 2005, 123).

Bhima's anger, after hearing Maya's story, mirrors her granddaughter's rage and she perceives Viraf as a 'child killer' (Umrigar 2005, 282). Bhima's sentiments seem to be in keeping with the convictions of early American feminists such as Susan Anthony and Alice Paul, who considered abortion 'infanticide' and 'the ultimate exploitation of women' (see Whitehead 2011), as well as contemporary feminists like Andrea Dworkin (1983) and Catharine MacKinnon (1987), who contend that abortion is a convenient means for men to take advantage of women without assuming responsibility for their actions. According to MacKinnon (1987, 99), 'the availability of abortion removes the one real consequence men could not easily ignore, the one remaining legitimate reason that women have had for refusing sex besides the headache'. Umrigar's novel also underscores the injustice that marks the very different destinies of Viraf's 'legitimate' baby that his wife Dinaz is carrying and the 'illegitimate' child that was not allowed to live:

> How does he feel, she wonders … to know that one child of his has been destroyed, even as his wife is ready to give birth to another? Does he consider that a sign of ill luck, the shadow of his dead child falling across the belly of his wife's happiness? Or does he care so little about his bastard child that he sleeps undisturbed at night, seeing in his dreams only the child, the son who will inherit his father's looks, his charm, his wealth, his power. (Umrigar 2005, 282)

Despite this apparent condemnation of abortion, Umrigar does not suggest that keeping the baby would have been the ideal solution to Maya's dilemma, either in religious or moral terms. Even the anger that Bhima feels towards her granddaughter when she learns of her pregnancy is rooted less in the fear of dishonour, but more in her concern about Maya's young age and the financial consequences of the pregnancy: 'Behind the anger is fear, fear as vast and gray as the Arabian Sea, fear for this stupid, innocent girl who stands sobbing before her, and for this unborn baby who will come into the world to a mother who is a child herself and to a grandmother who is old and tired to her very bones' (Umrigar 2005, 12).

Thus, rather than rejecting abortion as a solution to an undesirable pregnancy and romanticizing single motherhood, the author accentuates the emotional and physical suffering that may result from it. The abortion also frees Viraf of responsibility and allows him to erase all trace of his transgression, while the young woman's life is irremediably scarred.

Social Consequences and Strategies of Resistance

Roy's novel does not provide any details about the women who are sexually exploited by Chacko and the consequences of their 'relationship' with him. Rather, the text highlights the tolerance with which his behaviour is viewed, contrasting sharply with the price that Ammu and her children have to pay for her love for Velutha.

In *The Hottest Day of the Year*, the narrator evokes the damage to the reputation of the elite character and the deterioration in his physical appearance following Sudha's death at his residence. Sudha's suicide lends itself to a number of interpretations: should it be read as an essentially passive gesture of a helpless victim or as an act of defiance? The 'necroidealist' approach that I noted in *The End of Innocence* in an earlier chapter is also evident here, since in death the status of heroic martyr seems to be conferred onto the subaltern. Moreover, when Sudha's body is discovered, a neighbour notices traces of dried blood on her thighs, suggesting one of two things: either Sudha attempted to abort the foetus by herself, or she was menstruating at the time of her suicide (Charry 2003 [2001], 2). The latter would open up the possibility that Sudha killed herself knowing that she was not pregnant, making her death reminiscent of Bhuvaneswari Bhaduri's suicide; as Spivak (1988, 271–313) explains, Bhaduri purposely killed herself while she was menstruating so as to exclude any suspicion of an illicit pregnancy. Perhaps Sudha deliberately ended her life while she was menstruating, as Remedios (2007, 44) contends, 'in order to expose the hypocrisy of the Brahmin community in Thiruninravur' in general and of her former lover in particular.

Whether she died after having performed the abortion herself or while she was menstruating, Sudha, realizing the futility and powerlessness of her words, seems to have used her body to compel Sundar to listen to her. As Khair (2008, 12) has pointed out, if the body is 'inscribed into subalternity', it can also exceed it. Moreover, by refusing to go back to her parents and committing suicide at Sundar's house, Sudha prevents him from denying his role in the pregnancy and shatters his facade of bourgeois respectability. As the following passage shows, the public scandal that breaks out once the neighbours learn of Sudha's death has a visible impact on Sundar:

> He stayed in his room all the time he was at home, coming down only for his lonely meals. He'd even stopped going to look over his land as often as he used to. One or two grey strands appeared at his temples and when he was kneeling down to buckle his sandals one day I noticed that the hair on his back was thinning. The neighbours would have little to do with him ... even the children stared and whispered when he passed them. (Charry 2003 [2001], 230)

He will eventually have no choice but to leave his house and move away from his home town. However, it is not Sudha's death that provokes feelings of shame and regret in Sundar, but rather the embarrassing police interrogation and loss of face within the bourgeois Brahmin community. The insult that Janaki directs at Sundar reveals the extent to which he fears the social stigma that will result from his affair becoming public: 'What are you afraid of? That people will talk about you—the man who slept with a little servant girl?' (Charry 2003 [2001], 219). Therefore, arguably, Sundar's sense of disgrace is still rooted in a logic of class superiority and he does not indicate remorse for his exploitative behaviour.

The reaction of the middle-class Brahmin community in Thiruninravur to Sudha's illicit pregnancy and suicide reveals two opposing aspects of Sudha's socially constructed sexual identity as a Brahmin domestic maid. On the one hand, her premarital relationship with Sundar is seen to confirm stereotypes about the unbridled sexuality of female servants. This classist construction of the sexuality of lower-class women as opposed to bourgeois women echoes the way the sexuality of black women as opposed to white women was constructed in the United States, where 'a myth was created that all black women were eager for sexual exploits, voluntarily "loose" in their morals and therefore, deserved none of the consideration and respect granted white women' (Lerner 1973, 163). On the other hand, Sudha's affair contradicts the idealized chastity and purity of the Brahmin woman, as is obvious in the following extract of a conversation between Sundar's female neighbours: '"You can never say. Some of these servant girls are more sly than any of us know." "But Sudha was a *brahmin* girl." Kamala said. Everyone was quiet for a minute' (Charry 2003 [2001], 199).

What the Brahmin community finds disturbing is that one of 'their' women, despite her economic inferiority, behaved like a 'whore' (Charry 2003 [2001], 198). The women are particularly unforgiving towards the dead maid, hastening to condemn in a bid to underscore their own moral superiority: '"And just think of it—a brahmin girl. That's what makes it so terrible." "Yes, my father-in-law was saying that if the women of the community begin to behave this way we are in trouble. It is we who uphold the deepest values of the culture," Vaishnavi said importantly. The others nodded at that' (Charry 2003 [2001], 198).

As bell hooks (2000, 43) has argued, 'male supremacist ideology encourages women to believe we are valueless and obtain value only by relating to or bonding with men'. In the conversations that Nithya overhears, she discovers that posthumously the maid is even deprived of the social clemency that her young age may have elicited: 'What do you mean "child"? A whore—that's what she was' (Charry 2003 [2001], 198). Charry, in depicting Janaki's and the neighbours' hostility towards Sudha, underlines the role that women play in the reproduction and perpetuation of patriarchal values and class discrimination: colluding with patriarchy and adopting a bourgeois male language allows them to feel 'the illusion of power', a power that they use against other women (Ashok 2009, 2).

It is worth pointing out that Charry's novel seems to ultimately encourage a somewhat 'optimistic' reading of Sudha's death. While Sundar does pay a personal price for his callous treatment of Sudha, it, of course, does nothing to change the fact that Sudha is dead. The scandal does, however, weaken his authority within the family allowing Janaki to regain control of her finances and eventually marry her lower-caste admirer. Effectively, it is Sudha's death that shakes Janaki out of her listless existence, gives her the courage to defy Sundar and ultimately results in her liberation. Furthermore, in the child narrator's conscience, the two women seem to merge, and their hostile interaction the day before the maid killed herself is suddenly forgotten in the text, as if Janaki's new found freedom is meant to symbolically resurrect the dead maid: 'Sudha and Janaki, Janaki and Sudha. They were both important to me and I couldn't take sides with either and I didn't see any need to. They had blended into something grand and new' (Charry 2003 [2001], 234).

Despite depicting in detail Janaki's antagonism towards Sudha before her suicide, and the hostility of the female neighbours after her death, towards the end of the text the author nonetheless seems to have chosen to emphasize Brahmin male misogyny as personified by Sundar, who exploits both Sudha and Janaki. Victor Li (2009, 275) has observed that often in literary texts, the dead subaltern 'is perfected as a concept so pure no living referent can contradict or complicate it. As in utopian thinking, it is the subaltern's non-existence that ensures the possibility of its conceptualization as a critical alternative to existing hegemonies'. In Charry's novel, the portrayal of the subaltern's death certainly does work to contest patriarchal hegemony. However, the distance that class hegemony creates between women, which is explored earlier in the text, disappointingly fades into the background as the novel draws to a close, with no alternatives explored. Unconvincingly, Janaki, who showed complete indifference towards Sudha's plight and then cruelly exhorted her to commit suicide, now stands up for her: "'[Sudha] was a fool to trust you. Both of us have been fools," Janaki said' (Charry 2003 [2001], 242). This amnesia in the text about Sudha and Janaki's hostile confrontation is perhaps meant to advance sisterhood and 'woman bonding' as a mode of resistance to patriarchal oppression, but it results in an oversimplification of the politics of relationships between women and all that can divide them (hooks 2000, 44). As hooks (2000, 44) warns us, 'divisions will not be eliminated by wishful thinking or reverie despite the value of highlighting experiences all women share'.

While Umrigar's novel underscores the grim future awaiting Maya and Bhima after Sera dismisses the latter, it also evokes the strategies of resistance that they deploy and the ideological emancipation of the subaltern characters. As discussed, initially Bhima is quick to blame her granddaughter for the pregnancy and mouths patriarchal 'truths' which hold the Other woman responsible when a husband commits adultery. Moreover, like the cook in *The Inheritance of Loss*, who earnestly believes that 'most of the time it is the servant that steals' (Desai 2007 [2006], 19), Bhima is also perpetuating class stereotypes: in this case the cliché that paints lower-class women in general and female servants in particular as amoral temptresses. Sudha appears to resign herself to such a categorization; for instance, when Nithya informs her, after she becomes pregnant, that Janaki has forbidden her from associating with the maid, Sudha does not contest the aunt's decision: 'Your Janaki Chitti is right—you shouldn't spend too much time with me' (Charry 2003 [2001], 130). Maya, however, refuses to see herself as morally corrupt, challenging the classist and patriarchal ideologies that her grandmother has internalized. Significantly, she exposes to Bhima the flaws in her logic which compel her to feel eternally indebted to Sera. Maya also forces Bhima to abandon her belief in Sera's selfless generosity and moral superiority and reminds her that their relationship is above all an economic one: Sera pays her for services rendered and her salary is not an act of charity. She compels her grandmother to recognize that her blind servility towards Sera is creating a rift within her own family and damaging her personal interests:

> 'Why are you so fast to blame me for what happened, Ma-ma?' Maya says, her chest heaving with emotion. 'Why this rush to make your granddaughter into the only sinner here? What about what he did? Or must every member of his family remain a saint in your mind? Is it only your family that you must curse and blame for every act of wickedness and shame? … You just assumed that I was the one who did the evil deed. Why Ma-ma? Why do you love their family even more than you love your own?' (Umrigar 2005, 270)

In this scene, Maya is fighting not only against bourgeois perceptions of lower-class women, but also her own grandmother's lack of class consciousness. Bhima is struck by Maya's words and she now understands that her insistence that Sera accompany her to the clinic on the day of the abortion was an act of defiance. Despite herself, she is filled with admiration for her granddaughter: 'Maya had made sure that the Dubash family was implicated in her child's death, that some of the dark blood stained their hands forever ...' (Umrigar 2005, 282). According to E.P. Thompson (1963, 9), 'class happens when some men, as a result of common experiences (inherited or shared), feel and articulate the identity of their interests as between themselves, and as against other men whose interests are different from (and usually opposed to) theirs'. Disregarding the masculine markers in the citation, if like Thompson we consider class to be a process rather than a thing, then in Umrigar's text class 'happens' when Bhima begins to identify with her granddaughter and comes to acknowledge the chasm between her interests and Sera's.

As for the elite character, Viraf's actions do not have any serious consequences for him, apart perhaps from losing Sera's trust. In order to protect Sera and Dinaz's feelings, Bhima decides to initially hide the truth from them and consoles herself with the thought of divine retribution by imagining Viraf being eaten away by guilt, which would result in his losing his good looks: 'She has a sudden flash of prescience in which she sees Viraf as a jowly, white-haired man, fat and old before his time, a long-ago guilt making his eyelids droop and the flesh under his chin grow' (Umrigar 2005, 289). But Viraf, like Sundar, appears to feel no remorse over his actions and instead accuses Bhima of theft, urging Sera to dismiss her. Since maintaining appearances within her class has always been a priority for Sera, in all likelihood she would do her best to conceal the entire episode from her daughter and her circle of friends. Thus, at worst, Viraf would have to contend with Sera's quiet disappointment and distrust.

These novels openly contest dominant ideologies in depicting the abuse of power by elite men and their hypocritical attitudes towards women who are economically dependent on them. The three authors underscore the exploitative nature of such sexual relationships even when no physical force or other form of coercion is deployed during the act and even if the subaltern woman does derive temporary pleasure from it. More importantly, they expose, albeit with uneven consistency, the systematic denigration of the sexuality of lower-class women who are considered both corruptible and corrupting, and hence expendable, not just by bourgeois men and women, but also, in some cases, by other women belonging to their own class (and caste).

◆

5

National or Class Allegories?

Romance in *Rich Like Us* and *The Inheritance of Loss*

[B]oth nationalism and romantic love are based on fantasies, often very elaborate fantasies, of what one wants but does not have.

—Laura Fair*

Frederic Jameson (1986, 65–9) has (in)famously described 'all third-world texts' as 'national allegories', with the name of the country returning 'again and again like a gong'; he deems this especially true of texts whose 'forms develop out of predominantly western machineries of representation, such as the novel'. Even while possessing a private, 'properly libidinal dynamic', he sees these literary works as necessarily projecting 'a political dimension in the form of national allegory' (Jameson 1986, 69). Since its publication, this thesis has drawn considerable criticism notably from Aijaz Ahmad (2008 [1992]) and Rosemary Marangoly George (1996) who have contested, among other aspects of Jameson's argument, his use of the term 'third-world' and the totalizing word 'all'. However, as Saikat Majumdar (2013, 137) has argued, the Jamesonian argument does appear to have a 'peculiar applicability' when confined to a 'specific segment' of Indian literature: namely, the Indian English novel since the publication of Rushdie's *Midnight's Children* in 1981.

Sahgal's *Rich Like Us* and Desai's *The Inheritance of Loss*, the two novels examined in this chapter, grapple not only with the national question, but also with the daily challenges experienced by a cross-class couple over time, moving beyond external or familial obstacles to the couple's union and happiness. The romance between Ram,

* Quoted in Fair (2009, 79).

a wealthy Hindu, and Rose, a working-class Englishwoman, in *Rich Like Us* begins before Partition, with the later years of the marriage embedded in a national crisis in India: the state of Emergency under Indira Gandhi. The romantic relationship between Sai and Gyan in *The Inheritance of Loss* crosses both class and ethnic boundaries. Sai is the orphaned granddaughter of a Gujarati Babu judge living in Kalimpong and Gyan is her Nepali tutor from a lower-class background, who becomes involved in the Gorkha nationalist movement.

The libidinal element in these texts seems inextricably linked to collective politics, to be read, as Madhava Prasad (1992, 78) writes, not only in relation to 'particular nations but especially to particular classes', and can perhaps be seen as 'a class allegory'. In this chapter, I will evaluate the ways in which, and the extent to which, cross-class relationships in the two texts get cast in nationalist terms, with intimate class relations seemingly being subsumed by the 'national situation' (Jameson 1986, 65). I shall also examine the identity politics informing the depiction of inter-class, inter-cultural/inter-ethnic romance in these novels, and consider whether this entails the privileging of one identity marker over another.

Experiencing and Negotiating Class Differences

The class differences between Gyan and Sai and between Rose and Ram are not as marked as those between Ammu and Velutha in *The God of Small Things* and Mariam and Masood in *Salt and Saffron*. Gyan has been educated at a university whereas Rose was born and raised in London and, although is not university-educated, has had some formal schooling. Notably, both the subaltern and the upper-class lovers speak English, the language of the elites. As Sai realizes when she visits Gyan's house at the end of the novel, his family had to make enormous financial sacrifices to ensure that he received an expensive, English-language education: 'Every single thing his family had was going into him and it took ten of them to live like this to produce a boy, combed, educated, their best bet in the big world' (Desai 2007 [2006], 256). Both the novels grapple in depth with the challenges of a romantic cross-class relationship, which manifest themselves in various arenas of everyday life.

At the beginning of her marriage to Ram, both cultural and socio-economic differences between them are a source of discomfort for Rose, on whose point of view (alongside Sonali's) the novel primarily focuses. She struggles to become accustomed to her 'co-wife' Mona and the reality of being part of a traditional Hindu family which calls for living with her in-laws. Rose has to abandon the dream of living with Ram in a house 'surrounded by a garden with English flowers in it, a blessed English privacy enclosing them' (Sahgal 1999 [1985], 62). But the main disparities arise from their divergent class positionings. While Rose, of course, speaks English, she does have a Cockney accent which stays with her even after forty years of living with Ram in India. Her accent contrasts sharply with the impeccable English spoken by her husband; in fact, he often corrects her grammatical mistakes. Ram's intellectual life is shown to be far richer than his wife's: he and his friends quote the Greeks and canonical English poetry with as much ease as Persian verse and are great admirers of Mughal miniature paintings.

The chasm between Rose and Ram becomes even more pronounced with the appearance in their lives of Marcella—the English aristocratic woman with whom Ram falls in love. Despite their common racial and national identity, Rose feels no affinity with Marcella: she sees her as the Other not only because she is a romantic rival, but also because of her class identity. Marcella shares Ram's cultural tastes, making Rose feel 'common' and 'little' in their company (Sahgal 1999 [1985], 110). Born into an extremely privileged milieu, both Marcella and Ram share a sense of entitlement that is completely foreign to Rose: 'It was the way they sat, their limbs arranged that way for centuries of being in command of situations. It was their grammar, yet it didn't matter what they were talking about or if they were talking at all' (Sahgal 1999 [1985], 110). In becoming his wife, Rose has gained access to certain privileges and comforts of Ram's class (for instance domestic servants, trips abroad, and stays in luxurious hotels), but her upward mobility is an example of marital mobility, which does not bring in its wake a perceptible change to her cultural capital.

Rose's lack of refinement manifests itself not only in her 'common' accent, but also in how she perceives and articulates her opinion about art. The following passage, for example, illustrates the divergent class vocabulary and pronunciation of the two women when discussing a play that they had both seen:

> 'The extraordinary clarity of her voice,' Marcella was saying.... Rose did think the leading actress's voice had been nice and clear, she didn't know about ex-straw-nry cla-rity. Marcella's upper-class accent had spent quite ten minutes ballet-dancing around two words when all she was saying was that the girl who had played Lady Windermere had a nice voice. A regular hullaballoo around syllables, making such a production out of pronunciation. (Sahgal 1999 [1985], 110–11)

This difference in their vocabularies can be understood in terms of Bourdieu's (2010 [1984], 24) discussion of 'high' and 'popular' aesthetics: Rose's 'popular' aesthetic sensibility manifests itself in her deployment of short phrases and simple adjectives. Moreover, Rose understands that 'a manner of speaking was an unscalable wall of steel and concrete between half the world and the other half' (Sahgal 1999 [1985], 111). As Bourdieu (2010 [1984], 58–9) explains, 'knowing that "manner" is a symbolic manifestation whose meaning and value depend as much on the perceivers as on the producer, one can see how it is that the manner of using symbolic goods, especially those regarded as the attributes of excellence, constitutes one of the key markers of "class" and also the ideal weapon in strategies of distinction'.

Moreover, Rose represents the honest 'outspokenness' of the working classes in the novel, which contrasts with the gratuitous verbosity of the elites. The text emphasizes Rose's wholesome simplicity, concerned with 'substance' rather than 'appearance' (Bourdieu 2010 [1984], 250). Unlike her husband, 'she was the kind of person who put a relationship to a tablecloth to use and didn't mind it looking messy and darned and might have been suspicious of one that wasn't' (Sahgal 1999 [1985], 255). It is difficult not to detect here a certain element of romanticization in Sahgal's portrayal of Rose's character and her working-class roots. Pranav Jani (2010, 182) too has pointed out the 'fetishization' of Rose's working-class anti-intellectualism within the narrative; this, as we will see later, seems to make it easier for Rose's character to uphold a simplified form of (petty) bourgeois nationalism which, paradoxically, rests on a glossing over of class disparity within and beyond the nation (state).

In Rose's eyes, Marcella and Ram form a natural and 'legitimate' couple, making Rose 'the outsider' (Sahgal 1999 [1985], 128). She finds their romance inevitable, resigning herself to the thought that 'there's some that do the ordering and others that take orders' (Sahgal 1999 [1985], 257). But if Rose feels excluded from the sophisticated pleasures that Ram and Marcella enjoy, she also pities Ram's inability to access common, popular joys which for her are unadulterated entertainment (Sahgal 1999 [1985], 137). Thus, the text brings to the fore how the process of exclusion between classes based on tastes works in both directions. It is worth noting that Rose's acceptance of Ram's love for Marcella also, problematically, signifies an acceptance of class divisions and their supposed inevitability, despite Rose's often vocal critique of the exercise of class power during the Emergency years.

Class differences between the lovers in *The Inheritance of Loss* too are explored more in an individual rather than a familial context. As the following passage illustrates, an activity as simple as sharing a meal brings the class differences between the lovers sharply into focus:

> Gyan had used his hands without a thought and Sai ate with the only implement on the table—a table spoon, rolling up her roti on the side and nudging the food onto the spoon with it. Noticing this difference, they had become embarrassed and put the observation aside. 'Kishmish,' he called her to cover it up, and 'Kaju' she called him, raisin and cashew, sweet, nutty and expensive. (Desai 2007 [2006], 141)

Food is, in fact, as Paul Jay (2010, 128) explains, 'culturally coded in the novel; what and how one eats regularly carries symbolic import among the characters'. In this passage, Gyan and Sai are propelled by ideals of tolerance and eager to set aside these differences in manner, which are rooted in and effectively symbolic of the socio-economic differences between them: 'Eating together they had always felt embarrassed—he unsettled by her finickiness and her curbed enjoyment, and she, revolted by his energy and his slurps and smacks' (Desai 2007 [2006], 176). In Desai's novel, the dining table is an important arena where class differences seem to manifest themselves with every bite and her depiction of Gyan's manner of eating echoes Bourdieu's (2010 [1984], 192) observation that the working classes' eating habits reveal a lack of formality, or 'plain eating' (like 'plain speaking'). Both Desai and Sahgal capture the impatience that the subaltern character feels when confronted with the beloved's attitude towards food, 'making the meal a social ceremony, an affirmation of ethical tone and aesthetic refinement' (Bourdieu 2010 [1984], 194).

The stunning landscape of the picturesque town of Darjeeling, one of the foremost honeymoon destinations in India, initially seems to provide Sai and Gyan with class-neutral spaces where their romance can flourish outside the confines of bourgeois domesticity: 'Because new love makes sightseers out of couples even in their own town, they went to the Mong Pong Nature Reserve, to Delo Lake; they picnicked by the Teeta and the Relli … they took the toy train and went to the Darjeeling zoo and viewed in their self-righteous, modern love, the unfree and ancient bars, behind which lived a red panda …' (Desai 2007 [2006], 141).

However, this extract also gestures to the lovers' awareness of their romance flouting class laws: they perceive their relationship as an act of emancipation which is a testimony to their open-mindedness. As Barbara Augustin (1985, 67) points out in her sociological study of mixed marriages, since such unions are socially reproved, they become a valued private act: the couple sees itself as experiencing an impossible love in the manner of Romeo and Juliet, separated by, yet succeeding to overcome social, national, religious, and racial frontiers. But this tacit awareness of the transgressive nature of their love paradoxically also draws attention to their differences. For instance, Sai does not mention to her boyfriend that her father was part of the space programme in Russia lest he feel inferior to her family (Desai 2007 [2006], 141). Therefore, the 'neutrality' of public spaces where Gyan and Sai live their relationship is created and maintained through their conscious decision to be impervious to economic inequalities. Notably, some spaces are excluded from this configuration: Gyan, for instance, never invites Sai to his house or neighbourhood. And it is only towards the end of the novel, when Sai goes looking for an estranged Gyan, that these two worlds collide. By then, their relationship is already in crisis, with Gyan having verbally attacked her for her 'Western' manners and habits, and Sai has already caught sight of him among the Gorkha protesters at the local Gymkhana Club. While waiting for him outside his house, for the first time since meeting him, she is compelled to come to grips with the material differences between them:

> It was a small, slime-slicked cube; the walls must have been made with cement corrupted by sand, because it came spilling forth from pockmarks as if from a punctured bag ... there were houses like this everywhere, of course, common to those who had struggled to the far edge of the middle-class—just to the edge, only just, holding on desperately—but were at every moment being undone, the house slipping back not into the picturesque poverty that tourists liked to photograph but into something truly dismal. (Desai 2007 [2006], 256)

Her reaction to this 'lower-class' sight is one of both disgust and shame, for in loving Gyan she had unconsciously become associated with his milieu. She feels cheated and, indeed, almost betrayed, when confronted with the gap between Gyan's family's 'economic capital' and Gyan's 'cultural capital', in Bourdieusian terms (1986), where the former is 'immediately and directly convertible into money' and the latter takes the form of educational qualifications. Sai is startled to realize that the house 'didn't match Gyan's talk, his English, his looks, his schooling. It didn't match his future' (Desai 2007 [2006], 256). But her reaction to Gyan's living quarters also entails a certain idealization of her own living situation. Her grandfather's house is neglected and ramshackle, with Sai having to use a 'rotted' tablecloth as a bed sheet (Desai 2007 [2006], 34).

However, she consoles herself with the thought of the house's former glory to which she seems doggedly to attach her class positioning: 'Cho Oyu might be crumbling, but it had once been majestic, it had its past if not its future and that might be enough' (Desai 2007 [2006], 257). Only when she witnesses the judge's cruel beating of the cook at the end of the novel will she fully comprehend the ugliness of Cho Oyu. Indeed, for the greater part of the novel Sai can be seen as a member of a bourgeoisie which imagines itself belonging to a 'private community of individuals', rather than defining itself territorially (Prasad 1992, 75). But as Prasad goes on to point out, not all classes find 'that position of free, self interested citizen as hospitable as the bourgeoisie', a discrepancy which becomes the root of Sai and Gyan's conflict. While the cook's beating and Biju's return to India can be seen as part of the novel's indictment of class inequalities, Sai's resolve to leave Cho Oyu, as we shall see later, has serious implications for how the novel perceives, and arguably rejects, collective action against social privilege and its abuses, whether understood in class or nationalist/territorial terms.

If Rose, as Ram's wife, becomes inevitably assimilated in elite spaces, she is also marginalized within these private and public spaces. In fact, I would argue that she consciously maintains her spatial alterity as an act of independence and a means to maintain a link with the class culture of her childhood. For instance, when Ram has a new family house built, Rose's room stands out against the minimalist elegance of the living quarters with their predominance of shades of black and white: her personal space, described as 'an island off the mainland of the house', highlights both its link to and alienation from her upper-class surroundings (Sahgal 1999 [1985], 36). It is decorated with 'the flowered chintz, frills and flounces, pastel blues and baby pinks' that she had seen and appreciated in magazines as a young girl in London (Sahgal 1999 [1985], 36). Rose's room is a testimony to her desire not to be subsumed by Ram's class culture and to keep her past alive. Sahgal accentuates the relationship between Rose's feelings of being out of place and her awareness of class differences when she describes Rose's visit to London, her birthplace, several years after her marriage to Ram. Her feelings of alienation in her own city stem not only from the sight of destruction of the neighbourhood she grew up in during the Second World War bombardments, but also because of the chasm that separates the London she knew and inhabited and the London frequented by Ram and his friends—the London of luxurious hotels, art galleries, and fine restaurants: 'But it was Ram's London, all this. Her own had been simpler, buried in the blitz, along with her parents, two of the sixty thousand and five hundred civilians cold figures said had been killed in air raids' (Sahgal 1999 [1985], 226). This portrayal of a divided London ostensibly suggests that in *Rich Like Us*, the ultimate dividing line between human beings is neither race nor nationality, but class.

The body and physical beauty work as a site for class differences in Ram and Rose's marriage, particularly as the two grow older. Rose is aware that Ram's primary interest in her had been for her looks. As she ages and gains weight, she increasingly deems herself to be an unsuitable wife for Ram:

> She worried constantly and was positively certain now that she was the wrong wife for Ram, who needed someone with a proper vocabulary, and a la-di-da accent that curled at the top and uncurled at the bottom, and fashionable flatness beside him to advertise the elegance he sold. She didn't have the refinement, she never would, and she was getting fat. (Sahgal 1999 [1985], 204)

Sahgal's novel reveals how attitudes towards the ageing body are emblematic of class differences: Rose's 'working-class' attitude entails accepting the ageing process, contrasting sharply with that of Ram, who meticulously touches up 'his hair and his new moustache, leaving a speckle of patrician silver at his temples' (Sahgal 1999 [1985], 209). If Bourdieu (2010 [1984], 204) primarily examines the attitude of upper-class women towards their bodies in distinction to lower-class women, in *Rich Like Us* we see that Ram too derives a 'double assurance' from his physical appearance: he believes in the 'value of beauty' as well as 'the value of the effort to be beautiful, and so associating aesthetic value and moral value'; he feels superior both in the 'intrinsic, natural beauty of his body' and in the art of 'self-embellishment' (Bourdieu 2010 [1984], 204). This art for Ram, and by extension for the aristocratic classes in the novel, is equal to 'a moral and aesthetic virtue which defines "nature" negatively as sloppiness' (Bourdieu 2010 [1984], 204). Beauty then is 'simultaneously a gift of nature and a conquest of merit, as much opposed to the abdications of vulgarity as to ugliness' (Bourdieu 2010 [1984], 204). Ram chastises Rose for letting herself go, and once more the text underscores the focus among the elites on appearance rather than substance. Rose's acceptance of the ageing process, her refusal as an older woman to 'embellish' her body, is intended to indicate her simple honesty (which, echoes the romanticization of Rose's working-class background that I discussed earlier).

In *Rich Like Us*, Sahgal reveals not only the cultural, but also the serious material limitations informing Rose's upward mobility resulting from her marriage. Indeed, Sahgal's novels often show, as Jackson (2010, 30) has pointed out, 'that economic inequality operates not just between social classes, but also within families, so it is gender-based as well as class-based', with 'many of her supposedly privileged female protagonists', including Rose, being 'controlled and manipulated by the men on whom they depend for financial support'. After Ram becomes paralysed, Rose finds herself penniless and vulnerable, since he had taken no measures to ensure her financial independence. She finds herself at the mercy of her stepson Dev, to whom the family house belongs, and who forges his father's signature to access his money. But Dev's behaviour invites no anger or indignation on the part of Ram's friends and family; on the contrary, they believe that, given her class origins, Rose does not deserve a more egalitarian treatment:

> 'I'd say on the whole Rose has done pretty well for herself,' Neel said, 'considering her origins and so forth. It's hard to see why Uncle Ram got hitched up with her. Of course in those days only the landlady's daughters or that class of person was available but why did he have to marry her? She's probably been nothing but an embarrassment to him since. I've felt sorry for him at times.' (Sahgal 1999 [1985], 259)

The belittling comments made by Neel, an acquaintance of Ram's, rely on racist as well as classist stereotypes according to which only a lower-class English woman would deign to have a romantic relationship with a man of colour. As France Winddance Twine (2010, 34) explains, 'this reflects an attempt to position these women outside of middle-class norms and to establish a symbolic and class-inflected boundary between "respectable" middle-class women and hypersexual, irrational, working-class women'. Rose's supposed intrinsic 'lowliness' provides a pretext and even a justification for Ram's family to continue exploiting her, and even after forty years of marriage she is perceived as an intruder in her husband's milieu and her social 'ascension' as undeserved.

The cross-couple in Desai's novel, during moments of romantic harmony, see themselves as completely independent of their families and their socio-economic milieus, whereas in moments of discord they both resort to essentializing each other. The act of essentialization, according to Pnina Werbner (1997, 228), entails positing 'a falsely timeless continuity, a discreteness or boundedness in space, and an organic unity. It is to imply an internal sameness and external difference or otherness'. Class essentialization, then, has distinct echoes of the 'us–them distinction' which is 'so essential' to nationalist thought (Mayer 2002, 288). Certain critics appear to draw a contrast between what they perceive as Sai's cosmopolitan hybridity and Gyan's essentialist attitude: according to Menon (2009, 105), Desai has shown positive aspects of hybridity by depicting Sai's perfect ease in diverse class and cultural settings, and Spielman (2010, 78) posits that she 'does not reject Indian culture or want to elevate herself above others by advertising her background'. I would argue instead that Sai's hybridity entails a clear, class-driven hierarchy of languages and tastes. As we have seen earlier, she is profoundly uncomfortable in non-bourgeois spaces, and her conception of the Other, like Gyan's, entails recourse to reductive clichés. The insults that she directs at Gyan specifically target his poverty and class culture: 'Low-class family, uncultured, arranged-marriage types ... they'll find you a silly fool to marry you and you'll be delighted all your life to have a dummy' (Desai 2007 [2006], 261). Like Aliya's cousin Samia in *Salt and Saffron*, Sai evokes the practice of arranged marriages as the 'natural' preference of the lower classes and proof of their backwardness. Moreover, Sai's class prejudices, despite her having grown up without any adult of her class taking sustained interest in her, indicate the extent to which class socialization occurs passively.

Contesting Nations and Nationalisms

The endings of the two novels move away from the conventional happy or tragic endings of love stories in literature and film. As both narratives draw to a close, sociopolitical events (the separatist Gorkha movement in *The Inheritance of Loss* and the state of Emergency in Sahgal's *Rich Like Us*) come not only to define the private, libidinal relationship, but also to push it into the background.

According to Kirpal (1996, 173), the beginning to Rose and Ram's romance is reminiscent of a typical first meeting in a Mills & Boon novel: *Rose, the poor, pretty saleswoman/princess is rescued by the handsome, rich, Indian prince … and carried off to his Kingdom/India.* But marriage in *Rich Like Us* is not constructed as the happy ending of a romantic novel: Ram, as we know, already has a wife from an arranged marriage when he starts wooing Rose; therefore Rose and Ram as a couple do not subscribe to the conventional model of romantic love which has monogamy as its cornerstone. Moreover, implicit in this portrayal of the relationship is a condemnation of patriarchal power. For instance, as we have seen, Ram does not take any measures to secure Rose financially, despite her considerable involvement in running the family business. Moreover, long before he became paralysed and incapable of coherent speech, Rose was finding it difficult to have a conversation with Ram, especially when it concerned his son. She has a marginalized position within the family, not only because of her class origins, but because she is seen as 'a failed womb', not having given birth to a child (Sahgal 1999 [1985], 206).

But I would contend that, on occasion, both the anti-elitist and the feminist projects of the text lack consistency and coherence. For instance, during the course of her marriage, Rose discovers that she has to share her husband with several other women, and not just Mona. Furthermore, she realizes that, despite being married to him for over thirty years, she does not really know him (Sahgal 1999 [1985], 242). However, in spite of Ram's philandering and his patriarchal attitudes, Rose cannot imagine leaving him (Sahgal 1999 [1985], 245). She perceives their life together as an adventure, allowing her to experience things she would never have known had she remained in London: 'Rose could no longer have abandoned her marriage than an exploration of the Antarctic in mid-ocean, or a mid-story, never knowing what was going to happen next and next' (Sahgal 1999 [1985], 65). This depiction of Ram as a 'magnetic' and 'mysterious' force, almost not a 'a person', I would argue, is reminiscent of orientalist clichés which construct India as an inscrutable entity, casting a spell on Europeans: 'He was a pull, luring her out from behind the counter, and she had never looked back' (Sahgal 1999 [1985], 245). More problematically, it contributes to Rose's construction as a 'remarkably passive' figure, which is confirmed by her death at the end of the novel (Jackson 2010, 13).

It is important to point out here that the novel is set during the Emergency years under Indira Gandhi, and the text, through liberal use of analepsis, sheds light on the various phases of Rose's marriage. Soon after her marriage, Rose is witness to the political upheaval of Partition, and her perception of Mahatma Gandhi echoes Sahgal's Gandhian nationalist politics. She notes the 'magic' of Gandhi, whose civil disobedience movement brought together 'all sorts of classes of Hindus and Muslims' (Sahgal 1999 [1985], 142–3). Rose observes that it is the first time, not only since her arrival in India, but in course of her entire life, that she is seeing 'people high and low mixed up like this' (Sahgal 1999 [1985], 143). These observations made by Rose invite a reading of the anti-colonial nationalist struggle as a classless movement, downplaying its elitist nature and erroneously suggesting that during the civil disobedience movement all of 'India's constituent groups fought equally for equality for all' (Mann 1993, 107). Her portrayal of the Gandhian nationalist politics contradicts Sahgal's depiction of the divisive class differences between Rose and Ram that I have discussed in detail earlier. Indeed, 'the moralism of Gandhian politics', as Pranav Jani (2001, 228) explains, 'is a key component of how Sahgal conceptualizes resistance in India'; it is very much within the bounds of this model, which is 'based on mass mobilization, elite leadership, and a hostility to class-based struggle', that Sahgal conceives of collective action in *Rich Like Us*.

In the narrative, Rose emerges as a spokesperson against the state of Emergency and the abuses of power by its exponents. At the outset of the novel, she finds herself in conflict with Dev, who is closely connected with the government, notably the unnamed prime minster's son—a barely veiled reference to Sanjay Gandhi, who acquired a reputation for crooked business ventures during Indira Gandhi's Emergency rule. Dev is shown to be working in collaboration with the prime minister's son, misappropriating public funds to manufacture a non-existent 'people's car' (Sahgal 1999 [1985], 4). While the conflict between Rose and Dev arises primarily because Dev is illegally expropriating Ram's money, the differences between them are fundamentally ideological and moral, engaging with the ideas of patriotism and national duty. As Pranav Jani (2010, 179) has also pointed out, 'Rose's interventions reveal a sharp class analysis; they function as a vibrant counter discourse that challenges Dev and rips through the façade of the Emergency as a benevolent, necessary dictatorship'. One of the foremost election pledges made by Indira Gandhi in 1971 had included the eradication of poverty, but as Rudolph and Rudolph (1977, 390) explain, her strategy was to 'talk left and act right'. Found guilty of electoral malpractice, Indira Gandhi suspended constitutional liberties, declaring a state of national emergency in June 1975 which lasted until March 1977. The regime's anti-labour bias was evident from, among other things, the arrest of several union leaders, the freezing of salaries and the reduction of the number of man-days lost in industry 'forcibly achieved by cutting down strikes', while the government showed 'unmistakeable tenderness' towards employers and management (Gupta 1978, 334–5). The regime made it easier for private company owners to import goods and diversify their production without seeking the permission of public authorities (Jaffrelot 2005, n.p.).

According to Patrick C. Hogan (1999, 180), a 'national allegory broaching the issue of class is almost necessarily critical, for class is international. Class binds the workers of India or Trinidad or Ireland with one another and with the workers of England' and not to 'the industrialists and landlords of their own national place'. But if Rose articulates a vehement critique of the corrupt elites of the Emergency years and their abuse of class power, she is quite clearly not calling for a proletariat revolution. The nationalism that she preaches is a resolutely capitalist, rather than pro-labour. Rose makes a clear distinction between the crony capitalism of the Emergency years and the kind of capitalism practised by Ram's father, whose small business grew into a large textile company without recourse to corrupt practices. For Rose, Lalaji's activities embody honest and simple commerce, indeed a more authentic era: '[A] proper business man down to 'is toes, who knew everything there was to know about whatever 'e was 'andling, not like nowadays when business is minding itself and you're sitting pretty with the loot. And there's some businesses more like the 'at trick' (Sahgal 1999 [1985], 6). In this passage, we see Rose paying homage to the idealized, almost Protestant work ethic of the petty bourgeoisie who incarnate the role of both the owner and the worker. Rose's symbolic class positioning within the text varies and fluctuates, allowing her to speak in turn for subalterns (such as male domestic servants, beggars, and impoverished women), and also for the petty bourgeoisie that was marginalized by Indira Gandhi's regime in favour of big business. Indeed, Sahgal's condemnation of the Emergency years in the novel echoes Mahatma Gandhi's (1940) approach to capitalism: 'Capital as such is not evil, it is its wrong use that is evil.' Even if Sahgal hints at a critique of the collusion of 'Gandhi's pacifism with bourgeois capitalism', it is swiftly dismissed within the narrative by Sonali and Kishori Lal (Mann 1993, 107).[1]

The real love story in Sahgal's novel, then, is not between Ram and Rose in defiance of class boundaries, but between Rose and India, a reading which corroborates Sahgal's own observation about her writing: 'I have never written from any specific ideological viewpoint. If I have, I have a nationalistic viewpoint' (quoted in Mann 1993, 104). Even before the Emergency years, we can catch glimpses of Rose's nationalist inclinations when she becomes involved in managing Ram's business and persuades him to sell Indian-produced textiles at the family shop, instead of only imported goods which he favoured. Her predilection for Indian aesthetic sensibilities—for instance, she finds English cloth 'tame' in comparison to the 'fabulous colours' of Indian fabric—foreshadows the strong nationalist position that she will occupy later in the text (Sahgal 1999 [1985], 130).

Buchanan (2006, 176) has pointed out that 'nowhere in Jameson's paper does he state that Third World writers are only or can only be nationalists'. Indeed, insisting that for literary texts to work as

[1] I would like to thank Pranav Jani for helping me to work through the ambivalence of Rose's ideological class positioning in *Rich Like Us* (personal email correspondence, September 2011).

national allegories they must entail an 'advocacy of nationalism' is a misreading of Jameson's thesis, as Lazarus (2011, 240) also warns us. I would argue that a concern with the national situation does not have to, but certainly *can*, take the form of a nationalist position. Gandhian nationalist values are articulated and upheld in Sahgal's novel not only by Rose, but also by Sonali, an upper-class civil servant and Rose's friend, who refuses to become party to the corrupt bureaucratic practices of the Emergency era. Rose's and Sonali's opposition to Indira Gandhi's dictatorship also involves a certain idealization of the state of corruption and a glossing-over of the suffering of the marginalized classes in India after Partition and during the years preceding the Emergency period. As Jani (2001, 200–24) explains:

> Sahgal's bourgeois-nationalist vision reads the Emergency as an aberration caused by a shift away from Nehruvian and Gandhian values. Viewing the Emergency as a historical problem with historical solutions, Sahgal's project comes to restore the lost meaning of 1947 as opposed to Rushdie's attempt to expose its emptiness.... In effect, by representing the Emergency as a period existing outside the normal operation of bourgeois democracy, the structural oppression of the subaltern within bourgeois democracy remains unexamined.

Rose's murder, at the end of the text, carried out by men contracted by Dev, makes her a martyr, a sort of sati—not as Ram's wife, but for her nationalist ideals: Sahgal (1988, 101) herself has referred to Rose as a 'modern-day suttee'. This terminology, according to Mann (1993, 109), has disturbing implications for the gender politics of the text, since it reproduces in Rose's person conventional patriarchal constructions of womanhood. Rose is cast as the most traditionally 'Indian' of women: her sati-like death seems to have been constructed to underscore not only her *Indianness*, despite her English roots, but a stereotypically constructed *female* Indianness, marked by passivity and self-sacrifice. Moreover, this depiction of Rose's death also camouflages her shifting (ideological) class identities.

If in *Rich Like Us*, the Emergency does not directly contribute to the disintegration of Rose and Ram's marriage, in *The Inheritance of Loss* Sai and Gyan's romance breaks down primarily following, what appears to be, Gyan's political, 'nationalist' awakening. From 1986 to 1988, the Gorkha community led an insurrection in the district of Darjeeling against the economic and political dominance of the Bengali community. They demanded 'the separation of the northern districts of West Bengal and the creation of separate Gorkhaland state' (Minahan 2002, 679). Majumdar (2013, 138) argues that Desai's novel, like Roy's *The God of Small Things*, does not function as a national allegory since it engages 'in a far more immediate and sensual apprehension of private, regional sensibilities, existing in greater independence from the nationally constructed public space that the national allegory allows'. However, I would contend that in her portrayal of the Gorkha protesters, Desai demonstrates how the vocabulary deployed for a regional struggle by the protestors nevertheless engages with the nation state and national history. Desai also seems to have left the Gorkha territorial claims deliberately vague, not excluding the demand for a nation state: 'They wanted their own country, or at least their own state, in which to manage their own affairs' (Desai 2007 [2006], 9).

Moreover, in consciously echoing the language of the anti-colonial nationalist fight against the British, the Gorkha leaders, as depicted in Desai's novel, appear to be seeking to lend credibility to their political struggle by insisting that it is *not* a parochial, provincial movement:

> Gyan remembered the stirring stories of when citizens had risen up in their millions and demanded that the British leave. There was the nobility of it, the daring of it, the glorious fire of it—'India for Indians. No taxation without representation. No help for the wars. Not a man, not a rupee. British Raj Murdabad!' If a nation had such a climax in its history, its heart, would it not hunger for it again? (Desai 2007 [2006], 158)

The Gorkha leaders are calling for their struggle to be understood in the context of India as a nation state—both as a (formerly) colonized entity and a colonizing force. As Oana Sabo (2012, 390) explains, 'nations in the Global South, such as India and Nepal, also replicate the power asymmetries between neo-imperial powers and smaller countries. In this sense, India is in a position to Orientalize Nepal as much as both India and Nepal are Orientalized by Western powers'. The novel by no means suggests that 'Western' imperialism has declined or faded away. The sections of the novel that narrate

Biju's stay in New York, as a member of the 'shadow class' (Desai 2007 [2006], 102), also bring to the fore the economic exploitation of the poorest citizens of a country like India within advanced capitalist countries, thereby complicating the very idea of a 'Third-World' as well as a 'First-World' and compelling the reader to look at poverty as a transnational, rather than an Indian or, by extension, a 'Third-World' problem. As the narrator of Desai's novel points out, 'profit could only be harvested in the gap between nations, working one against the other' (Desai 2007 [2006], 205). These nations, I contend, can be both nation states and nations *within* a nation state like India.

When the novel opens, Gyan is working as a private tutor for Sai because he is unable to find employment elsewhere despite having given numerous interviews: one particularly painful memory for him is a failed trip to Calcutta in the hope of finding work (Desai 2007 [2006], 158–9). Understandably, then, the call for an independent Gorkha state resonates intensely with him: 'We must unite under the banner of the GNLF, *Gorkha National Liberation Front*. We will build hospitals and schools, we will provide jobs for our sons' (Desai 2007 [2006], 158). While provincial within Indian geography, the Gorkha movement nonetheless has at the heart of its claim the idea of a nation struggling against a more powerful collectivity. Indeed, in Desai's novel, as Priyamvada Gopal (2009, 183) argues, 'if individual characters like the judge struggle with the profound self-hatred that is their inheritance from colonialism, the Nepali disenfranchised now confront an India that appears to be a colonizing power in its own right, occupying land and capable of inflicting its own humiliations and hurt'.

Once his political passions are sufficiently roused, Gyan directs his vituperative anger at his non-Nepali, anglicized girlfriend, who lives in a large house, while his own family seems forever condemned to an impoverished existence. As Paul Jay (2010, 128) points out, 'Desai takes great care to link the fate of their love affair to the politics of the insurgency and the long history it is connected to'. The conflict in the romantic relationship echoes and reflects the ethnic conflict between the two communities and the disparity in their economic positionings within the nation state. Moreover, Gyan begins to perceive his ties with Sai as aberrant and a betrayal of the separatist movement as well as of his masculinity. Having attended a protest organized by the Gorkha liberation army, he sees himself as part of a noble and virile struggle and is overcome with shame as he recalls his participation in, what he now sees as, 'effeminate' activities with Sai: 'It was a masculine atmosphere and Gyan felt a moment of shame remembering his tea parties with Sai on the veranda, the cheese toast, queen cakes from the baker, and even worse, the small warm space they inhabited together, the nursery talk—It suddenly seemed against the requirements of his adulthood' (Desai 2007 [2006], 161).

This extract hints at how class cultures may themselves be gendered constructions: Gyan subscribes to a patriarchal hierarchy of values which deems socially constructed masculine activities superior to what are perceived as female or feminine preoccupations. The insults that he directs at Sai (much like Sai's criticisms of Gyan) entail essentializing and grossly simplifying socio-economic and cultural realities: 'You are like slaves, that's what you are, running after the West, embarrassing yourself. It's because of people like you *we* never get anywhere' (Desai 2007 [2006], 163; italics mine). It is worth noting that Gyan's Othering discourse shifts between defining Sai's alterity in terms of her class, ethnicity, and a narrow, arbitrary definition of a national 'Indian' culture, but also, at times, in terms of an amalgam of the three. I would argue that in the excerpt quoted earlier, when he berates Sai for her 'Western' ways, Gyan does not deploy the pronoun 'we' to ally himself with the Gorkha community or with the Indian lower classes; rather, he is upholding a pan-Indian identity based on the Gandhian notions of swaraj (self-rule) and swadeshi (self-reliance). Gyan perceives Sai's anglicism and westernized eating habits as symptomatic of a mental dependence on former colonizers and indicative of a deficiency of nationalist feeling and Indianness. Paradoxically, he sees his participation in the Gorkha movement, despite the separatist claims of its exponents, as proof of his authentic Indian credentials. His use of 'we' and 'they', or 'us' and 'them', harks back to historical rather than immediate realities, focusing on a 'foreign' imperial enemy rather than the contemporary Gorkha contention with the state of India.

To prove to himself the depth of his commitment to the movement, Gyan betrays Sai, putting her in danger by revealing to the insurgents that the judge possesses a number of firearms, even though, or perhaps *because* he understands only too well that Sai is merely a convenient scapegoat for his anger: 'She was defining his hatred, he thought' (Desai 2007 [2006], 174). He seeks to quell his doubts, however, and justifies his betrayal by cataloguing, what he perceives to be, her offences against a pan Indian 'national' culture. 'We live in India', Gyan reminds her (Desai 2007 [2006], 258), while berating her for her supposedly 'unIndian ways'. In the following passage, Sai comes to represent for Gyan not only the 'West', but also the privileged Indian upper classes:

> She who could speak no language but English and pidgin Hindi. She who could not converse with anyone outside of her tiny social stratum. She who could not eat with her hands, could not squat down on the ground on her haunches to wait for a bus, who had never been to a temple but for architectural interest, never chewed a paan and had not tried most sweets in the mithaishop. (Desai 2007 [2006], 176)

Despite her sympathetic portrayal of the economic marginality of the Gorkha community in the region, Desai questions the validity of the nationalist movement. As Jill Didur (2011, 57) points out, when the GNLF protesters intimidate Sai and her family into 'repeating the Gorkha movement slogans "Jai Gorkha" and "Gorkhaland for Gorkhas", they unwittingly undermine the conviction associated with these chants, emptying them of political or nationalist significance'. Desai's ironic depiction of the insurgents' activities and their lack of genuine commitment to the ideals upheld by the movement can also be seen to serve an allegorical function, as it implies 'that their political immaturity mirrors Indian society's own immaturity' (Girardin 2009, 297). The Gorkha rebels' forceful and illegal possession of the dilapidated local Gymkhana Club too arguably serves a symbolic function since the violation of a British emblem 'even in its ruined state, stands as the ultimate gesture of rebellion in a postcolonial state that has not allowed all Indians to be equally empowered' (Girardin 2009, 297). But the short-lived nature of Gyan's nationalist sentiment negates not only his commitment to the insurgent movement, but also the rationality of the movement itself which becomes increasingly violent. Thus, the novel, as Vanessa Guignery (2009, 313) explains, 'reveals the contingency and constructedness of notions of identity and nationality, which are nevertheless appealed to in order to legitimate terrible acts of violence and rebellion'. Once his ties with the Gorkhas are severed, Gyan attempts a reconciliation with Sai. But the novel, and the love story, end on a note of mitigated happiness. Its qualified tone of hopefulness (echoed by Biju's reunion with his father) has more to do with Sai's destiny as an individual young woman than with the couple as a unit or indeed with the nationalist movement. Having spent an entire year ignoring the world around her, suddenly its terrible injustices come sharply into focus for Sai. In particular, the cook's beating by her grandfather compels her to recognize the earlier narrowness of her concerns: 'Never again could she think that there was but one narrative that belonged only to herself, that she might create her own tiny happiness and live safely within it' (Desai 2007 [2006], 323).

The Gorkha nationalist movement is mocked by Desai not because it challenges the Indian nation state, but because of the essentializing processes that characterize most, if not all, nationalist movements. It is worth noting here that in postcolonial literary studies the realist mode in novels such as Seth's *A Suitable Boy* is seen to ideologically secure 'the idea of India as a single *nation*' as well as build 'a consensus around this area among the anglicised bourgeois readers who are the ruling elite of the postcolonial era', while magic realism is often seen as a narrative mode that is particularly amenable to contesting the supposed homogeneity of the nationalist project (Singh 1996, 166). Desai's novel, however, challenges reductive nationalist projects within the parameters of realism. But the realization that Sai reaches at the end of the novel, gestures also to an inevitability of inequality and its many manifestations: 'The fact was that one was empty-handed. There was no system to soothe the unfairness of things; justice was without scope; it might snag the stealer of chickens, but great evasive crimes would have to be dismissed because, if identified and netted, they would bring down the entire structure of the so-called civilization' (Desai 2007 [2006], 200).

Unlike Sahgal, Desai pointedly does not take sides, 'suggesting that nation-states and nationalities are artificial constructs' (Deshmane 2013, 192). In fact, the anonymous narrator contests the idea of a nation in the opening chapter of the novel by underscoring the vagueness and arbitrary nature of national borders and boundaries: 'A great amount of warring, betraying, bartering had occurred; between Nepal, England, Tibet, India, Sikkim, Bhutan; Darjeeling stolen from here, Kalimpong plucked from there—despite, ah, despite the mist charging down like a dragon, dissolving, undoing, making ridiculous the drawing of borders' (Desai 2007 [2006], 9; see also Didur 2011, 57–8). It is obvious that, while concerned with nations and nationalism, Desai very clearly does not write from a 'nationalist' point of view. However, because the Gorkha community's discontentment is tied in with its socio-economic marginality, I would argue that rejecting its territorial nationalism ultimately also eclipses the need to address class inequalities through collective action. In underscoring the tenuousness of the nationalist movement, the novel problematically invites a rejection of the role of class in collective identity formation and social struggle.

If Sahgal's text links the heroine's fate to the nation's destiny, Desai's appears to seriously challenge the efficacy of both nationalist sentiment *and* romantic love as a means of spiritual liberation, highlighting instead the importance of individual independence and personal determination, while problematically downplaying the significance of class in this process. Gyan's character too, even while he is involved in the Gorkha movement, experiences moments of scepticism about its leaders and their intentions: 'He asks himself, "Were these men entirely committed to the importance of the procession or was there a disconnected quality to what they did? Were they taking their cues from old protest stories or from the hope of telling a new story? Did their hearts rise and fall to something true? Once they shouted, marched, was the feeling authentic?"' (Desai 2007 [2006], 157). As David Spielman (2010, 83) points out, Gyan's doubts disconnect 'him from the crowd and the experience that temporarily affirms his selfhood, even though he wants to be part of the group and feel the way they do'. This could be read as a rejection of national as well as class allegorization, not as Majumdar argues, because of the private, regional nature of the struggle, but because of the text's refusal to let 'the private individual destiny' represent 'public political events' (Jameson

1986, 69). As Patrick C. Hogan (1999, 181) explains 'allegories are concerned with individual actions insofar as they manifest or represent larger social developments', while in Desai's novel, the journey towards selfhood appears to entail, even *require*, a dismissal of collective social identities.

Ostensibly, classes and nations, but not necessarily *classed nations*, are central concerns in both *The Inheritance of Loss* and *Rich Like Us*. These novels are rare in their preoccupation with how socio-economic differences can affect romantic relationships on a quotidian basis, but at the same time the romantic relationship very clearly becomes secondary in the two texts. Rose and Ram's marriage and Sai and Gyan's relationship come to be defined by political events even if, as in the case of Desai's novel, the narrative questions the nationalist sentiments propelling these events. The obvious nationalist stance of *Rich Like Us* demotes in importance and eventually contradicts Sahgal's portrayal of the significance of class differences in human relationships. Rather than a character's class status, it is nationalist sentiment—or the lack thereof—that emerges as the principal identity marker in the novel. Desai's text brings to the fore the destructive consequences of inequality, both between and within nations, but it proves pessimistic not only about the fruitfulness of crossing class and national boundaries, but also about any collective action based on an individual's national or class positioning.

◆

6

Speaking Back

The Politics of Cross-Class Dialogue

After all, the language we choose to write in (or that chooses us) imposes a set of possibilities, tensions and problems—and the creativity of the author is revealed in the way she negotiates the relationship of her language with the realities of her narrative and world.

—Tabish Khair*

The use of an 'elitist' language of colonial origin by postcolonial literary writers continues to draw considerable criticism, particularly with reference to the dialogue attributed to socio-economically subaltern characters in works of fiction. Ngugi wa Thiong'o (1994 [1986], 22), for instance, refers to the 'English-speaking (or French or Portuguese) African peasantry and working class' in postcolonial African fiction as a 'clear negation or falsification of the historical process and reality'. In South Asia today, despite the growing perception that English should now be considered a 'vernacular' rather than a foreign language, it remains primarily the language of the urban elite or the Babu classes.[1] Aijaz Ahmad's (2008 [1992], 77) observation about the status of the English language in India applies also to Pakistan:

> English is simply one of India's own languages now, and what is at issue at present is not the possibility of its ejection but the mode of its assimilation

* Quoted in Khair (2015, n.p.).

[1] According to Trivedi (1995 [1993], 20), 2 per cent of the Indian population knows English. A 'non-verified' estimate based on a literacy rate of 42.7 per cent suggests that 4 per cent of the population in Pakistan speaks the language (Mahboob and Ahmar 2004, 1005).

into our social fabric, and the manner in which this language, like any other substantial structure of linguistic difference, is used in the process of class formation and social privilege, here and now.

This privileged positioning of the language in the region has serious implications for the narration in literary works of verbal exchanges between subaltern and elite characters for whom English is not a shared tongue. Sociolinguistic differences within a monoglossic society are often portrayed in fiction by the deployment of different registers in the dialogue; however, as Robert Fraser (2000, 46) explains, in addition to various registers, the postcolonial anglophone author is confronted by the juxtaposition of different languages. Moreover, these languages are often perceived in hierarchical terms—as is the case with English with respect to (other) vernacular languages in India and Pakistan.

The purpose of my analysis in this chapter is not to denigrate or call into question the 'authenticity' of fiction from South Asia, which 'dares' to grapple with the 'impossible' task of depicting non-English-speaking characters in conversation with anglophone characters, but to draw attention to the complexity of narrating in the English language verbal exchanges between the haves and the have-nots in this part of the world. Moreover, I consider how the issue of linguistic difference is addressed by the characters and/or narrator within the text. In particular, I am seeking to evaluate the ways in which the techniques deployed to render cross-class dialogue may confirm or challenge socio-economic hierarchies as well as hierarchies within the narrative.

I conduct my examination of cross-class dialogue through the prism of the ten novels analysed in the preceding chapters, including the portrayal in these texts of intimate cross-class relationships not previously examined—notably, Sai's bond with the cook in *The Inheritance of Loss*, Masood and Aliya's friendship in *Salt and Saffron*, the narrator Nithya's friendship with the maid Sudha in *The Hottest Day of the Year*, and the twins' friendship with Velutha in *The God of Small Things*. The questions that I address are as follows: what linguistic and literary techniques do the writers employ to narrate conversations between the elite and subaltern characters which could not have taken place in English, especially in the context of profoundly unequal relationships, for instance, between a servant and her mistress? How is the direct speech of non-English-speaking subaltern characters 'translated' in these texts? Do the authors adopt different 'translation' strategies when narrating in English the speech of an upper-class character that is supposed to have taken place in a 'vernacular' language, such as Hindi or Urdu? In carrying out such an analysis, I am echoing Rashmi Sadana's (2012, 158) call for,

> a new politics of reading Indian English literature that is grounded in the very languages that it seeks to represent, and the places where those languages come from. To do so is to understand the politics of where English itself resides. To recognize that English emerges and exists alongside other languages in an intensely multilingual society is to repoliticize and territorialize Indian novels rather then read merely in their transnational 'isolation'.

It is worth noting that most of the novels that I have examined underscore within the narrative the hegemonic position of 'upper-class' English language in India and Pakistan and its implications for human intimacy. For example, in *Salt and Saffron*, Aliya the narrator explicitly states that 'English is the language of advancement in Karachi' (Shamsie 2000, 59) and regrets not offering to teach it to Masood, the family cook, who had so often said that 'he wanted to learn to read and write English' (Shamsie 2000, 150). Desai in *The Inheritance of Loss* depicts how an elitist language creates an insurmountable communication gap between Sai and the cook who raised her, precluding the possibility of genuine intimacy: '[S]omething about their closeness being exposed in the end as fake, their friendship composed of shallow things conducted in a broken language, for she was an English-speaker and he was a Hindi-speaker. The brokenness made it easier never to go deep, never to enter into anything that required an intricate vocabulary' (Desai 2007 [2006], 19). In *The God of Small Things*, as Christine Vogt-William (2003, 401–3) points out, Malayalam is as important to the twins as English, and it can be argued that this shared language contributes to the strength of their relationship with the non-English-speaking Velutha.

Apart from Khaleel, Gyan, Rose, and possibly the college-educated Maya (though this is never discussed in the novel), none of the other subaltern characters examined in the preceding chapters speak English. Some, like Bhima in *The Space Between Us*, are illiterate. In the majority of the cross-class relationships, the reader quickly gathers, even without being explicitly informed by the narrator, that the verbal exchange between the subaltern and the elite character is 'technically' taking place in an Indian or Pakistani language other than English. This gives rise to a number of linguistic and potentially ethical challenges as it requires a kind of 'pseudo translation' (Guilhamon 2009, 229). This kind of 'translation' is, as Neelam Srivastava (2007, 145) explains, 'not a translation at all, in the sense that the dialogues and free indirect speech in other Indian languages which are rendered in English, or Indian English in the text, are renditions of an "original" which does not exist'. In the texts just examined we can identify two primary ways to render non-English speech in English. The first of these is the use of a 'highly stylized' or 'staged' version of Indian or Pakistani Englishes (Khair 2001, 102). The second technique entails deploying Standard or 'neutral' English.

An English-speaking subaltern does appear to obviate the need to 'translate', as is the case of Khaleel in *Salt and Saffron* and Gyan in *The Inheritance of Loss*. Rose in *Rich Like Us*, as we know, is English and so by default speaks the language of the Indian elite, despite her working-class origins. As Jani (2010, 180) points out, 'undoubtedly, Rose is a fascinating character because her presence among elite Westernized Indians problematizes the neat binary oppositions that might pair nationality with language and/or social status (English/Indian; English-speaking/non-English-speaking, rich/poor)'. However, as pointed out in Chapter 5, the English that is attributed to her in the text is nevertheless marked by a Cockney accent and grammar, setting it sharply apart from Ram's flawless English. To quote a conversation between Rose and Ram when they first meet in London: '"I see I'll have to court you properly." "'Ow d'you mean, court me proper?" "-ly", he corrected. "Oh you, teaching me my own language. What'll you be teaching me next?"' (Sahgal 1999 [1985], 39).

Rose's Cockney English remains more or less unchanged in the text, even after being married to Ram and living in India for several decades. It seems that Sahgal has deliberately maintained Rose's linguistic alterity to indicate her distance from Ram's socio-economic milieu even if she is his wife; in other words, the author *does* use a form of stylized dialogue as a class marker within the narrative.

Stylized English

Before I begin my analysis of the stylized English deployed by authors such as Sidhwa and Umrigar, it may be useful to make a distinction between the English used to narrate the direct and indirect speech of the characters, and the actual Indian or Pakistani Englishes as they exist 'in the real world'.

The Indian subcontinent today is home to multiple varieties of English, from pukka, Babu English to the pidgin English of shopkeepers (Renouard 2008, 25). Regional linguistic differences are also a consideration as various regional languages influence the way English is spoken in a specific geographic area (Renouard 2008, 25). The Englishes spoken in Pakistan are similar to those spoken 'in contiguous regions of northern India', sharing the characteristic of 'rhoticity and its syllable-timed nature' (Hickey 2004, 551). Moreover, English speakers in South Asia often speak a combination of English and one or more vernacular languages on a daily basis. Anjali Gera Roy (2013, 21–2), for instance, points out that, in addition to Hinglish (a mixture of Hindi and English), 'new mixes with other Indian languages' have emerged in recent years including 'Tamlish', 'Punjlish', and 'Bonglish', produced from a combination of English with Tamil, Punjabi, and Bengali, respectively. Members of the lower classes are more likely to speak an English that is marked by vernacular idioms and regional inflections than are members of the highest socio-economic stratum of society, whose English is often relatively close to the Standard British in terms of both accent and lexicon (Guilhamon 2009, 225).

The English used by some Indian and Pakistani novelists in their works of fiction, on the other hand, is a strictly 'poetic' idiom which has been forged to meet specific expressive needs (Guilhamon

2009, 226). It is important to acknowledge the artificial quality of this English, which is meant to echo the language spoken in the real world and therefore to 'craft a mimesis of authenticity' (Muthiah 2009, 3). Its artificiality becomes particularly worthy of analysis when stylized English is deployed to narrate the direct speech of characters who do not speak English at all. Among the texts included in my analysis, *Ice-Candy-Man*, *The Space Between Us*, and *The Inheritance of Loss* deploy stylized, staged English, entailing the extensive use of techniques such as code-mixing which consists of the presence of Hindi or Urdu words 'in the dialogues and/or the narrative voice' (Srivastava 2007, 146). Other techniques include a literal translation of local idioms and proverbs and the superimposition of the grammatical structures of the 'source language' on English (Gane 2006, 574). Yet another device is the provision of a translation in English after having quoted the dialogue in the local language.

In Umrigar's and Sidhwa's novels, stylized English is used for the direct speech in case of upper- and lower-class characters. The following extracts from *The Space Between Us* are examples of how the conversation between Sera, an upper-class Bombayite, and her maid Bhima is rendered in the text: '"Chal ne, Bhima," she says in mock impatience: "How long does it take to decide which bags to take with you?" … "God knows, once the baby is born she'll have no time for friends-schends"' (Umrigar 2005, 285, 295). 'Friends-schends' is an example of echo words, often identified as a distinctive feature of Indian English (Bhatia and Ritchie 2004, 780). And '*Chal ne*' is a Hindi expression, an interjection, indicating that the mistress is exhorting her servant to hurry up and 'get going'. As for the servant Bhima's direct speech, the following is taken from the scene where Sera, a victim of domestic violence, asks her servant if her husband beats her too. 'Bhima snorted. "Beat me? Arree, if that fool touched me once, I would do some jadoo on him and turn his hands into pillars of wood…. No, bai, With God's grace, my Gopal is not like the other mens [*sic*]"' (Umrigar 2005, 111).

Upon closer examination we can detect a difference between the type of Indianized English used to render the mistress's speech and the kind used for the servant. Certainly, variations exist in how a language—whether it is English or another vernacular language—is spoken by members of various classes. As Barthes (1990, 81) has pointed out, 'within a national norm such as French, forms of expression differ in different groups, and every man is a prisoner of his language: outside his class, the first word he speaks is a sign which places him as a whole and proclaims his whole personal history'. In Umrigar's novel, the rendition of the indirect and direct speech of the mistress, when conversing with the maid, does include a large number of Hindi words, but the grammatical structure remains that of Standard English, even though as a Bombay Parsi, Sera's mother tongue is more likely to be either Parsi-Gujarati ('the community's identified language') or English, rather than Hindi (Luhrmann 1996, 37). However, to render the maid's speech, Umrigar not only does a literal translation of South Asian expressions such as 'do some *jadoo*' which is a Hindi/ Urdu expression (*kisi pay jadoo karna*), meaning to cast a spell on someone to get your own way. Could we attribute this manipulation of English grammar in Umrigar's novel, and in Desai's (as we will see later), as a reflection of the realist sensibility of the text? Are the narrators seeking to indicate the variations in how a vernacular language is 'actually' spoken, depending on the speaker's level and quality of education (the two being inextricably tied in with class in South Asia)? But this does not explain the introduction of grammatical errors ('not like other mens') in Bhima's speech and the Standard, grammatically correct English used to render Sera's speech, even while the conversation is ostensibly taking place in Hindi, which is the maid's mother tongue, but in all probability the mistress's third language.

As in *The Space Between Us*, in Sidhwa's novel too the direct speech of both elite and subaltern characters is rendered in stylized English. As an example of the direct speech of an upper-class character, this is what Lenny's godmother says to Ice-candy-man when she confronts him about his treatment of the Hindu Ayah: 'You would have your own mother carried off if it suited you! You are a shameless *badmash! Nimakharam!* Faithless!' (Sidhwa 1989 [1988], 248). But while the elite character's English consists primarily of lexical pointers, on several occasions in the text Ayah's speech exhibits distorted grammar and/or syntax which echoes and accentuates the subaltern's lack of understanding of current affairs and hence seems to indicate a certain lack of intelligence. For example, Ayah tells Lenny that the Partition of India would entail 'crack[ing]' it with 'a long, long canal' (Sidhwa 1989 [1988], 93). The repetition of the adjective 'long' is meant to mimic the Hindi language, as repetition 'is a marked characteristic of Hindi idiom' (Kellog and Bailey 1955, 492). However, I would argue that this technique has the effect of further infantilizing Ayah's explanation and thereby subordinating her to the elite characters within the text, even if she is seemingly at the heart of the novel: in fact the explanation that Ayah proffers is contemptuously dismissed by Lenny's cousin, an upper-class male child.

It is worth noting that Ayah's speech rendered in English is not consistently stylized in the narrative. It appears to have been distorted in scenes when political events are being discussed, but not when emotions are explored, suggesting that her intelligence is restricted to the so-called 'feminine'/'private' sphere. Notably, when Lenny and her godmother visit Ayah in Lahore's red-light area, she utters only a few sentences, but the English deployed is devoid of the traces of Pakistanized/Indianized idiom: 'I want to go to my family … I will not live with him … I have thought it over … I want to go to my folk' (Sidhwa 1989 [1988], 261–2). Just as the stylized elements of her speech infantilized her earlier in the text, here the absence of these elements allows her to acquire a degree of dignity; it underscores her resolution to leave Ice-candy-man and return to her family in India. These divergent effects also demonstrate that the use of stylized English is not an ideologically neutral choice.

Indeed, it is the *inconsistent and unequal* use of stylized Indian/Pakistani English which makes it particularly ideologically charged. Muthiah (2009, 15), in her doctoral thesis entitled 'Fictionalized Indian English Speech and the Representations of Ideology in Indian Novels in English', argues that the unequal distribution of the traits of Indian English among the Indian characters in literary works has profound ideological consequences, particularly since 'Indian English', or rather stylized Indian English, is subordinated and presented as inferior to Standard English within the text:

> By distributing IndE (Indian English) features to either all or almost all their characters, the four authors implicitly gesture to the Indian quality

of their characters, their settings and their motifs. By reserving a higher percentage of IndE features to accentuate the vilification, comicality, or lower socio-economic status of specific characters, the authors ideologically rationalize 'a set of beliefs' about IndE—that it is only good enough to function as a subordinating tool.

The 'subordinating' aspect of the uneven use of stylized English is especially stark in Desai's novel. Sai, the young protagonist, has a limited grasp of the Hindi language. She seems to have internalized the colonial hierarchy of languages, taste, culture, and religions: a hierarchy that is reinforced by her grandfather and which becomes a bone of contention with her lower-class boyfriend Gyan, as we saw earlier. Sai has learnt at the convent where she grew up that 'cake was better than laddoos, fork, spoon, knife better than hands.... English was better than Hindi' (Desai 2007 [2006], 30). While Desai's text points to the perils of perceiving one culture or one language as superior to another by highlighting the pernicious effects of the judge's Anglophilia, it unwittingly reaffirms this hierarchy in employing the cook's broken English to comic effect. To quote an example, his accent turns 'bed tea' into 'baaad tea', provoking Sai's laughter (Desai 2007 [2006], 61). The cook's broken English echoes and accentuates his intellectual inferiority within the narrative. For instance, while discussing Gyan's competence as a tutor, he affirms that the intelligence of a people is directly linked to its consumption of fish which elicits Sai's contempt and exasperation:

> 'Everyone knows,' said the cook. 'Coastal people eat fish and see how much cleverer they are, Bengalis, Malayalis, Tamils. Inland they eat too much grain, and it slows the ingestion—especially millet—forms a big heavy ball. The blood goes to the stomach and not to the head....' 'Go and eat some fish yourself,' Sai said. 'One stupid thing after another from your mouth.' (Desai 2007 [2006], 73)

Sai's, Gyan's, and the judge's exchanges in the novel are narrated in Standard English, while the cook's direct speech often contains entire phrases in Hindi (*hamara kya hoga, hai hai*) and is rendered in a highly stylized English (Desai 2007 [2006], 8). This works to produce humour and contempt, with the risk of ridiculing the lower-class character. When analysing the following extract, taken from another conversation between the cook and Sai, we notice the absence of the direct object at the end of the sentence: 'You cannot believe' (Desai 2007 [2006], 56). Once when Sai returns home late, having spent the day with her sweetheart, the cook reacts as follows: 'I've been waiting, waiting.... In this darkness you have not come home!' (Desai 2007 [2006], 142). The 'Indianized' aspects of his speech in this example are repetition ('waiting, waiting') as well as 'fronting for focus' (Muthiah 2009, 165) which here consists of placing the direct object or the prepositional phrase ('in this darkness') before the verbal phrase ('you have not come home')—accentuating Sai's tardy arrival and the cook's anxiety. But the structure of the sentence, ostensibly meant to echo Hindi syntax, has the effect of bestowing the cook with a kind of childish petulance. As Khair (2001, 104) points out, 'the gap between English and other languages may be one of the reasons why Indian transcriptions of local languages into English so often sound (and read) childish, and even retarded'.

The technique of 'translating' subaltern speech with grammatically incorrect or distorted English becomes even more problematic when the elite character's speech is rendered in 'Standard', that is, grammatically correct English, such we saw in *The Space Between Us*. Let us consider a few examples of Sai's speech when in conversation with the cook. When the cook's hut is subjected to a search by the police after the theft of firearms from the judge's house, Sai reacts with indignation: 'How dare they behave this way to you!' We also see her asking him questions about her grandfather's past: 'Did he really love her so very much? ... How did the servants know, then?' (Desai 2007 [2006], 60). As these examples show, the direct speech attributed to Sai when she 'speaks' in Hindi is devoid of any syntactical or morphological distortions, even when the text explicitly states that Sai speaks a 'broken Hindi' (Desai 2007 [2006], 19). Therefore, the text essentially deploys Standard English to render Sai's broken Hindi, and distorted English to narrate the cook's speech while he is theoretically speaking his mother tongue. In addition to its comic effect, the cook's broken English arguably creates a distance between anglophone readers and the lower-class character, while the Standard English used to render Sai's broken Hindi ensures her centrality in the text.

Sai's speech is problematic in another respect also. The 'brokenness' of her Hindi tests the reader's credibility as, since she was nine years old, the Hindi-speaking cook has been her chief companion and confidant. In the novel his socio-economic inferiority seems to exclude the possibility of his exercising any influence on the upper-class child's linguistic learning. It is somewhat unrealistic for a linguistic distance of this sort to be maintained over eight years, especially given that Sai was only a child when she arrived at Cho Oyu and was virtually raised by the cook rather than by her anglicized grandfather. It is worth recalling, as Alison Blunt (1999, 434) points out, that during British Raj in India, according to the colonizers, one of the undesirable consequences of having native ayahs caring for British children was that they were likely to speak 'an Indian language earlier and better than English'. Instead of exploring the possibility of a shared language attenuating rigid class differences, Desai's novel seems to insist that class differences necessarily entail a permanent linguistic gap. The text freezes Sai's linguistic (and consequently socio-economic) positioning, thereby emphasizing the cook's social subalternity within the narrative. Indeed, this portrayal belies both the fluidity of languages and the affection between Sai and the cook.

Standard/Neutral English

The use of stylized English in 'postcolonial' literary works presents, as Khair (2001, 125) points out, 'the problem of superior reportage, of appropriation from a position of dominance. The greatest danger ... is that a stylized Indian English and a refusal to face the problems of employing English in India are liable to twist any narrative into passing off alien discourses under false pretexts. This would merely repeat earlier structures of occlusion, dominance and exploitation.'

The second common poetic technique used to narrate cross-class dialogue is to employ neutral/Standard English, which appears to be a means of avoiding these perils. Crystal (1994, 24) describes 'the Standard English of an English-speaking country as a minority variety (identified chiefly by its vocabulary, grammar, and orthography) which carries most prestige and is most widely understood'. In the context of the subcontinent generally, and South Asian anglophone fiction specifically, I am here taking this to mean American and British Standard Englishes, in terms of syntax and grammar, which nonetheless display certain, though limited, lexical signs indicating the sociocultural context of the work, particularly for which equivalents in Standard American or British English do not exist. These signs may include the name of Pakistani or Indian dishes (momo, chapatti, dal), familial or other social relationships (akka, ammi, tai) or names of places (chawl).

In *The End of Innocence* and *The Hope Chest*, the authors deploy Standard English for both the direct and indirect discourse of lower- and upper-class characters, and the use of Urdu words is limited largely to titles (for example, begum, Nani Ma). We can detect the use of Standard English in *The Hottest Day of the Year* and in *The Binding Vine* as well, where the elite and subaltern characters have Tamil and Marathi in common, respectively. To quote an example of the direct speech attributed to Shakuntala, the subaltern character, when speaking to Urmila: 'She is very smart, that's how she got that job in the shop. Kalpana even learnt to speak English.... When she wants something, she goes after it, nothing can stop her. She's stubborn, you can't imagine, how stubborn she is' (Deshpande 2001 [1993], 92). Moreover, Urmila is the only upper-class character in this study who does not belong to the Babu class. Urmila, her family and friends speak Kannada and Marathi during the course of their daily lives, and as is the case in Roy's *The God of Small Things* which I discuss later, Deshpande's novel does not advance a hierarchy of languages with English on top.

As Amit Chaudhuri (2008, 116) has pointed out, since it is often believed that the postcolonial Indian is characterized by a hybrid identity, there exists an expectation that 'the language of the postcolonial too must be hybrid, with a scattering of untranslated Indian words and phrases and odd sentence constructions'. As a consequence of this, 'what is perceived to be or even constructed as, standard English is seen to be linked to an alien sensibility and to the verbal traditions of colonialism, and [is] perhaps less adequate to the hybrid, multilingual nature of post-colonial, Indian consciousness' (Chaudhuri 2008, 116). But as Chaudhuri goes on to explain, hybridity 'can frequently enter texts in subtly disruptive, rather than obvious ways; it need not be worn like a national costume'.

These subtle methods that Chaudhuri mentions and that Mohsin, Ahmad, Deshpande, and Charry deploy are examples of what Neelam Srivastava (2007, 146) has called the 'symbolic use' of the indigenous language. Standard English works in the text as Urdu, Marathi, or Tamil and the variation in linguistic competence is reflected in a variation of register. The verbal exchanges between the servant girl Rani and Laila are rendered in Standard English without any modification of the syntax or grammar. To quote an example from *The End of Innocence*, which narrates a conversation between Rani and Laila after their visit to the cinema to watch the Punjabi film *Heer Ranjha*: 'I wish I was Heer. I wish I were beautiful like her so someone would fall in love with me as deeply as Ranjha did with her. I want to be adored and sung to and smiled at' (Mohsin 2006, 33). Despite the Standard English deployed here, readers never forget that the conversation between Rani and Laila is not taking place in English, nor do we lose sight of the Pakistani context of the relationship.

But if the use of staged/stylized English carries its perils, the use of neutral English comes with its 'own charge of discursive meanings' and potential pitfalls (Khair 2001, 117). In Mohsin's text, this technique entails a simplification of the linguistic diversity of Pakistan. The spatial backdrop of Mohsin's novel is a fictive village in Punjab, but the novel glosses over the divergent social value attached to Urdu and Punjabi, respectively, in contemporary Pakistan. It is as though the only difference of import is between 'indigenous' languages and English: the hierarchical relationship between (other) Pakistani languages is camouflaged, which overlooks the fact that Urdu, conjointly with English, often works as an elitist language in contemporary Pakistan. As Huma Ibrahim (2001, 46) points out, while the marginalization of Punjabi had begun 'as a colonizing principle', in the newly created Pakistan it was reinstituted by the Punjabis themselves, with children from Punjabi-speaking families learning in school that 'the way they speak at home is coarse and economically disadvantageous and very soon they adopt Urdu as the medium of communication—which undermines Punjabi language and literature'.

Moreover, while staged English carries the risk of further subordinating the subaltern character within the narrative, the use of neutral English does not automatically render the text subaltern-centred or the portrayal of the cross-class relationship more egalitarian. Other narrative hierarchies also need to be considered, in particular those pertaining to point(s) of view and focalization. Mohsin's novel is narrated in the third person, almost solely from the point of view of the elite child Laila, who is the protagonist of the text, with the narrative focused for the most part, though not exclusively, on her thoughts and consciousness while those of the subaltern character remain secondary. Similarly in *The Hottest Day of the Year*, while the maid's conversations with the upper-class child narrator are rendered in a neutral English, Sudha's character is nonetheless infantilized within the narrative. For example: '"Why do you call them *bindis*. They are *pottus*." "It's the Hindi word. It means the same thing." "*Bindis*." she giggled. "It sounds strange." "It's just another language, that's all." I said sternly' (Charry 2003 [2001], 33).

Sudha is shown to have trouble grasping the notion that in a foreign language familiar objects carry a different name from that in Tamil, her mother tongue. If, unlike Nithya, Sudha does not speak English and did not attend an elite missionary school in Bangalore, she nevertheless is a twenty-year-old woman who has had formal schooling in Tamil. However, in her conversations with Nithya, Sudha's intellectual capacities are shown to be far inferior to those of the convent-educated elite child. For instance, Nithya reports that 'Sudha was overwhelmed by any length of time longer than twenty years. The Indus Valley civilisation is 5,000 years old, I liked to tell her, and it is nearly 2,000 years since the birth of Christ, and the British left 39 years ago. Her eyes would widen' (Charry 2003 [2001], 48–9). Such an observation by the upper-class narrator creates a disturbing hierarchy between English and Tamil by rendering intelligence and intellectual sophistication dependent on the knowledge (or lack thereof) of a specific language.

The English used for the direct speech of the subaltern and elite characters in Ahmad's *The Hope Chest* is also more or less Standard English with what Khair (2001, 105) calls 'a restrained use of the vernacular'. But, unlike Mohsin's novel (and Shamsie's, as we will see later), Ahmad's text does reflect the complex linguistic reality of Lahore, where the bulk of the action takes place. The text allows readers to gather that when Reshma is with her Pathan family the 'source' language of the dialogue is Pashto, and when she speaks to her friend Shehzadi the conversation takes place in Urdu without a change in the grammatical or syntactic structure, even though certain lexical markers are at times present. As the following examples demonstrate, there is a minimal manipulation of grammar in the direct speech of subaltern and upper-class characters. In the first citation, Reshma asks her friend to make arrangements for a sterilization procedure at the hospital where Shehzadi works: 'But please, Shehzadi, do this little job for me, *haan*?' (Ahmad 1996, 210). Here the author makes use of the invariant tag question in Urdu 'haan?' (will you?), placed after a phrase, which can be taken in both the affirmative and the negative. It is interesting to note that Reshma's direct speech becomes more stylized towards the end of the text, when she is sent away by her husband and expelled from the marital home. The following extract describes her entrance interview for midwifery school: 'Matron looked at her doubtfully, "But you can read and write, can't you? At least in Urdu?" "*Jee, jee*, I can; very well in Urdu, also a little in English. And I finished *Quran-e-Pak* when I was twelve"' (Ahmad 1996, 283).

The use of the Urdu word for 'yes' (jee), the implied intonation through repetition, the missing definite article before *Quran-e-Pak* and the syntactic structure of Reshma's speech echo Urdu, the 'source' language of the conversation. As we saw in the first chapter, at the end the novel Ahmad rejects the possibility of a sustainable friendship between Reshma and Shehzadi because of the immense class differences between them. I would argue that the use of stylized English here does not work to subordinate or ridicule the lower-class character, but instead draws our attention to the social distance that separates Reshma from Shehzadi as well as from the Babu readership, and consequently highlights the subaltern character's independence and agency.

As mentioned earlier, in *The Hottest Day of the Year* Sudha's speech is infantilized and therefore subordinated in the text, despite the use of neutral English to render her speech. Similarly, in a text like *The Binding Vine*, even though the author allows both Urmila and Shakuntala to speak Standard English, the subaltern's speech, while not subordinated by a staged, erroneous English, is nonetheless rendered secondary to Urmila's. This is either because the subaltern is shown to be unable to speak (due to her grief) or because she silences herself by deferring to the upper-class character's supposedly better judgement. Clearly, the politics of Standard or stylized English cannot be considered in isolation from other aspects of the literary work, in particular the silences that may exist in the narrative.

Cross-Class Dialogue in *The God of Small Things* and *Salt and Saffron*

I consider the cross-class dialogue in *The God of Small Things* and *Salt and Saffron* separately from the other literary works, not because the techniques that the authors deploy are radically different from those discussed earlier, but because the distinctive nature of the politics of these techniques in the two novels calls for closer examination.

In Roy's novel, in addition to words, and indeed entire sentences in Malayalam, the author makes use of both Indianized and neutral/Standard English to render the direct speech of her characters—whether upper- or lower-class. In her linguistic analysis of the dialogue in this novel, Shobhana Chelliah (2006, n.p.) argues that 'the least sympathetic characters' use 'the most Indian English features' in their speech, notably the child-molester Orangedrink Lemondrink Man and the self-serving Comrade Pillai; consequently, Roy, not unlike other authors such as Rohinton Mistry, reinforces the 'inferior' status of Indian English in comparison with Standard English, which remains the prestigious dialect. According to Chelliah (2006, n.p.), readers sympathize with the characters who speak a 'prestigious variety' of English, and the use of Indianized English in novels by Indian authors 'reinforces the status of Indian English as a substandard variety'. The drink vendor, for example, pronounces 'pocket money' as 'porketmunny' (Roy 1997, 102). Likewise, in the direct speech attributed to Pillai we can detect a number of features of Indianized English. The following example makes use of an article before a mass noun ('nonsense') as well as the zero article before the noun 'masses': 'For you what is *a nonsense* for [ ]

Masses it is something different' (Roy 1997, 279; italics mine). To quote another example: '*I think so* you are in *Amayrica* now?' (Roy 1997, 129; italics mine). In Standard English, the adverb proform 'so', standing in for an elliptical clause, is used for complementation of verbs such as 'say' and 'think' (Pearce 2007, 148). However, Pillai uses 'so' with the verb 'think', despite it being followed by a clause. Moreover, he pronounces 'America' with highly 'Indianized' accent; his accent also transforms 'divorce' into 'die-vorce' (Roy 1997, 130) and 'minute' into 'mint' (Roy 1997, 134).

The direct speech of the bourgeois characters in Roy's novel bears few traces of Indian English and echoes cultural conventions rather than modification of the grammatical rules of Standard English. For instance, at the cinema, when speaking to Estha, Ammu refers to the drinks vendor as 'Uncle'. In the Indian subcontinent, the title of 'Uncle' or 'Aunty' is often used by a younger person referring to an older individual, while the use of a title such as Mister or Missus may be interpreted as a sign of rudeness (Sailaja 2009, 86). The conversation between Velutha and the twins and his exchanges with Ammu 'take place' in Malayalam. For instance, Ammu and Velutha name the spider found on the banks of the river '*Chappu Thamburan*' ('Lord Rubbish') (Roy 1997, 339). The text ends, as we know, on a promise made by the lovers and uttered in Malayalam: the tomorrow that will never come. 'She had a dry rose in her hair. She turned to say it once again: "Naaley." Tomorrow' (Roy 1997, 340).

In the following extract of a conversation between the twins and Velutha, they ask him to repair a boat that they have found:

'I don't want you playing any silly games on this river.'
'We won't. We promise. We'll use it only when you're with us.'
'First we'll have to find the leaks …' Velutha said.
'Then we'll have to plug them!' the twins shouted, as though it was the second line of a well-known poem.
'How long will it take?'
'A day,' said Velutha.
'A day! I thought you'd say a month!' (Roy 1997, 213)

Indeed, attributing Standard, neutral English to Velutha, a lower-caste, lower-class subaltern, is not an ideologically neutral poetic device. As Christine Vogt-William (2003, 402) points out:

Velutha, an Untouchable, would not have had access to the kind of English Roy uses in his speech. Yet Roy reports his thought patterns and lends his speech a certain dignity by using a more or less standard variety of English. This of course contributes to the reader's perception of Velutha not just as an Untouchable, but rather as a person with rights.

However, despite the use of these two kinds of English, the dialogue in *The God of Small Things* does not subscribe to a binary approach, whereby Standard English is attributed only to sympathetic and/or upper-class characters, while Indianized English is used for the speech of unsympathetic and/or lower-class ones. Arguably, the least sympathetic character in the book, Baby Kochamma, speaks a standard variety of English devoid of any trace of Indianisms. She quotes Shakespeare in her daily conversations and is keen to differentiate her accent from that of other 'inferior' Indians. But Baby Kochamma's proficiency in English and her pronounced Anglophilia are not at all presented as a positive quality in the text. In a similar vein, despite his illustrious academic qualifications and years spent at Oxford, the heavily anglicized Chacko is portrayed as an upper-class man who blatantly exploits the subaltern women working for him, as well as his sister, and is for the most part an indifferent uncle who does not hesitate from callously reminding the twins that their presence is unwanted in Ayemenem.

Let us not forget the significant presence of Malayalam in *The God of Small Things*, which, in certain cases, Roy does not even translate into English. If, like other postcolonial writers, Roy 'assumes the role of interpreter for her non-Malayalam-speaking readers' by translating specific words, on certain occasions she refuses to translate at all and does not even italicize the words in Malayalam to signal their foreignness (Tickell 2007, 8). For example: 'Chacko was driving. He was four years older than Ammu. Rahel and Estha couldn't call him Chachen because when they did, he called them Chetan and Cheduti. If they called him Ammaven he called them Appoi and Ammai. If they called him Uncle he called Aunty, which was embarrassing in Public. So they called him Chacko' (Roy 1997, 37). As Alex Tickell (2007, 8) explains, this passage not only emphasizes Roy's 'interest in names and naming (and the power of language to construct meaning and identity)', but also 'partially alienates Roy's non-Malayalam readers and underlines the fact that cultural differences cannot, and should not, always be easily translated or explained'. Roy's refusal to translate appears to reaffirm her refusal to present the English language as intrinsically superior to (other) Indian languages and to render every aspect of the text comprehensible for a Western readership, or even for an Indian readership that does not speak or read Malayalam. Moreover, in the text Estha and Rahel play with the English language, question and breach its laws, for instance by reading backwards or 'breaking the semantic unity' of words (such as '*Lay tar*' or '*Bar Nowl*'), which echoes their other social transgressions (Clarke 2007, 137).

Ammu and the twins, despite their Anglophilia, speak Malayalam; this language is crucial to their imaginative lives and arguably contributes to their transgressive relationship with Velutha. In fact, initially for the twins, the English language is associated with the malevolent discipline imposed upon them by Baby Kochamma. In particular, during the week preceding their cousin Sophie Mol's arrival, she 'eavesdropped relentlessly on the twins' private conversations, and whenever she caught them speaking in Malayalam, she levied a small fine which was deducted at source. From their pocket money' (Roy 1997, 36). The fondness that Estha and Rahel later develop for English contrasts with Baby Kochamma's obsequious obsession with the language, which echoes her belief in the superiority of Christianity and the white race. Therefore, if Roy demonstrates how English can work as a tool of oppression within societies (and families), through the twins' speech, she also reveals how it can give rise to a model of linguistic hybridity that is not hierarchical, but instead gestures to, as Clarke (2007, 140) explains, 'amalgamation rather than contestation'. The following humorous exchange between Velutha and Rahel, while rendered in Standard English, nevertheless draws attention to the linguistic plurality and disjunction characterizing cross-class interactions; but in evoking the paralinguistic aspects of human interaction (the act of smiling), Roy reveals the commonality between the two languages, and by extension the possibility of humour and genuine intimacy between disparate classes: '"See, you're smiling!" Rahel said. "That means it was you. Smiling means, 'It was you.'" "That's only in English!"

Velutha said. "In Malayalam my teacher always said, 'Smiling means it wasn't me'"' (Roy 1997, 178).

Shamsie's *Salt and Saffron* provides us with a limited number of cross-class verbal interactions. In endowing Mariam's character with a fantastical mutism and situating their post-elopement story off-stage, the text forbids the depiction of (audible) exchanges between her and Masood, apart from the daily menu that Mariam announces to the cook. The narrator Aliya is shown to share a close bond with Masood and recalls several distinct conversations that they shared. As the following example shows, a refined, almost poetic English is deployed to narrate the cook's direct speech in the text, accentuated by his use of the literary word *aftab* in Urdu to refer to the sun, rather than the colloquial *sooraj*:

> 'The sun can climb or it can burn,' he said more than once. 'The first stages of the sun's ascent are the more sheer and slippery. It's like climbing K2. So Aftab Sahib climbs the sky and does nothing but climb. By the time he is near the top it's as easy as climbing the hill, so his attention can wander and then he starts seeking out kitchens and angles his rays through the windows.' (Shamsie 2000, 95)

To quote another example, Masood gives the following response when Aliya once asks him impatiently how much longer it will take for him to prepare a dish: '"How much time ?" I heard Masood's voice, incredulous. "How can I tell how much time it'll take? When the spices and the meat dissolve the boundaries between them and the flavours seep, one into the other, then it is time"' (Shamsie 2000, 58–9). These verbal exchanges, which could only have taken place in Urdu, somewhat try the credibility of the reader, especially an Urdu-speaking reader, in several respects. To begin with, in the novel Aliya confesses her lack of proficiency in the Urdu language. She confuses the words *umeed* (hope) and *umrood* (guava), a very common fruit in South Asia, for instance (Shamsie 2000, 94). However, as the protagonist–narrator, Aliya also 'translates' for the reader her cross-class conversations with Masood, which are characterized by an elegant vocabulary and style. The narration of such conversations would presuppose a strong bilingualism on the narrator's part, which Aliya admits she lacks. As Spivak (1992, 185) warns us, 'to decide whether you are prepared enough to start translating, then, it might help if you have graduated into speaking, by choice or preference, of intimate matters in the language of the original'. It could perhaps be argued that *Salt and Saffron* is not a realist text, and therefore verisimilitude of dialogue should not be a pressing concern: the 'fabulous' events in the text include, as mentioned earlier, Mariam's fantastical refusal to speak as well as a series of unlikely events preceding Khaleel's arrival in Karachi at the end of the novel. But the desire to create an illusion of 'Pakistani' realities through language is very much present in the novel. Even when an elevated English is deployed for the dialogue, the author has recourse to code-switching in the form of interjections, such as *suno* (listen), *arré* (hey), and *'eh ehmuk'* (you idiot), to indicate the 'Pakistani' identity of the characters, even those who belong to the aristocratic and highly anglicized Dard-e-Dil clan.

Moreover, the inter-class dialogue in *Salt and Saffron* seems to make a binary equation between socio-economic milieu and language: if a mastery of the English language is a hallmark of the upper classes in the text, Urdu subsequently becomes associated with the lower classes. Masood's direct speech, as we saw, rendered in a literary English, suggests a scholarly Urdu as the 'source' language of the 'translated' dialogue, even though the text does not indicate that Masood has had anything more than a rudimentary schooling, if that. I would contend that whether *Salt and Saffron* is described as a realist or magical realist text, it is nonetheless very attentive to differences in linguistic proficiency in English as class markers. The linguistic *non-anglophone* realities of Pakistan, however, become homogenized in the novel. For instance, in the following passage, Aliya wonders about the possible causes of Mariam's voluntary mutism: 'Did she refrain from speech because speech betrays accent, and accent betrays everything? But then, why speak of food?' (Shamsie 2000, 157). When Mariam did speak, it was to specify the day's menu *in Urdu*. But Aliya's self-questioning seems to exclude the possibility that Mariam's accent in Urdu could possibly reveal her social origins, as if a variation in accents or in proficiency exist only with respect to the English language. Furthermore, in casting Urdu as the language of the subalterns, *Salt and Saffron*, like *The End of Innocence*, glosses over the linguistic conflicts within Pakistan and the significance of regional languages.

Urdu is the mother tongue of 'only 8 per cent' of the Pakistani population who are concentrated in the cities (Weightman 2002, 140). As discussed, Urdu functions as an elitist language alongside English and this has resulted in the subordination of languages such as Punjabi. Since the 1950s the city of Karachi has witnessed several periods of rioting against the marginalization of the Sindhi language with respect to the hegemonic position of Urdu. Sindhi first came under threat after Partition, with the arrival of Urdu-speaking immigrants (Muhajirs) from India who began to replace the Sindhis economically. Despite Urdu and Sindhi being declared the 'official' languages of the province of Sindh, the language question remains a thorny one, often leading to violent confrontations between Sindhis and Muhajirs (Ayres 2003, 52–6). In *Salt and Saffron*, Masood's character is shown to be from a village, in all probability from the province of Sindh, but instead of Sindhi or Saraiki (spoken in rural southern Punjab), the 'translated' dialogue suggests that he speaks a refined Urdu, with his linguistic identity bearing little relationship to his regional roots, which are not evoked in the text at all.

Language in Shamsie's novel, as in Desai's, appears to be a rigid entity, entwined with what are constructed as immutable and inevitable class differences. Even while explicitly recognizing the importance of English as the language of socio-economic mobility in Pakistan, the narrative seems to reject the possibility that the subaltern's knowledge of the language could alleviate class differences. In the following passage, Aliya and her cousin Sameer discuss the prospect of meeting Masood on an equal footing after his elopement with Mariam, but eventually reject the possibility that even a shared elitist language would help bridge class differences (Shamsie 2000, 185):

> 'But suppose.... Remember he used to say he wished he could read English? What if Mariam Apa taught him? What if he's read, I don't know ...'
> 'Frantz Fanon?' Sameer made a dismissive gesture. 'Are you saying it's all about education? The great leveller. You think that if you read John Ashbery all differences cease to matter. Come on, Aliya. You're smarter than that.'

Sameer's opinion about the immutability of the relationship between class differences and language is not challenged by Aliya, and this works to erode the 'happy' nature of the ending of the two love stories in the text.

Clearly, the linguistic devices deployed to render the dialogue between the rich and the poor in anglophone Indian and Pakistani literature are intimately tied in with the class politics of a text. In particular, the inconsistent or unequal use of certain translation strategies has serious ideological consequences. However, as we have seen, contradictory political ramifications can and do arise from the use of broadly similar linguistic techniques; one particular 'type' of English, therefore, cannot be designated as being inherently subaltern-friendly or hostile to the subaltern viewpoint(s). An examination of the dialogue across class in English must be considered together with other formal aspects, and with the way in which the social reality of the English language itself is constructed within the narrative, especially in the context of other languages, to arrive at a better understanding of the language and class politics of a literary work.

◆

Conclusion

Intimacy Across Class—Modes of Elitist Narration?

Texts are protean things, they are tied to circumstances and to politics, large and small, and these require attention and criticism … reading and writing texts are never neutral activities: there are interests, powers, passions, pleasures, entailed no matter how aesthetic or entertaining the work.
—Edward Said*

Homi Bhabha (1990, 7) has asserted that magical realism is 'the literary language of the emerging postcolonial world'. However, even a cursory overview of the literary works in English produced by South Asian writers since the publication of Rushdie's *Midnight's Children* in 1981 provides ample proof that the realist mode has persisted and flourished alongside more obviously experimental ones. Significantly, it is the women writers who have favoured realism, with only Shamsie's *Salt and Saffron*, among the novels examined in this book, deploying certain fantastical elements in the narrative while otherwise still subscribing to the realist mode. *The God of Small Things* has been designated as an example of magical realism, for instance by Lane (2006, 97) and Podgorniak (2002). But as Tickell (2007, 57) points out, what are considered to be surreal aspects of the novel can be explained by the 'heightened, imaginative perceptions' of the child protagonists. And as Roy herself has protested:

I don't understand when readers assume that Indian writers are 'magical realists' and suddenly I'm a 'magical realist,' just because Salman Rushdie or other Indian writers are 'magical realists.' No, what I am writing is what the characters are experiencing. What the reader is reading is the

* Quoted in Said (1994 [1993], 385).

character's own perceptions. Those images are driven by the characters. It is never me invoking magic! This is realism, actually, that I am writing. (Jaana 1997, n.p.)

It seems that the temptation to classify a text like *The God of Small Things* as 'magical realist' stems from a recognition among critics of its deeply subversive class, caste and gender politics, and from the widely shared perception in postcolonial criticism that realism 'is almost necessarily conservative, and non-realistic forms are inherently somehow more postcolonial—and therefore subversive' and less elitist (Moss 2000, 158). In particular, feminist domestic realism, according to Rajeswari Sunder Rajan (1993b, 81), seems 'unlikely to attempt to transgress the structure of separate spheres even where home, marriage, family—the private sphere—is perceived as most repressive'; and Anuradha Roy (1999, 144) argues that the choice of realism by Indian women authors indicates a lack of courage 'in the use of narrative modes to challenge patriarchal ideology'. But such an observation underestimates the experimentation that realism allows as well as ignores the fact that it has many varieties—as Leslie Esther (2010, 158) has pointed out, 'realism is as flexible as the reality it attempts to mirror'. In fact, each of the ten novels that I have examined exhibits characteristics associated with two or more kinds of realism. These include: 'critical realism' as a form of literary representation which is 'socially engaged' and 'depicts social reality so as to analyze and critique' it (Vargas 2011, 29), the 'subjective' form of realism which allows for the 'depiction of dreams, fantasies, flights of the imagination as part of its conception of the real' (Felski 1989, 82), as well as domestic realism, exploring 'issues of home and family, courtship and marriage, interwoven with gender, power and class conflict' (Dabundo 2012, 371). Significantly, a focus on the bourgeois domestic sphere and the figure of the domestic servant in a realist text powerfully underscores the artificial nature of the divide between the private and public spheres, and brings to the fore the role played by the home and the family in the construction of gendered and class identities.

As we saw in the preceding chapters, realist novels by women writers do have the capacity to contest patriarchal oppression as well as to challenge the socially constructed logic of economic stratification. In the texts examined, the realist narrative may ultimately underscore the inevitability of class boundaries, such as in *The Inheritance of Loss*, or allow gender to take precedence over class as an identity marker towards the end of the novel as I discuss later, but the textual engagement with the role of class in human relationships is undeniable. As Julian Markels (2003, 47–8) explains: 'The realist novel is no more committed to class a priori than any other sort of novel, but in its simulacrum of social experience it must open itself up to class as other novels may choose not to do, just insofar as class is understood as a process of producing, appropriating and distributing surplus labor that makes social experience intelligible.'

Realism shares an affinity with third-person, omniscient narration (Fraser 2000, 35), which is often characterized by a 'pretence of objective truth' (Kanaganayakam 2002, 117). But this mode of narration too can be deployed successfully, especially with the use of shifting points of view, to present both elite and subaltern perceptions of reality, for instance, as Ahmad does in *The Hope Chest* and Umrigar in *The Space Between Us*. Moreover, the notion of objective truth can also be explicitly questioned by a realist text using third-person narration. We can recall, for example, the epigraph of *The God of Small Things* ('Never again will a single story be told as though it's the only one'), as well as the realization that Sai reaches at the end of *The Inheritance of Loss* about the pitfalls of believing in the primacy of a single narrative, and her recognition that 'life wasn't single in its purpose … or even in its directions' (Desai 2007 [2006], 323). Coupled with a 'disjunctive chronology' in the two novels, these observations invite a reflection on the possible multiplicity of narratives and realities, material or otherwise (Scanlan 2010, 270).

While operating broadly in the realist mode, the ten novels adopt different, sometimes widely divergent, approaches to the question of cross-class intimacy. Nevertheless, they share the commonality of compelling us to come to grips with the multifaceted nature of socio-economic subalternity and privilege, and to engage with the problematic 'processes of power across overlapping and uneven social arenas' in contemporary Pakistan and India (Jani

2010, 141). Class in these novels intersects in complex ways with other hierarchies pertaining not only to gender, but also to caste, age, and ethnicity. We saw in the analysis of Shamsie's *Salt and Saffron* and Umrigar's *The Space Between Us*, among others, how the implicit codes that inform relationships across class echo the more structured and explicit codes dictating relationships between members of disparate castes. However, intersecting hierarchies also create divided loyalties and uneasy tensions not only between the characters, but also between the formal and ideological aspects of a given text. These tensions can result in textual silences or 'a certain absence' as Macherey (2006 [1978], 95) calls it, which is why I have been concerned as much with what is said in a narrative about cross-class intimacy, as with what is not.

No less than six of the texts examined in this book grapple with the thorny relationship between gender and class identities and how this complicates the idea and possibility of 'universal' female friendship. In *That Long Silence* (Deshpande 1988, 52), a novel by Deshpande, not considered in this book, Jaya, the upper-class female protagonist, reflects on the suffering of her maid Jeeja and acknowledges the complicity of bourgeois women in the exploitation of their lower-class counterparts:

> Poor Jeeja, we said all of us women who employed her, but I knew, if I thought of it, that I wouldn't have had her life any different. All of those happy women with husbands in good jobs, men who didn't drink and beat their wives, those fortunate women whose kitchen shelves gleamed with brass and stainless steel vessels—they were of no use to me. It was Jeeja and her like I needed, it was those women who saved me from the hell of drudgery. Any little freedom I had depended on them.

If the denouement of *The Binding Vine, The Hope Chest*, and *The Space Between Us* echoes Jaya's observation, and seems to reject the possibility of long-lasting female solidarity across class, the issue of class differences dividing women becomes camouflaged and silenced in *Ice-Candy-Man, The Hottest Day of the Year*, and *The End of Innocence*. It does not seem a coincidence that this 'absence' of class towards the ends of these three novels is paralleled by a heightened focus on not only gendered violence and oppression, but also on female solidarity as a strategy of resistance. This entails a problematic simplification of the complexity characterizing women's relationships with each other. Such a technique also ultimately accords the power to act or to tell the subaltern's story to an upper-class female.

Edward Said's (1994 [1993], 95) observation that the 'capacity to represent, portray, characterize and depict is not easily available to just any member of just any society', holds particularly true within the context of anglophone fiction from the Indian subcontinent. Significantly, depicting cross-class intimacy necessarily calls for the portrayal of mostly non-English speaking subalterns. Representations of members of an 'oppressed group' by 'members of privileged groups' run the risk of carrying 'projections and fantasies through which the privileged reinforce a complimentary image of themselves' (Young 1997, 350). Indeed, the act of representation can work to keep 'the subordinate subordinate, the inferior inferior' (Said 1994 [1993], 95). Therefore, a reading of narratives with lower-class or non-anglophone characters requires an engagement with how social hierarchies are challenged or reaffirmed within the English-language text, while also allowing for the very real possibility that a privileged language does not *necessarily* result in elite-centred texts, with no agency accorded to the subaltern character.

In the novels examined in this study, one of the ways that a text attempts to attenuate—but with variable success as we saw in Chapter 1—the privilege that is inherent in the act of narration is by deploying the figure of the elite child. *Ice-Candy-Man* and *The Hottest Day of the Year* both have an upper-class female child narrator, whereas *The End of Innocence* and *The God of Small Things* use third-person narration but focus on the consciousness of children. The upper-class child's distance from the adult world can signal the narrative's desired distance from dominant class ideologies, even if this desire is complicated and weakened by other aspects of the text, such as the insistence on the 'innocence' of the child narrator in Mohsin's novel which ultimately allows a silence to build around the 'adult' question of inequality. Furthermore, even if an anglophone literary work is ostensibly speaking to the privileged classes, to the exclusion of others, it is capable of making such a choice ironically so as to condemn, rather than legitimize and justify, the abuse of class power. For instance, as Jani (2010,

176) points out, 'the very title of the book, *Rich Like Us*, works by asking the implied audience to read against the grain of an uncritical elite perspective'.

Thus, despite the elitist positioning of English in the region, the (realist) fiction written in this language cannot be assumed to be inevitably complicit with the status quo, nor can it be assumed that it reinforces social marginality through the subordination of lower-class characters within the narrative. Indeed, the growing number of works, by both female and male writers from India and Pakistan, which have a subaltern character as their protagonist, and various manifestations of inequality as a central theme, is a testimony to this observation. To cite only a few recent novels by male authors, consider Aravind Adiga's *The White Tiger* (2008), Mohammed Hanif's *Our Lady of Alice Bhatti* (2011), Jeet Thayil's *Narcopolis* (2012), and Mohsin Hamid's *How to Get Filthy Rich in Rising Asia* (2013).

It is hoped that this study has succeeded in raising as many questions as it has attempted to answer, and that it will lead to a sustained engagement with the theme of class relations in postcolonial literary criticism. I chose to focus on the portrayal of cross-class female friendship and heterosexual desire and romance, but other examples of human intimacy, such as platonic friendship between men and women and same-sex relationships across class are equally of interest. It might also be worth examining the ways in which the depiction of intimacy across class by women writers from India and Pakistan contrasts with the treatment of this theme in works by South Asian male writers. Specifically, how do male writers address transgressive class relationships in spaces that are conventionally deemed 'feminine' and 'female'? Do they construct the subalternity of male and female domestic servants differently from female authors?

Finally, in dealing with the challenges and also the possibilities of narrating cross-class verbal exchanges in the English-language novel, I hope I have succeeded in inviting a reflection on how literary fiction in the other languages of the region has grappled with instances of social interaction and dialogue between characters belonging to divergent classes. An examination of the literary portrayal of cross-class intimacy in languages such as Urdu, Bengali, Marathi, and Malayalam, among others, would shed light on whether, and to what extent, these tongues and their narrative modes are inherently 'less racist, less sexist, less class- and caste-conscious' than English (Namjoshi 2000, 109).

◆

Bibliography

Primary Texts

Adiga, Aravind. 2008. *The White Tiger*. New York: Free Press.

Ahmad, Rukhsana. 1996. *The Hope Chest*. London: Virago Press.

Charry, Brinda. 2003 [2001]. *The Hottest Day of the Year*. London: Black Swan.

Desai, Kiran. 2007 [2006]. *The Inheritance of Loss*. London: Penguin.

Deshpande, Shashi. 1988. *That Long Silence*. London: Virago Press Limited.

———. 1990. *The Dark Holds No Terror*. New Delhi: Penguin.

———. 2001 [1993]. *The Binding Vine*. New York: Feminist Press.

Hamid, Mohsin. 2000. *Moth Smoke*. New York: Picador.

———. 2013. *How to Get Filthy Rich in Rising Asia*. New York: Riverhead Books.

Hanif, Mohammed. 2011. *Our Lady of Alice Bhatti*. Noida: Random House.

Mohsin, Moni. 2006. *The End of Innocence*. New Delhi: Penguin.

Namjoshi, Suniti. 2000. *Goja*. North Melbourne: Spinifex Press.

Roy, Arundhati. 1997. *The God of Small of Things*. New Delhi: IndiaInk.

Rushdie, Salman. 2008 [1981]. *Midnight's Children*. London: Vintage.

Sahgal, Nayantara. 1999 [1985]. *Rich Like Us*. New Delhi: HarperCollins.

Shamsie, Kamila. 2000. *Salt and Saffron*. Karachi: Oxford University Press.

Sidhwa, Bapsi. 1989 [1988]. *Ice-Candy-Man*. New Delhi: Penguin.

Thayil, Jeet. 2012. *Narcopolis: A Novel*. New York: Penguin.

Umrigar, Thrity. 2005. *The Space Between Us*. New York: William Morrow.

Secondary Readings

Abel, Elizabeth. 1981. '[E]Merging Identities: The Dynamics of Female Friendship in Contemporary Fiction by Women', *Signs*, 6(3): 413–35.

Adams, Kathleen and Sara Dickey (eds). 2000. *Home and Hegemony: Domestic Service and Identity Politics in South and Southeast Asia*. Ann Arbor: University of Michigan Press.

Ahmad, Aijaz. 2008 [1992]. *In Theory: Classes, Nations, Literatures*. London and New York: Verso.

———. 2007. 'Reading Arundhati Roy *Politically*', in Alex Tickell (ed.), *Arundhati Roy's The God of Small Things: A Routledge Study Guide*, pp. 110–19. London: Routledge.

Ahmed, Rehana. 2002. 'Unsettling Cosmopolitanisms: Representations of London in Kamila Shamsie's *Salt and Saffron*', *World Literature Written in English*, 40(1): 12–28.

Ahmed, Sara. 1996. 'Beyond Humanism and Postmodernism: Theorizing a Feminist Practice', *Hypatia*, 11(2): 71–93.

———. 2000. *Strange Encounters: Embodied Others in Post-Coloniality*. London: Routledge.

Amin, Shahid and Dipesh Chakrabarty (eds). 1997. *Subaltern Studies: Writings on South Asian History and Society*, vol. 9. New Delhi: Oxford University Press.

Anand, Divya. 2005. 'Inhabiting the Space of Literature: An Ecocritical Study of Arundhati Roy's *The God of Small Things* and O.V. Vijayan's *The Legends of Khasak*', *Interdisciplinary Studies in Literature and Environment*, 12(2): 95–108.

Aristotle. 2014. *Nicomachean Ethics*, tr. C.D. Reeves. Indianapolis: Hackett Publishing Company.

Armstrong, Nancy and Leonard Tennenhouse (eds). 2014 [1987]. 'The Literature of Conduct, the Conduct of Literature, and the Politics of Desire: An Introduction', in *The Ideology of Conduct: Essays on Literature and the History of Sexuality*, pp. 1–24. Oxon and New York: Routledge.

Ashok, Savitri. 2009. 'Gender, Language, and Identity in *Dogeaters*: A Postcolonial Critique', *Postcolonial Text*, 5(2): 1–14.

Augustin, Barbara. 1985. *Mariages sans frontières*. Paris: Le Centurion.

Ayres, Alyssa. 2003. 'The Politics of Language Policy in Pakistan', in M.E. Brown and S. Ganguly (eds), *Fighting Words: Language Policy and Ethnic Relations in Asia*, pp. 51–80. Cambridge: MIT Press.

Azzam, Julie Hakim. 2007. 'The Alien Within: Postcolonial Gothic and the Politics of Home', PhD dissertation, University of Pittsburgh.

Bahri, Deepika. 2003. *Native Intelligence: Aesthetics, Politics, and Postcolonial Literature*. Minneapolis: University of Minnesota Press.

Banerjee, Swapna M. 2004. *Men, Women and Domestics: Articulating Middle-Class Identity in Colonial Bengal*. New Delhi: Oxford University Press.

Barthes, Roland. 1990. *Writing Degree Zero*, trs Annette Lavers and Colin Smith. New York: Hill & Wang.

Bernikow, Louise. 1980. *Among Women*. New York: Harmony Books.

Beverley, John. 1999. *Subalternity and Representation: Arguments in Cultural Theory*. Durham: Duke University Press.

———. 2004. *Testimonio: On the Politics of Truth*. Minneapolis: University of Minnesota Press.

Bhabha, Homi K. (ed.). 1990. *Nation and Narration*. London and New York: Routledge.

Bhalla, Amrita. 2006. *Shashi Deshpande: Writers and Their Work Series*. Devon: Northcote House Publishers.

Bharucha, Nilufer E. 2001. 'Inhabiting Enclosures and Creating Spaces: The Worlds of Women in Indian and Pakistani Literature in English', in A. Hashmi, M. Lal, and V. Ramraj (eds), *Post Independence Voices in South Asian Writings*, pp. 93–107. Islamabad: Alhamra Publishing.

Bhatia, Tej K. and William C. Ritchie (eds). 2004. 'Bilinguism in South Asia', in *The Handbook of Bilingualism*, pp. 780–807. Malden: Blackwell Publishing.

Bhatnagar, Vinita Dhondiyal. 2001. *Readings in Indian English Literature: Nation, Culture, and Identity*. New Delhi: Harman Publishing House.

Bhattacharya, Rinki. 2004. *Behind Closed Doors: Domestic Violence in India*. New Delhi: SAGE Publications.

Bland, Lucy. 2005. 'White Women and Men of Colour: Miscegenation Fears in Britain after the Great War', *Gender & History*, 17(1): 29–61.

Blunt, Alison. 1999. 'Imperial Geographies of Home: British Domesticity in India, 1886–1925', *Transactions of the Institute of British Geographers*, 24(4): 421–40.

Bose, Brinda. 2007. 'In Desire and Death: Eroticism as Politics in Arundhati Roy's *The God of Small Things*', in Alex Tickell (ed.), *Arundhati Roy's The God of Small Things: A Routledge Study Guide*, pp. 120–31. London: Routledge.

Bourdieu, Pierre. 1976. 'Les modes de domination', *Actes de la recherche en sciences sociales*, 2(2–3): 122–32.

———. 1986. 'Forms of Capital', in J.G. Richardson (ed.), *Handbook of Theory and Research for the Sociology of Education*, tr. Richard Nice, pp. 241–58. New York: Greenwood.

———. 2001. *Masculine Domination*, tr. Richard Nice. Stanford: Stanford University Press.

———. 2010 [1984]. *Distinction: A Social Critique of the Judgement of Taste*, tr. Richard Nice. Abingdon: Routledge. Originally published in French as *La Distinction* in 1979.

Buchanan, Ian. 2006. 'National Allegory Today: A Return to Jameson', in C. Irr and I. Buchanan (eds), On *Jameson: From Postmodernism to Globalization*, pp. 173–88. Albany: State University of New York Press.

Carson, Anne. 1995. *Glass, Irony and God*. New York: New Directions.

Cawelti, John G. 1976. *Adventure, Mystery, and Romance: Formula Stories as Art and Popular Culture*. Chicago: University of Chicago Press.

Chakravarti, Uma. 2003. *Gendering Caste Through a Feminist Lens*. Calcutta: Stree.

Chanda, Tirthankar. 1997. 'Sexual/Textual Strategies in *The God of Small Things*', *Commonwealth Essays and Studies*, 20(1): 38–44.

Chandra, Vikram. 2000. 'The Cult of Authenticity', *Boston Review*, 1 February, http://bostonreview.net/BR25.1/chandra.html (accessed 25 January 2015).

Channa, Subhadra. 2013. *Gender in South Asia: Social Imagination and Constructed Realities*. Cambridge: Cambridge University Press.

Chaudhuri, Amit. 2008. *Clearing a Space: Reflections on India, Literature and Culture*. Oxford: Peter Lang.

Chaudhuri, Supriya. 2011. 'Dangerous Liaisons: Desire and Limit in the Home and the World', in Subha Mukherji (ed.), *Thinking on Thresholds: The Poetics of Transitive Spaces*, pp. 87–100. New York: Anthem Press.

Chelliah, Shobhana. 2006. 'The Representation of Indian English in Indian English Novels', handout distributed at the 26th South Asian Language Analysis Conference, Mysore, India, 19–21 December.

Choksy, Jamsheed K. 2003. 'To Cut Off, Purify, and Make Whole: Historiographical and Ecclesiastical Conceptions of Ritual Space', *Journal of the American Oriental Society*, 123(1): 21–41.

Chowdhury, Elora. n.d. '*The Space Between Us:* Reading Umrigar and Sangari in the Quest for Female Friendship', unpublished paper.

Chughtai, Ismat. 2004. *A Chughtai Collection*, trs Tahira Naqvi and Syeda S. Hameed. New Delhi: Women Unlimited.

Clarke, Anna. 2007. 'Language, Hybridity and Dialogism in *The God of Small Things*', in Alex Tickell (ed.), *Arundhati Roy's The God of Small Things: A Routledge Study Guide*, pp. 132–41. London: Routledge.

Conly, Sarah. 2004. 'Seduction, Rape, and Coercion', *Ethics*, 115: 96–121.

Crystal, David. 1994. 'What Is Standard English', *Concorde*, pp. 24–6.

Dabundo, Laura. 2012. 'Domestic Realism', in Frederick Burwick (ed.), *The Encyclopedia of Romantic Literature A–G.*, vol. 1, pp. 370–76. Malden: Wiley–Blackwell.

Davis, Lennard J. 1987. *Resisting Novels: Fiction and Ideology*. New York: Methuen.

Delap, Lucy. 2011. *Knowing Their Place: Domestic Service in Twentieth-Century Britain*. Oxford and New York: Oxford University Press.

Deshmane, Chetan (ed.). 2013. '"A Race of Angels": The Dialectic of Liminality in Kiran Desai's *The Inheritance of Loss*', in *Muses India:*

Essays on English-Language Writers from Mohamet to Rushdie, pp. 186–202. Jefferson and London: McFarland.

Deshpande, Ashwini and Prabirjit Sarkar. 1995. 'Structural Adjustment in India: A Critical Assessment', *Economic and Political Weekly*, 30(49): 3151–5.

Deshpande, Shashi. 1992. 'Of Kitchens and Goddesses', in Antonia Till (ed.), *Loaves and Wishes: Writers Writing on Food*, pp. 17–22. London: Oxfam.

DeVine, Christine. 2005. *Class in Turn-of-the-Century Novels of Gissing, James, Hardy, and Wells*. Aldershot: Ashgate.

Dickey, Sara. 2000a. 'Permeable Homes: Domestic Service, Household Space and the Vulnerability of Class Boundaries in Urban India', *American Ethnologist*, 27(2): 462–89.

———. 2000b. 'Mutual Exclusions: Domestic Workers and Employers on Labor, Class and Character in South India', in Kathleen M. Adams and Sara Dickey (eds), *Home and Hegemony: Domestic Service and Identity Politics in South and Southeast Asia*, pp. 31–62. Ann Arbor: University of Michigan Press.

———. 2010. 'Anjali's Alliance: Class Mobility in Urban India', in D.P. Mines and S. Lamb (eds), *Everyday Life in South Asia*, 2nd ed., pp. 192–205. Bloomington: Indiana University Press.

Didur, Jill. 2011. 'Cultivating Community: Counter Landscaping in Kiran Desai's *The Inheritance of Loss*', in E. Deloughrey and G.B. Handley (eds), *Postcolonial Ecologies: Literatures of the Environment*, pp. 43–61. New York: Oxford University Press.

Dimock, Wai Chee and Michael T. Gilmore. 1994. *Rethinking Class: Literary Studies and Social Formations*. New York: Columbia University Press.

Donaldson, Stephen. 1990. 'Eroticization of the Working Class', in Wayne R. Dynes, Warren Johansson, and William A. Percy (eds), *Encyclopedia of Homosexuality*, pp. 1405–6. New York: Garland Publishing Inc.

Driver, Edwin D. and Aloo E. Driver. 1987. *Social Class in Urban India: Essays on Cognitions and Structures*. Leiden: Brill Academic Publishers.

Dworkin, Andrea. 1983. *Right-Wing Women*. New York: Perigee Books.

Eagleton, Terry. 1976. *Marxism and Literary Criticism*. Berkley: University of California Press.

———. 1991. *Ideology: An Introduction*. London; New York: Verso.

———. 2013 [1994]. *Ideology*. Oxon: Routledge.

Ehrenreich, Barbara. 2003. 'Maid to Order', in Barbara Ehrenreich and Arlie Russell Hochschild (eds), *Global Woman: Nannies, Maids, and Sex Workers in the New Economy*, pp. 85–103. New York: Metropolitan Books.

Esther, Leslie. 2010. 'Interrupted Dialogues of Realism and Modern: "The Fact of New Forms of Life, Always Born and Active"', in Matthew Beaumont (ed.), *A Concise Companion to Realism*, pp. 153–59. Malden: Wiley–Blackwell.

Fair, Laura. 2009. 'Making Love in the Indian Ocean: Hindi Films, Zanzibari Audiences, and the Construction of Romance in the 1950s and 1960s', in Jennifer Cole and Lynn M. Thomas (eds), *Love in Africa*, pp. 58–82. Chicago and London: University of Chicago Press.

Felski, Rita. 1989. *Beyond Feminist Aesthetics: Feminist Literature and Social Change*. Cambridge: Harvard University Press.

Firestone, Shulamith. 1970. *The Dialectic of Sex: The Case of Feminist Revolution*. New York: Morrow.

Foucault, Michel. 1978. *The History of Sexuality: An Introduction*, vol. 1, tr. Robert Hurley. New York: Pantheon Books.

———. 1997. 'Friendship as a Way of Life', in Paul Rabinow (ed.), *Essential Works of Foucault: Ethics, Subjectivity and Truth*, vol. 1, tr. John Johnston, pp. 135–40. New York: New Press.

Fraisse, Geneviève. 2007. *Du consentement*. Paris: Éditions du seuil.

Fraser, Robert. 2000. *Lifting the Sentence: A Poetics of Postcolonial Fiction*. Manchester: Manchester University Press.

Gandhi, Leela. 2003. 'Novelists of the 1930s and 1940s', in Arvind Krishna Mehrotra (ed.), *A History of Indian Literature in English*, pp. 168–92. New York: Columbia University Press.

Gandhi, Mohandas Karamchand. 2001. *The Collected Works of Mahatma Gandhi [16 July 1940–27 December 1940]*, vol. 79. New Delhi: Ministry of Information and Broadcasting, Government of India.

Gane, Gillian. 2006. 'Postcolonial Literature and the Magic Radio: The Language of Rushdie's Midnight's Children', *Poetics Today*, 27(3): 569–96.

George, Rosemary Marangoly. 1996. *The Politics of Home: Postcolonial Relocations and Twentieth Century Fiction*. Cambridge: Cambridge University Press.

Giddens, Anthony. 2001. *Sociology*, 4th ed. Cambridge: Polity Press.

Girardin, Cécile. 2009. 'The Inheritance of Modernity: Insurgencies in Contemporary Indian Fiction', *Etudes anglaises*, 62(3): 292–304.

Gopal, Priyamvada. 2009. *The Indian English Novel: Nation, History, and Narration*. Oxford: Oxford University Press.

Gordon, April. 1996. *Transforming Capitalism and Patriarchy: Gender and Development in Africa*. Boulder: Lynne Rienner.

Gramsci, Antonio. 1971. *Selections from the Prison Notebooks of Antonio Gramsci*, trs Quintin Hoare and Geoffrey Nowell-Smith. New York: International Publishers.

Guha, Ranajit. 1982. *Subaltern Studies I: Writings on South Asian History and Society*. New Delhi: Oxford University Press.

Guignery, Vanessa. 2009. '"Step across This Line": Edges and Borders in Contemporary Indian Literature', *Etudes anglaises*, 62(3): 305–16.

Guilhamon, Lise. 2009. '*Indian English ou Masala English: Quelle variété d'anglais pour le roman indien Anglophone*', in A. Castaing, L. Guilhamon, and L. Zecchini (eds), *La modernité littéraire indienne: Perspectives postcoloniales*, pp. 210–36. Rennes: Presses Universitaires de Rennes.

Gupta, Jyotirindra Das. 1978. 'A Season of Caesars: Emergency Regimes and Development Politics in Asia', *Asian Survey*, 18(4): 315–49.

Hai, Ambreen. 2000. 'Border Work, Border Trouble: Postcolonial Feminism and the Ayah in Bapsi Sidhwa's *Cracking India*', *Modern Fiction Studies*, 46(2): 379–426.

———. 2014. 'Postcolonial Servitude: Interiority and System in Daniyal Mueenuddin's *In Other Rooms, Other Wonders*', *Ariel: A Review of International English Literature*, 45(3): 33–73.

Hartmann, Heidi. 2013 [1981]. 'The Unhappy Marriage of Marxism and Feminism: Towards a More Progressive Union', in C. McCann and S. Kim (eds), *Feminist Theory Reader: Local and Global Perspectives*, pp. 187–201. New York: Routledge.

Hecht, Tobias. 1998. *At Home in the Street: Street Children of Northeast Brazil*. New York: Cambridge University Press.

Hickey, Raymond (ed.). 2004. 'South Asian Englishes', in *Legacies of Colonial English: Studies in Transported Dialects*, pp. 536–58. Cambridge: Cambridge University Press.

Hogan, Patrick Colm. 1999. 'Revolution and Despair: Allegories of Nation and Class in Patrick Hogan's "Camps on the Hearthstone"', *The Canadian Journal of Irish Studies*, 25(1/2): 179–201.

hooks, bell. 1981. *Ain't I a Woman*. Boston: South End Press.

———. 1996. *Killing Rage: Ending Racism*. New York: H. Holt and Co.

———. 2000. *Feminism Is for Everybody: Passionate Politics*. Cambridge: Pluto Press.

Ibrahim, Huma. 2001. 'Transnational Migrations and the Debate of English Writing in/of Pakistan', in A. Hashmi, M. Lal, and V.J. Ramraj (eds), *Postindependence Voices in South Asian Writings*, pp. 33–48. Islamabad: Alhamra Publishing.

Illouz, Eva. 1997. *Consuming the Romantic Utopia: Love and the Cultural Contradictions of Capitalism*. Berkeley: University of California Press.

Jana, Reena. 1997. 'The Salon Interview', interview of Arundhati Roy, *Salon*, 30 September, http://www.salon.com/1997/09/30/00roy/ (accessed 14 March 2016).

Jackson, Elizabeth. 2010. *Feminism and Contemporary Indian Women's Writing*. Basingstoke: Palgrave Macmillan.

Jaffrelot, Christophe. 2005. '*L'état d'urgence en Inde [1975–1977]: La suspension de la démocratie, condition des réformes sociales?*' paper presented at the Eighth Congress of the Association Française de Science Politique, 14–16 September, http://www.afsp.msh-paris.fr/archives/congreslyon2005/communications/tr4/jaffrelot.pdf (accessed 11 March 2016).

James, Allison, Chris Jenks, and Alan Prout A. 1998. *Theorizing Childhood*. Cambridge: Polity.

Jameson, Fredric. 1986. 'Third-World Literature in the Era of Multinational Capitalism', *Social Text*, 15: 65–88.

Jani, Pranav. 2001. 'Before Rushdie: Cosmopolitanism and the National Question in the Post-colonial Indian English Novel', PhD dissertation, Brown University.

———. 2009. 'Beyond Anti-Communism: The Progressive Politics of *The God of Small Things*', in R. Ghosh and A.N. Tejero (eds), *Globalizing Dissent: Essays on Arundhati Roy*, pp. 47–70. New York: Routledge.

———. 2010. *Decentering Rushdie: Cosmopolitanism and the Indian Novel in English*. Columbus: Ohio State University Press.

Javed, Sajid Amin and Mohammad Irfan. 2012. 'Intergenerational Mobility: Evidence from Pakistan Panel Household Survey', *Poverty and Social Dynamics Paper Series*. Islamabad: Pakistan Institute of Development Economics.

Jay, Paul. 2010. *Global Matters: The Transnational Turn in Literary Studies*. Ithaca: Cornell University Press.

Johnson, Carol. 1996. 'Does Patriarchy Really Need Capitalism', *Women's Studies International Form*, 19(3): 193–202.

Jones, Gill. 1990. 'Marriage Partners and Their Class Trajectories', in Geoff Payne and Pamela Abbot (eds), *The Social Mobility of Women: Beyond Male Mobility Models*, pp. 91–109. London: The Falmer Press.

Kakar, Sudhir. 1990. *Intimate Relations in India: Exploring Indian Sexuality*. Chicago: University of Chicago.

Kanaganayakam, Chelva. 2002. *Counterrealism and Indo-Anglian Fiction*. Waterloo: Wilfrid Laurier University Press.

Kapoor, Dip. 2011. *Critical Perspectives on Neoliberal Globalization, Development and Education in Africa and Asia*. Boston: Sense Publishers.

Kapur, Cari C. 2010. 'Rethinking Courtship, Marriage and Divorce in an Indian Call Center', in D.P. Mines and S. Lamb (eds), *Everyday Life in South Asia*, 2nd ed., pp. 50–61. Bloomington: Indiana University Press.

Kellogg, Samuel Henry and Thomas Grahame Bailey. 1955. *A Grammar of the Hindi Language*. London: Routledge & Kegan Paul.

Khair, Tabish. 2001. *Babu Fictions: Alienation in Contemporary Indian English Novels*. New Delhi: Oxford University Press.

———. 2008. 'Can the Subaltern Shout (and Smash?)', *World Literature Written in English*, 38(2): 7–16.

———. 2015. 'The Bhashanglo Tangle: Questions the Nemade–Rushdie Spat Raises', *Outlook* (23 February 2015), http://www.outlookindia.com/magazine/story/the-bhashanglo-tangle/293383 (accessed 19 April 2016).

Kirpal, Viney. 1996. '*Rich Like Us*: Text, Context and Subtext', in Jasbir Jain (ed.), *Women's Writing: Text and Context*, pp. 167–79. Jaipur: Rawat Publications.

Korte, Barbara. 2010/2011. 'Can the Indigent Speak? Poverty Studies, the Postcolonial and Global Appeal of *Q & A* and *The White Tiger*', *Connotations*, 20(2–3): 293–317.

Kukreja, Veena. 2005. 'Pakistan's Political Economy: Misplaced Priorities and Economic Uncertainties', in V. Kukreja and M.P. Singh (eds), *Pakistan: Democracy, Development and Security Issues*, pp. 137–65. New Delhi: SAGE Publications.

Lal, Malashri. 1995. *The Law of the Threshold: Women Writers in Indian English*. Shimla: Indian Institute of Advanced Study.

Lane, Richard J. 2006. *The Postcolonial Novel*. Cambridge: Polity Press.

Lau, Lisa. 2010. 'South Asian Mistresses and Servants: The Fault Lines between Class Chasms and Individual Intimacies', *Pakistani Journal of Women's Studies*, 17(1): 33–58.

Lavalette, Michael (ed.). 1999. '"New Sociology of Childhood" and Child Labour: Childhood, Children's Rights and "Children's Voice"', in *A Thing of the Past? Child Labour in Britain in the Nineteenth and Twentieth Centuries*, pp. 15–43. Liverpool: Liverpool University Press.

Lazarus, Neil. 2011. *The Postcolonial Unconscious*. Cambridge: Cambridge University Press.

Lerner, Gerda. 1973. *Black Women in White America: A Documentary History*. New York: Vintage Books.

Lévinas, Emmanuel. 1971. *Totality and Infinity*, tr. Alphonso Lingis. Pittsburg: Duquesne University Press.

Li, Victor. 2009. 'Necroidealism or The Subaltern's Sacrificial Death', *Interventions*, 11(3): 275–92.

Ligaya, Mishan. 2006. 'The Clash of Caste', *New York Times Book Review*, 22 January, http://www.nytimes.com/2006/01/22/books/review/22mishan.html (accessed 11 March 2016).

Luhrmann, Tanya. 1996. *The Good Parsi: The Fate of a Colonial Elite in a Postcolonial Society*. Cambridge: Harvard University Press.

Macherey, Pierre. 2006 [1978]. *Theory of Literary Production*, tr. Geoffrey Wall. London and New York: Routledge.

MacKinnon, Catharine A. 1987. *Feminism Unmodified: Discourses on Life and Law*. Cambridge: Harvard University Press.

———. 1989. *Toward a Feminist Theory of the State*. Cambridge: Harvard University Press.

Mahboob, Ahmar and Nadra Huma Ahmar. 2004. 'Pakistani English: Phonology', in E.W. Schneider and B. Kortmann (eds), *A Handbook of Varieties of English: A Multimedia Reference Tool*, pp. 1003–16. Berlin: Mouton de Gruyter.

Majumdar, Saikat. 2013. *Prose of the World: Modernism and the Banality of Empire*. New York: Columbia University Press.

Mann, Harveen Sachdeva. 1993. 'Elliptic Feminism and Nationalism in Nayantara Sahgal's *Rich Like Us*', *International Fiction Review*, 20(2): 103–11.

Markels, Julian. 2003. *The Marxian Imagination: Representing Class in Literature*. New York: Monthly Review Press.

Marx, Karl. 1986 [1976]. *Capital: A Critique of Capitalist Economy*, vol. 1, tr. Ben Fowkes. Harmondsworth: Penguin.

Marx, Karl and Friedrich Engels. 2012 [1888]. *The Communist Manifesto: A Modern Edition*. London: Verso.

Mayer, Tamar. 2002. *Gender Ironies of Nationalism: Sexing the Nation*. London and New York: Routledge.

McBride, Theresa. 1978. 'As the Twig Bent: The Victorian Nanny', in Anthony S. Wohl (ed.), *The Victorian Family: Structure and Stresses*, pp. 44–58. London: Croom Helm.

Menon, Nirmala. 2009. 'Remapping the Postcolonial Canon', PhD dissertation, George Washington University.

Menon, Priya. 2010. 'Liminal Resistances: Local Subjections in *My Story*, *Vidheyan*, and *The God of Small Things*', PhD dissertation, Georgia State University.

Menon, Ritu and Kamla Bhasin. 1998. *Borders & Boundaries: Women in India's Partition*. New Delhi: Kali for Women.

Michie, Helena. 1991. 'Confinements: The Domestic in the Discourses of Upper-Middle-Class Pregnancy', in R.R. Warhol and D.P. Herndl (eds), *Feminisms: An Anthology of Literary Theory and Criticism*, pp. 57–75. New Brunswick: Rutgers University Press.

Minahan, James. 2002. *Encyclopedia of the Stateless Nations: D–K*. Westport: Greenwood Press.

Mirza, Maryam. 2010. 'Female Relationships Across Class Boundaries: A Study of Three Contemporary Novels by Women Writers from the

Indian Sub-Continent', *The Sri Lanka Journal of the Humanities*, 36(1 and 2): 11–18.

———. 2015. 'Intimacy across Caste and Class Boundaries in Arundhati Roy's *The God of Small Things*', in Judith Misrahi-Barak and Abraham Joshi (eds), *Dalit Literatures in India*, pp. 277–91. New Delhi: Routledge.

Mody, Perveez. 2007. 'Kidnapping, Elopement and Abduction: An Ethnography of Love-Marriage in Delhi', in Francesca Orsini (ed.), *Love in South Asia: A Cultural History*, pp. 331–44. New Delhi: Cambridge University Press.

Moore, Allison and Paul Reynolds. 2004. 'Feminist Approaches to Sexual Consent: A Critical Assessment', in M. Cowling and P. Reynolds (eds), *Making Sense of Sexual Consent*, pp. 29–44. Aldershot: Ashgate.

Moss, Laura. 2000. 'Can Rohinton Mistry's Realism Rescue the Novel?' in Rowland Smith (ed.), *Postcolonizing the Commonwealth: Studies in Literature and Culture*, pp. 157–66. Waterloo: Wilfrid Laurier University Press.

Murphy, Eamon and Aazar Tamana. 2010. 'State Terrorism and the Military in Pakistan', in Richard Jackson, Eamon Murphy, and Scott Poynting (eds), *Contemporary State Terrorism: Theory and Practice*, pp. 48–67. London and New York: Routledge.

Muthiah, Kalaivahni. 2009. 'Fictionalized Indian English Speech and the Representations of Ideology in Indian Novels in English', PhD dissertation, University of North Texas.

Namjoshi, Suniti. 1993 [1981]. *Feminist Fables*. North Melbourne: Spinifex Press.

Nath, Viswambhar and Surinder K. Aggarwal. 2007. *Urbanization, Urban Development, and Metropolitan Cities in India*. New Delhi: Concept Publishing Company.

Needham, Anuradha Dingwaney. 2005. '"The Small Voice of History" in Arundhati Roy's *The God of Small Things*', *Interventions*, 7(3): 369–91.

Omvedt, Gail (ed.). 1982. 'Class, Caste and Land in India: An Introductory Essay', in *Land, Caste and Politics in Indian States*, pp. 9–50. Delhi: Authors Guild Publication.

Ostrander, Susan. 1987. 'Women Using Other Women', *Contemporary Sociology*, 16(1): 51–3.

Pearce, Michael. 2007. *The Routledge Dictionary of English Language Studies*. Oxon: Routledge.

Pederson, Jean Elisabeth. 1998. '"Special Customs": Paternity Suits and Citizenship in France and the Colonies, 1870–1912', in Julia Clancy-Smith and Frances Gouda (eds), *Domesticating the Empire: Race,*

Gender and Family Life in French and Dutch Colonialism, pp. 43–64. Charlottesville and London: University Press of Virginia.

Philips, Amali. 2004. 'Gendering Colour: Identity, Femininity and Marriage in Kerala', *Anthropologica*, 46(2): 253–72.

Podgorniak, Alexandra. 2002. 'Magical Realism, Indian-Style; or, the Case of Multiple Submission: *The God of Small Things* by Arundhati Roy', in Gerhard Stilz (ed.), *Missions of Interdependence: A Literary Directory*, pp. 255–63. Amsterdam: Rodopi.

Pozzo, Barbara. 2008. 'A Suitable Boy: The Abolition of Feudalism in India', *Erasmus Law Review*, 1(3): 41–58.

Prasad, Madhava. 1992. 'On the Question of a Theory of (Third World) Literature', *Social Text*, 31/32: 57–83.

Pratt, Mary Louise. 1992. *Imperial Eyes Travel Writing and Transculturation*. London: Routledge.

Puri, Jyoti. 1999. *Woman, Body, Desire in Post-Colonial India: Narratives of Gender and Sexuality*. London: Routledge.

Qadeer, Mohammad A. 2006. *Pakistan: Social and Cultural Transformations in a Muslim Nation*. London: Routledge.

Qureshi, Irna. 2010. 'Destigmatising Star Texts: Honour and Shame among Muslim Women in Pakistani Cinema', in Shakuntala Banaji (ed.), *South Asian Media Cultures: Audiences, Representations, Contexts*, pp. 181–98. London: Anthem Press.

Rahman, Tariq. 2005. 'Passports to Privilege: The English-Medium Schools in Pakistan', *Peace and Democracy in South Asia*, 1(1): 24–44.

Rajan, Rajeswari Sunder. 1993a. *Real and Imagined Women: Gender, Culture and Postcolonialism*. London: Routledge.

———. 1993b. 'The Feminist Plot and the Nationalist Allegory: Home and World in Two Indian Women's Novels in English', *Modern Fiction Studies*, 39(1): 71–92.

Rajan, Sujeet. n.d. 'Indian Express Interview', interview of Thrity Umrigar, http://www.umrigar.com/interview/indian_express.html (accessed 25 November 2014).

Ray, Raka and Seemin Qayum. 2009. *Cultures of Servitude: Modernity, Domesticity and Class in India*. Stanford: Stanford University Press.

Reddy, Sunita Y.S. 2001. *A Feminist Perspective on the Novels of Shashi Deshpande*. New Delhi: Prestige Books.

Remedios, Karen Renee. 2007. 'Working Women, Re-Working Space: Representations of Women's Workplaces in Contemporary Indian Writing in English', PhD dissertation, Purdue University.

Renouard, Michel. 2008. *La littérature indienne anglophone*. Neuilly: Atlande.

Rollins, Judith. 1985. *Between Women: Domestics and Their Employers*. Philadelphia: Temple University Press.

Roopnarine, Jaipaul L., Ziarat Hossain, Preeti Gill, and Holly Brophy. 1994. 'Play in the East Indian Context', in J.L. Roopnarine, J.E. Johnson, and F.H. Hooper (eds), *Children's Play in Diverse Cultures*, pp. 9–30. Albany: State University of New York Press.

Roy, Anjali Gera. 2013. 'The Politics of Hinglish', in Lionel Wee, Robbie B.H. Go, and Lisa Lim (eds), *The Politics of English: South Asia, Southeast Asia and the Asia Pacific*, pp. 21–36. Amsterdam and Philadelphia: John Benjamins Publishing Company.

Roy, Anuradha. 1999. *Patterns of Feminist Consciousness in Indian Women Writers*. New Delhi: Prestige Books.

———. 2004. *An Ordinary Person's Guide to Empire*. Cambridge: South End Press.

Rubbo, Anna and Michael Taussig. 1983. 'Up Off Their Knees: Servanthood in Southwest Colombia', *Latin American Perspectives*, 10(4): 5–23.

Rudolph, Lloyd I. and Susanne Hoeber Rudolph. 1977. 'India's Election: Backing into the Future', *Foreign Affairs*, 55(4): 836–53.

Sabo, Oana. 2012. 'Disjunctures and Diaspora in Kiran Desai's *The Inheritance of Loss*', *Journal of Commonwealth Literature*, 47(3): 375–92.

Sadana, Rashmi. 2012. *English Heart, Hindi Heartland: The Political Life of Literature in India*. Berkeley and Los Angeles: University of California Press.

Sahgal, Nayantara. 1988. 'Nayantara Sahgal on Who She Is', in Harold G. Coward (ed.), *Peace, Development and Culture: Comparative Studies of India and Canada*, pp. 95–106. Calgary: Canada–India Conference on Comparative Studies.

Said, Edward. 1994 [1993]. *Culture and Imperialism*. London: Vintage.

Sailaja, Pingali. 2009. *Indian English*. Edinburgh: Edinburgh University Press.

Sarker, Sonita. 2001. 'Afterword: Legacies of Strength', in Shashi Deshpande, *The Binding Vine*, pp. 209–43. New York: The Feminist Press.

Scanlan, Margaret. 2010. 'Migrating from Terror: The Postcolonial Novel after September 11', *Journal of Postcolonial Writing*, 46(3–4): 266–78.

Shah, Saubhagya. 2000. 'Service or Servitude? The Domestication of Household Labour in Nepal', in K.M. Adams and S. Dickey (eds), *Home and Hegemony: Domestic Service and Identity Politics in South and Southeast Asia*, pp. 87–118. Ann Arbor: University of Michigan Press.

Sharma, Shalendra D. 1999. *Development and Democracy in India*. Boulder: Lynne Rienner.

Sharma, Siddhartha. 2005. *Shashi Deshpande's Novels: A Feminist Study*. New Delhi: Atlantic.

Singh, Jyotsna G. 1996. *Colonial Narratives/Cultural Dialogues: 'Discoveries' of India in the Language of Colonialism*. London and New York: Routledge.

Singh, Rashna B. 2008. 'Traversing Diacritical Space: Negotiating and Narrating Parsi Nationness', *The Journal of Commonwealth Literature*, 43(2): 29–47.

Singh, Sujala. 2006. 'The Child and the Nation in Contemporary South Asian Literature', in M. Ghosh-Schellhorn and V. Alexander (eds), *Peripheral Centres, Central Peripheries: India and its Diaspora(s)*, pp. 183–94. Muünster: Lit.

Smith, Adam. 2009 [1776]. *An Inquiry into the Nature and Causes of the Wealth of Nations*, vol. X. New York: Cosimo, Inc.

Spielman, David Wallace. 2010. '"Solid Knowledge" and Contradictions in Kiran Desai's *The Inheritance of Loss*', *Critique*, 51: 74–89.

Spivak, Gayatri Chakravorty. 1985. 'Subaltern Studies: Deconstructing Historiography', in Ranajit Guha (ed.), *Subaltern Studies IV*, pp. 330–63. New Delhi: Oxford University Press.

———. 1988. 'Can the Subaltern Speak?' in C. Nelson and L. Grossberg (eds), *Marxism and the Interpretation of Culture*, pp. 271–313. Urbana: University of Illinois Press.

———. 1992. 'The Politics of Translation in Destabilizing Theory', in M. Barrett and A. Philips (eds), *Contemporary Feminist Debates*, pp. 177–200. Oxford: Polity Press.

———. 1996. *The Spivak Reader: Selected Works of Gayatri Chakravorty Spivak*. New York: Routledge.

Sree, Sathupati Prasanna. 2003. *Woman in the Novels of Shashi Deshpande: A Study*. New Delhi: Sarup and Sons Ltd.

Srivastava, Neelam. 2007. *Secularism in the Postcolonial Indian Novel: National and Cosmopolitan Narratives in English*. London: Routledge.

Stiglitz, Joseph E. 2002. *Globalization and Its Discontents*. New York: W.W. Norton.

Steiner, George. 1969. *Language and Silence: Essays 1958–1966*. Harmondsworth: Penguin.

Stoler, Ann Laura. 1995. *Race and the Education of Desire: Foucault's History of Sexuality and the Colonial Order of Things*. Durham: Duke University Press.

———. 2001. 'Tense and Tender Ties: The Politics of Comparison in North American History and (Post) Colonial Studies', *The Journal of American History*, 88(3): 829–65.

———. 2002. *Carnal Knowledge and Imperial Power*. Berkeley: University of California Press.

——— (ed.). 2006. 'Intimidations of Empire: Predicaments of the Tactile and Unseen', in *Haunted by Empire: Geographies of Intimacy in North*

American History, pp. 1–22. Durham and London: Duke University Press.

Straub, Kristina. 2009. *Domestic Affairs: Intimacy, Eroticism, and Violence between Servants and Masters in Eighteenth-Century Britain*. Baltimore: Johns Hopkins University Press.

Tagore, Proma. 2009. *The Shapes of Silence: Writing Women of Colour and the Politics of Testimony*. Montreal and Ithaca: McGill-Queen's University Press.

Tate, Claudia. 1994. 'Toni Morrison', in Danille Kathleen Taylor-Guthrie (ed.), *Conversations with Toni Morrison*, pp. 156–70. Jackson: University Press of Mississippi.

Tax, Meredith. 2001 [1980]. *The Rising of the Women: Feminist Solidarity and Class Conflict, 1880–1917*. Urbana and Chicago: University of Illinois Press.

Thompson, Edward P. 1963. *The Making of the English Working Class*. Victor Gollancz: London.

Thiong'o, Ngugi wa. 1994 [1986]. *Decolonising the Mind: The Politics of Language in African Literature*. Nairobi: East African Educational Publishers Ltd.

Tickell, Alex (ed.). 2007, *Arundhati Roy's The God of Small Things: A Routledge Study Guide*. London: Routledge.

Tolen, Rachel. 2000. 'Transfers of Knowledge and Privileged Spheres of Practice: Servants and Employers in a Madras Railway Colony', K.M. Adams and S. Dickey (eds), *Home and Hegemony: Domestic Service and Identity Politics in South and Southeast Asia*, pp. 63–86. Ann Arbor: University of Michigan Press.

Trivedi, Harish. 1995 [1993]. *Colonial Transactions. English Literature and India*. Manchester: Manchester University Press.

Turner, Victor. 1969. *The Ritual Process: Structure and Anti-Structure*. Chicago: Aldine Publishing Co.

———. 1974. *Dramas, Fields, and Metaphors: Symbolic Action in Human Society*. Ithaca: Cornell University Press.

Twine, France Winddance. 2010. *A White Side of Black Britain: Interracial Intimacy and Racial Literacy*. Durham: Duke University Press.

UNICEF (United Nations Children's Fund). 2001. 'Early Marriage: Child Spouses', *Innocenti Digest*, no. 7. Florence: UNICEF Innocenti Research Centre, http://www.unicef-irc.org/publications/pdf/digest7e.pdf (accessed 11 March 2016).

United Nations Population Division. 2001. *Abortion Policies: A Global Review—Oman to Zimbabwe*, vol. III. New York: United Nations, Department of Economic and Social Affairs.

Vargas, Jennifer Hardford. 2011. 'Critical Realisms in the Global South: Narrative Transculturation in Senapati's *Six Acres and a Third* and Garcia Marquez's *One Hundred Years of Solitude*', in Satya P. Mohanty (ed.), *Colonialism, Modernity, and Literature: A View from India*, pp. 25–54. New York: Palgrave Macmillan.

Varma, Rashmi. 2012. *The Postcolonial City and Its Subjects: London, Nairobi, Bombay*. London: Routledge.

Vicziany, Marika. 2004. 'The Middle Classes of South Asia', in M. Bhattacharya, R. Smyth, and M. Vicziany (eds), *South Asia in the Era of Globalisation: Trade, Industrialisation and Welfare*, pp. 29–44. New York: Nova Science Publishers.

Virdi, Jyotika. 2003. *The Cinematic ImagiNation: Indian Popular Films as Social History*. New Brunswick: Rutgers University Press.

Vogt-William, Christine. 2003. '"Language Is the Skin of My Thought": Language Relations in *Ancient Promises* and *The God of Small Things*', in Christian Mair (ed.) *The Politics of English as a World Language: New Horizons in Postcolonial Cultural Studies*, pp. 393–404. Amsterdam: Rodopi.

Weber, Max. 2009. *From Max Weber: Essays in Sociology*, tr., ed., and with an intro. by H.H. Gerth and C. Wright Mills. Oxon: Routledge.

Weightman, Barbara A. 2002. *Dragons and Tigers: A Geography of South, East, and Southeast Asia*. New York: John Wiley.

Werbner, Pnina. 1997. 'Essentializing Essentialism, Essentializing Silence: Ambivalence and Multiplicity in the Constructions of Racism and Ethnicity', in P. Werbner and T. Modood (eds), *Debating Cultural Hybridity: Multicultural Identities and the Politics of Anti-Racism*, pp. 226–54. New York: Zed Books.

Whitehead, Deborah. 2011. 'Feminism, Religion, and the Politics of History', *Journal of Feminist Studies in Religion*, 27(2): 3–9.

Wiemann, Dirk. 2008. *Internationale forschungen zur allgemeinen und vergleichenden literaturwissenschaft: Genres of Modernity—Contemporary Indian Novels in English*, vol. 120. Amsterdam: Rodopi.

Wilson, Kalpana. 1998. 'Arundhati Roy and the Left: For Reclaiming "Small Things"', *Liberation*, January, http://www.cpiml.org/liberation/year_1998/january/books.htm (accessed 2 September 2012).

Wright, Erik Olin. 2000. *Class Counts: Student Edition*. Cambridge: Cambridge University Press.

Young, Iris Marion. 1997. 'Asymmetrical Reciprocity: On Moral Respect, Wonder, and Enlarged Thought', *Constellations: An International Journal of Critical and Democratic Theory*, 3(3): 340–63.

Index

About the Author

Maryam Mirza received her PhD in English Studies from Aix-Marseille University, France, and is currently working as a BeIPD-COFUND postdoctoral research fellow at the University of Liège, Belgium. Her work has appeared in journals such as the *Journal of Commonwealth Literature* and *Gender, Place & Culture: A Journal of Feminist Geography*, as well as in anthologies. She has taught at several colleges and universities in Pakistan, including Kinnaird College for Women, Lahore. In June–July 2015, she held a Charles Wallace Pakistan Trust Visiting Fellowship at Newcastle University, UK. Her main research interests include South Asian anglophone fiction, gender studies, economics and postcolonial literature, and sociology.